Brazil's Indians and the
Onslaught of Civilization

Brazil's Indians and the Onslaught of Civilization

The Yanomami and the Kayapó

LINDA RABBEN

University of Washington Press
Seattle and London

Originally published in 1998 under the title *Unnatural Selection* by Pluto Press, London, U.K., and University of Washington Press

The 2004 edition titled *Brazil's Indians and the Onslaught of Civilization* is a revised and expanded edition of the original book.

Printed in the United States of America
10 09 08 07 06 05 04 5 4 3 2 1

Design by Dennis Martin

University of Washington Press
PO Box 50096, Seattle, WA 98145, U.S.A.
www.washington.edu/uwpress

Library of Congress Cataloging-in-Publication Data

Rabben, Linda,
Brazil's Indians and the onslaught of civilization: the Yanomami and the Kayapó /
Linda Rabben.
p. cm.
Rev. ed. of: Unnatural selection. c.1988.
Includes bibliographical references and index.
ISBN 0-295-98362-0 (pbk.: alk. paper)
1. Yanomamo Indians—Social conditions. 2. Yanomamo Indians—Ethnic identity. 3. Yanomamo Indians—Cultural assimilation. 4. Cayapo Indians—Social conditions. 5. Cayapo Indians—Ethnic identity. 6. Cayapo Indians—Cultural assimilation. 7. Social change—Brazil. 8. Brazil—Ethnic relations. 9. Brazil—Social policy. I. Rabben, Linda, Unnatural selection. II. Title.
F2520.1.Y3R33 2004
305.898´4—dc21   2003053945

The paper used in this publication meets the minimum requirements of American National Standard for Information Sciences—Permanence of Paper for Printed Library Materials, ANSI Z39.48-1984.

Jacket photo by Cristiana Isidoro/Agência JB, May 1992.

In memory of Berta Ribeiro, 1924–1997

Pioneira

Contents

List of Abbreviations

AAA	American Anthropological Association
ABA	Associação Brasileira de Antropologia—Brazilian Anthropology Association
APOINME	Articulação dos Povos Indígenas do NE/MG/ES—Linkage of Indigenous Peoples of the Northeast/Minas Gerais/Espírito Santo
AVA	Associação Vida e Ambiente—Life and Environment Association
CAPOIB	Coordenação de Articulação dos Povos e Organizações Indígenas no Brasil—Council Linking Indigenous Peoples and Organizations in Brazil
CCPY	Comissão Pró-Yanomami—Pro-Yanomami Commission
CEDI	Centro Ecumênico de Documentação e Informação—Ecumenical Information and Documentation Center
CIMI	Conselho Indigenista Missionário—Missionary Indigenist Council
CIR	Conselho Indígena de Roraima—Indigenous Council of Roraima
COIAB	Coordenação das Organizações Indígenas da Amazônia Brasileira—Coordination of Indigenous Organizations of the Brazilian Amazon
CPT	Comissão Pastoral da Terra—Pastoral Land Commission
FMV	Fundação Mata Virgem—Rainforest Foundation of Brazil

FNS	Fundação Nacional de Saúde—National Health Foundation
FUNAI	Fundação Nacional do Índio—National Indian Foundation (federal agency)
FUNDAFACI	Fundación para la Ayuda de la Familia Campesina y Indígena—Foundation for Assistance to the Peasant and Indigenous Family
GTA	Amazon Working Group
IBAMA	Instituto Brasileiro do Meio-Ambiente—Brazilian Environmental Institute (federal agency)
IDB	Inter-American Development Bank
ILO	International Labor Office
ILRC	Indian Law Resource Center
INPARQUES	Venezuelan Parks Institute
ISA	Instituto Sócioambiental—Socio-Environmental Institute
MDB	Multilateral development bank
MNDH	Movimento Nacional de Direitos Humanos—National Human Rights Movement
NDI	Núcleo de Direito Indígena—Indigenous Rights Unit
NGO	Nongovernmental organization
RADAM	Radar in Amazonia
RFF	Rainforest Foundation
SEJUP	Serviço de Justiça e Paz
SPI	Serviço de Proteção ao Índio—Indian Protection Service
UFRJ	Federal University of Rio de Janeiro
UNCED	United Nations Conference on Environment and Development
UNI	União das Nações Indígenas—Union of Indigenous Nations
WGBH	PBS television affiliate in Boston, Massachusetts

Acknowledgments

I could not have written this book without the example and help of friends and colleagues in Brazil, the United States, and other countries who have dedicated themselves to defending the human rights of Brazil's most vulnerable people. Among the many who have inspired me are Claudia Andujar, Vilma Barban, Valéria de Brito, Larry Cox, Pedro Wilson Guimarães, Maria José Jaime, Michael Mary Nolan CSC, Iara Pietricovsky, Ana de Souza Pinto, William Reinhard OMI, Fr. Ricardo Rezende, Joe Rozansky OFM, Herbert de Souza (Betinho), Sr. Rebecca Spires and Marcos Terena.

Organizations that provided indispensable assistance to me included the Pro-Yanomami Commission (CCPY), Missionary Indigenist Council (CIMI), the Roraima Indigenous Council (CIR), the Pastoral Land Commission (CPT), the Socio-Environmental Institute (ISA), the National Human Rights Movement (MNDH), the Rainforest Foundation, Survival International, and Amnesty International (especially the Brazil team at the International Secretariat).

Thanks go also to the following people who consented to be interviewed: Bruce Albert, Claudia Andujar, Ana Valéria Araújo, Dr. Ulisses Confalonieri, Dep. Salomão Cruz, Dr. Deise Francisco, Kanyonk Kayapó, Marco Lazarin, leaders of the Pataxó Hã-Hã-Hãe and Xucuru peoples, Sérgio Leitão, Roberto Liebgott, Bishop Aldo Mongiano, Paulinho Payakan, Dr. Marcos Pellegrini, Alcida Rita Ramos, Aurélio Rios, Dr. Douglas Rodrigues, Dep. Elton Rohnelt, Márcio Santilli, and Marcos Terena.

Several anthropologists have helped me tread unfamiliar ground, *quebrando o galho* (breaking the branch), as the Brazilians say. Terence Turner's dedication to indigenous people and his substantive efforts on their behalf have profoundly influenced and heartened me; he responded generously to many requests for help, advice, and information. Gail Goodwin Gomez gave me the idea for the book and encouraged me along the way. Alcida Ramos, Bruce Albert, Marco Lazarin, and Gilberto Azanha shared their insights about indigenous people. I am also grateful to Thomas Holloway for reading a chapter draft. Any errors in this book are my own responsibility.

Friends have shown me great kindness. Margrit de Marez Oyens of Rio de Janeiro has offered crucial moral support over the years. Jo-Marie Griesgraber helped at a critical moment. Other friends who have provided hospitality and help include Moyra Ashford, Vilma Barban, Donna Hurwitz, Maria José Jaime, Jan Rocha, and Alison Sutton.

Berta Ribeiro, to whose memory the book is dedicated, made a distinguished career as an interpreter of indigenous material culture. She was born in Romania in 1924. After migrating to Brazil in the 1930s, she and her family experienced great hardship and political persecution. Her father was deported to Europe and died in the Holocaust. As a teenager she was left to fend for herself in São Paulo. This period was so painful to recall that fifty years later she could not bear to discuss it.

In 1948 she began working with the renowned anthropologist Darcy Ribeiro. That year she accompanied him to Kadiweu, Kaiwá, and Terena villages in southern Mato Grosso. The couple did field work with the Kadiweu for about eight months. In 1951 they did research in Kaingang and Xokleng villages in Paraná and Santa Catarina.

Berta Ribeiro received a bachelor's degree in geography and history in 1953 from the then University of the Federal District. During the 1950s she established herself as an expert in indigenous material culture at the Indian Museum and the National Museum in Rio de Janeiro. When Darcy Ribeiro moved to the new capital of Brasília in 1958, to establish the federal university there, she went with him. The couple continued their collaboration with *The Indians and Civilization* and *The Americas and Civilization*.

In 1964, when a military regime took over the Brazilian government, Darcy Ribeiro was one of the first opponents to be jailed. After publication of *The Americas and Civilization* was suspended and all copies of the book were destroyed in 1968, the couple went into exile in Uruguay, Venezuela, Chile, and Peru. Berta Ribeiro returned to Brazil in 1974 and continued working on indigenous material culture. She completed her Ph.D. in anthropology at the University of São Paulo in 1980, at age fifty-six.

The 1980s marked the peak of her career as a researcher and teacher. She published eight books and some fifty articles; participated in innumerable working groups, seminars, and congresses; did field research; worked at the Indian Museum; and supervised graduate students at the Federal University of Rio de Janeiro (UFRJ).

In the midst of all this activity, she found time to organize the exhibition "Amazônia Urgente: Cinco Séculos de História e Ecologia" (Essential Amazon: Five Centuries of History and Ecology) and produce a 270-page guide. The exhibition opened at the Brazilian Congress in 1989. During the 1992 Earth Summit, the exhibition was displayed in a subway station in downtown Rio, where thousands of people saw it.

Berta Ribeiro did field work with indigenous peoples in the Upper and Middle Xingu, Mato Grosso, Pará, and the Upper Rio Negro. Her most beautiful work is the lavishly illustrated bilingual book, *Arte Indígena, Linguagem Visual/Indigenous Art, Visual Language* (1989). Her other books include *O Índio na Cultura Brasileira* (The Indian in Brazilian Culture) and *Diário do Xingu* (Xingu Diary).

Berta Ribeiro not only studied indigenous people, she collaborated with them as equals and did everything she could to defend their interests. A scrupulous and ethical scholar and a steadfast friend, she inspired the respect and deep affection of the people of many cultures who were privileged to know her.

Brazil's Indians and the Onslaught of Civilization

Introduction

MAY 1992—A WARM AND GOLDEN AUTUMN IN BRAZIL.
For some reason, the state government of Rio de Janeiro has provided
the grounds of a *manicômio*—a prison farm for the criminally insane—to
the organizers of the international indigenous conference. The farm is
located on the periphery of Rio, not far from Riocentro, the convention
center that serves as the site of the United Nations Conference on Environment and Development (UNCED), also known as the Earth Summit.

Indians from central Brazil arrived weeks ago, to build a *maloca* (communal house) of timber and palm thatch. The maloca is about sixty feet
long, meticulously finished, and very photogenic. But its entry is rather
small, and only men seem to go in and out.

Across from the maloca is the center of conference activity, a large shelter thatched halfway down to the ground, where indigenous people from all
over the world meet in formal sessions for five days. Mapuches from Chile
chat with Sami from Finland; a Zuni from New Mexico gives an interview
to a Brazilian journalist while a British photographer snaps Guarani danc-
ers in elaborate feather headdresses. Many of the sessions feature dancing,
rather than talking, and some of the sessions are closed to nonindigenous
people. Language is a problem, since there are not enough translators to
go around, and electronic translation is out of the question. Perhaps that is
why dancing becomes such an important part of the meetings: For many of
the participants, it is the most efficient and eloquent means of communicat-
ing across linguistic and cultural barriers.

The Brazilian Indians tend not to go to the sessions for South American
Indians, which are conducted in Spanish. Besides, the meeting participants
are drafting written documents, and many of the Brazilian Indians are il-

4

Kayapó Indians demonstrating in Brasília. Photo by Beto Ricardo, courtesy of Instituto Sócioambiental.

literate, or barely literate, in Portuguese. For them, words written on a piece of paper are not important, and spending hours arguing over phrases holds no interest. They talk quietly with one another or with nonindigenous visitors until it is time to dance.

One afternoon Davi Kopenawa takes the floor. His translator announces that he and a young warrior will perform the most sacred and important of Yanomami dances, to fight evil spirits. Davi pushes powder into a thin, yard-long wooden tube. The young warrior wears delicate feather decorations on his arms and ears and a red woven loincloth. At a signal from Davi he puts the end of the tube to his nose. Davi blows the powder through the tube as the young man inhales. I feel I am watching something I should not be seeing, something intimate. The crowd quiets as the young warrior dances and chants for about twenty minutes.

As he dances, a Venezuelan journalist steps into the circle and films him with a video camera, sometimes moving directly into his path, thrusting the camera into his face. His actions seem blasphemous, although the dancer, deep in trance, seems oblivious to the intruder. For a few moments we were journeying to a far-off place with the dancer, but now we are pushed back into a meaning-starved world without respect or compunction, the world some of us traveled thousands of miles to escape. The audience gasps, then mutters resentfully, but the warrior keeps dancing. He is confronting the enemies of us all.

At the end of the gathering, some of the participants produce a one-page declaration in English, Spanish, and Portuguese that reaffirms indigenous demands for basic human rights, especially land rights. It is presented to the press and, perhaps, to some of the government delegates at the Riocentro. More important is the gathering itself, a manifestation of indigenous solidarity that defines what the diverse participants have in common: their identity as the original inhabitants of whatever land they come from; their denunciation of the terrible persecutions they have suffered for their differentness; their connection with what those estranged from nature call nature; and their insistence on enduring.

A few days later, Paulinho Payakan's face appears on the cover of Brazil's leading news magazine. Above the painful close-up of his unsmiling face is a bright red headline: "The Savage." Payakan has been accused of raping a young white woman in the frontier town of Redenção, Pará. That night on nationwide television, Payakan somewhat sheepishly says, "I did it, but I can't remember because I was drunk." Is it coincidental that this story appears on the day the Earth Summit begins?

Despite having met Payakan, Davi and many other Brazilian Indians and followed their stories, I am an outsider to all this. A middle-class kid from Philadelphia, I became an anthropologist but did not study Indians. Instead I did research on urban elites. After almost two years' field research in Rio in 1978 and 1979, I kept returning to the big cities, in love with the community movements that were trying to transform Brazil. The Brazil I came to know was not beaches, carnival, and *futebol* but a darker world of social and economic injustice on a massive scale—and the determined people who were struggling to change it.

By the mid-1980s I realized that to understand urban Brazil, I had to understand rural Brazil. My travels took me to daub-and-wattle shacks in the northeastern backlands, indigenous villages in the Amazon and the rainforest near Xapuri, Acre, where Chico Mendes waged his fatal battle on behalf of the rubber tappers and the forests that provided their sustenance.

Back in Washington, D.C., I met indigenous leaders who were traveling the world to call attention to the situation of their people in Brazil. The hot summers of 1987 and 1988 spurred international concern about Amazon deforestation as a contributor to global warming. Politically canny environmentalists touted the Indians as protectors of the rainforests. Meanwhile, coalitions of nongovernmental organizations (NGOs) pressured Northern governments and banks to stop lending money to Brazil and other developing countries for environmentally destructive "mega-projects."

Early in 1988 Paulinho Payakan came to Washington for the first time, to denounce Brazilian hydroelectric projects that, if funded by the World Bank, would flood the homeland of his people, the Kayapó. Later that year, on a trip to Belém, at the mouth of the Amazon, I met Payakan and Darrell Posey, an American anthropologist then living in Brazil. Payakan seemed guarded, uncomfortable, suspicious. The normally ebullient Posey suddenly found himself in a great deal of trouble after accompanying the two Kayapó to the United States and translating for them when they visited the World Bank. Along with Payakan and another young Kayapó leader, he was indicted under the Brazilian Foreigners Law, a grim relic of the military dictatorship. After an international campaign, the charges were dropped, but Posey's life changed greatly. He left his job in Brazil and went on to Oxford University, to work on the more general issue of intellectual property rights for indigenous peoples.

I wrote an article about Posey's troubles for the American Anthropological Association's newsletter, and other articles about what was going on in Brazil for the publication of the Brazil Network, a small NGO I coordinated for almost three years. Through all these activities I became familiar with the Brazil of land conflicts, death squads, and environmental devastation.

The Brazilian activists I encountered kept asking, "If you go home and write about us, what good will that do us?" One can never be sure what effect one's work will have. But it is clear that the hundreds of books, articles, Urgent Action Appeals, and other documents published during the past two decades have helped Brazil's indigenous people in their struggle to survive and preserve their traditional ways of life. The resulting international attention and pressure have made a positive difference to the Kayapó, the Yanomami, and other groups.

Nobody has expressed this more eloquently than Davi Kopenawa, who has traveled the world on behalf of his people. In Rio in 1992, he told film-maker Geoffrey O'Connor:

> People a long way from here hear what we say and support us. They really support us. You people here [filming] are also helping us. If we weren't supported like this, we would think, "Are we going to die?" That's what we wonder: "Are we all going to disappear?" And a lot of white people take our words round the world. Many people heard these words; they became well known. The Brazilian government tried to hide us, but they can't do that anymore; our words are known everywhere. Help from the white world is important to us.

In October 1990 I went to London to work as a researcher for Amnesty International. For a year I toiled over the files of Brazil's threatened, the tortured, the killed, and the "disappeared." Working for Amnesty made me feel not only useful but accepted by the Brazilian activists I admired. As a result I met and collaborated with people to whom I had had no access before.

In the late 1980s, after traveling around the world with Raoni, a charismatic indigenous leader, the British rock star Sting had started the Rainforest Foundation to fulfill his promises to Raoni's people, the Kayapó of central Brazil. At the invitation of the foundation's director, I joined the foundation in October 1991. For the first time in my career I was working on indigenous issues and in frequent contact with indigenous people. The few Brazilian Indians I had met before were world travelers, and we met in New York, London, Brasilia, or Washington. Some had spent many years in cities and were far from their places and cultures of origin. Their constituencies were other indigenous leaders, professional activists, and supporting intellectuals, in Brazil and beyond.

During my year at the Rainforest Foundation, I met Indians in Brasilia who still lived in reserves and traveled only rarely to the city. In preparing for UNCED, I read a great deal about the Kayapó and other Brazilian indigenous groups, met prominent Kayapó including Raoni and Payakan, and learned about the international indigenous movement. As a result of these experiences, I came to appreciate how ingeniously and persistently indigenous people strive to protect and preserve their culture in the face of great obstacles and dangers. And I started to work on this book.

In 1993 I visited an indigenous reserve in the Western Amazon as an Amnesty International volunteer. The journey seemed long and complicated, though nothing compared to the marathon treks of some anthropologists: a plane from Manaus to the frontier town of Tabatinga, a 45-minute motorboat ride over the unexpectedly rough waters of the Solimões (upper Amazon) River to the town of Benjamin Constant, another boat ride on the Javari River to the Ticuna reserve, and long walks along slippery tree trunks and muddy paths to four Ticuna villages. There I visited the survivors of a 1988 massacre, committed by the hired guns of a Brazilian logger greedy for Ticuna land, in which fourteen Ticuna, including several children, were killed. Twelve years after the massacre, those responsible finally were brought to justice in the second case of genocide to reach the Brazilian courts.

The Ticuna were hospitable and kind, but communication was difficult. The widows and mothers of the massacre victims did not speak Portuguese, so my Ticuna hosts (who lived in town) interpreted. Each time I met one of the survivors, I shook her hand; each survivor giggled, whether out of embarrassment or amusement I could not tell.

After a long day of visits and walks between villages, we returned to Benjamin Constant. The leading news story on television that night was the massacre of sixteen Yanomami on Brazil's frontier with Venezuela. At five the next morning I telephoned Amnesty in London with the news. "Oh, we already know about that," my colleague said. "CNN called for our comment."

The massacre had happened about six weeks earlier, and it had taken all that time for the report to reach the outside world, via a letter from a Brazilian nurse who lived and worked in Yanomami territory. The justice minister had thought it important enough to make the announcement himself on nationwide television—quite a contrast with earlier government reaction (or lack thereof) to the plight of the Yanomami. The ensuing flurry of government activity resulted from constant international pressure on behalf of the Yanomami over several years. In the case of the Ticuna and scores of other indigenous groups, however, international attention has been sporadic or transitory. Consequently, most of Brazil's indigenous people live in a state of silent deprivation. When they do call for help, few hear them.

In 2002 I returned to Brazil to find out what had happened to its indigenous groups since the publication of the first edition of this book. I was aware of important events, like the 1997 burning of Galdino dos Santos, a Pataxó Hã-Hã-Hãe activist, as he slept in a bus shelter in Brasilia, and the indigenous protest in 2000 against the official commemorations of the 500th anniversary of the Portuguese arrival in Brazil.

But other news, not widely publicized outside the country, seemed equally important: Brazil's 2000 census reported that the indigenous population (that is, the number of Brazilians identifying themselves as Indians) had doubled since 1990. Demarcations of indigenous areas with international support had increased the amount of land under indigenous control to 12 percent of the national territory. Indigenous groups throughout Brazil were organizing associations, creating sustainable development projects, fielding candidates for public office, opening schools with indigenous teachers, managing health services, and carrying out many other activities that would have seemed inconceivable just a few years before. Brazilian indigenous groups were entering a new and promising phase of activism, mobilization, and self-governance.

Meanwhile, the original subjects of this book, the Kayapó and Yanomami, had become emblematic figures for millions of people throughout the world. Thanks to Sting's efforts, the Kayapó leader Raoni became internationally famous in the late 1980s, along with his kinsman Payakan. The Yanomami are well known to those who have read Napoleon Chagnon's book, *Yanomamö: The Fierce People*, as an assigned text in anthropology courses since the late 1960s. In recent years Davi Kopenawa has journeyed to North America and Europe to call for action to save his people, whose plight became generally known after 40,000 gold miners invaded their lands in the late 1980s.

Many other indigenous groups in Brazil face similar threats to their cultural and physical survival, but the Kayapó and the Yanomami have gained the world's attention and sympathy. I try to show how and why in this book. For the second edition, I have also included information about other, less-known indigenous groups that are breaking new ground in the defense of their land and their traditional way of life.

Many anthropologists and other scholars have spent their careers studying indigenous people in Brazil and other countries. Without their work, the rest of us would know almost nothing about these groups, which might have disappeared without notice. The information and interpretations the anthropologists make available to the world undoubtedly help indigenous people in their struggle to survive and prosper. In researching this book, I have had the benefit of reading their articles and books, which have strongly influenced me, and of talking with them about their experiences and ideas.

Some of these scholars have become activists because of their sense of personal commitment to the people they study. They have moved from the classroom and the library to the arenas of political and economic power. Their dedication to both knowledge and action has inspired me. For example, Terence Turner (Cornell University) has studied the Kayapó for more than thirty years and has helped them become video chroniclers of their culture and history. Bruce Albert (French Institute of Scientific Research for Development in Cooperation) found the survivors of the 1993 Yanomami massacre and recorded their account of the killings. At some personal risk, Alcida Ramos (University of Brasilia) delivered emergency medical aid to the Yanomami. She and Kenneth Taylor, a British anthropologist, developed the first plan to create a Yanomami reserve in the early 1970s. She is now president of the Pro-Yanomami Commission. Darrell Posey risked his career to help the Kayapó gain international attention to their opposition to hydroelectric projects. Many others have given various kinds of material help. Some have testified as expert witnesses before congressional or parliamentary committees in the United States, Brazil, and Europe. Still others continue to gather, interpret, and publish information about indigenous people despite great practical and political difficulties. Their efforts reinforce the work of nonanthropologists, such as Claudia Andujar, who have dedicated themselves to defending indigenous interests.

Often the indigenous activists who visit us seem to stand alone against an uncomprehending and hostile world. But they could not reach us to convey their messages without the support of people like these, who share their concerns and their determination. They, too, are part of the story.

This book is neither a traditional ethnography, based on prolonged field research in an indigenous community, nor a theoretical work. It is, rather, an experiment in applied anthropology that draws on a wide variety of primary and secondary sources. The extensive ethnographic literature about the Kayapó and Yanomami has provided a great deal of detailed information that I have used to chronicle the history of the two groups. I have also consulted books, films and articles on development in the Amazon and other regions of Brazil, human rights reports from international organizations such as Amnesty International, Internet postings from indigenous and solidarity organizations in Brazil and other countries, and my own notes on more than a decade's work with Brazilian grassroots movements. Rather than focus narrowly on indigenous groups, as if they were self-contained, autonomous cultures, I seek to show their inevitable, crucial connections to the surrounding society and the rest of the world.

In this book I use the terms "North" and "South" to discuss developed and developing countries. "First World" and "Third World" lost their currency and usefulness with the end of the Cold War (and the disappearance of the "Second World"). The "civilization" in the book's title is the result of two millennia of colonization, imperialism, and globalization—a world economic, social, and political system that links accountants in Tokyo, Aborigines in the Australian outback, mahogany trees in the Brazilian Amazon, and mountain gorillas in Rwanda in a complex network of ideas, beliefs, hardware, software, weapons of mass destruction, and millions of other material objects. This civilization is not exactly western or eastern but has pretensions to universality.

To set the scene, chapter 1 surveys the dizzying changes that civilization has brought to the Amazon region. Road building, mining, ranching, logging, colonization, hydroelectric projects, deforestation, urban development—all came to the Amazon in a rush, and the results have overwhelmed both the environment and its traditional inhabitants. The region's indigenous people have become symbols of the most ancient ways of living in and with nature, even as they struggle to cope with and adjust to the modern world.

Our understanding of indigenous people (not to mention their understanding of us) is rooted in 500 years of tumultuous history. Chapter 2 examines some of the most important accounts—from the first description

of indigenous Brazilians in 1500 to twenty-first century scholarly and jour-
nalistic interpretations—that have defined them for the outside world.

The Kayapó have been in contact with outsiders for hundreds of years.
Chapter 3 recounts the history of their struggle to survive civilization. Their
persistence in preserving their traditional culture, their warlike behavior,
colorful appearance, and political exploits have made them especially visible. Their deals with gold miners, which made them wealthy, also had serious negative consequences, including mercury contamination of their land,
air, and water. As the richest indigenous group in Brazil, the Kayapó stand
at a crossroads, as they try to decide what kind of development will benefit
them most.

Chapter 4 recounts the rise and fall of the Kayapó leader Payakan,
who came into contact with whites as a teenage worker on a road-building crew in the Amazon. Throughout the 1980s he led young warriors in
symbolic confrontations with the Brazilian government. As a result of the
deals he and other leaders helped broker, the Kayapó became Brazil's richest indigenous group. He became famous as a world-traveling spokesman
for environmental conservation. But his career as an international figure
crashed in 1992, when he was accused of rape. Convicted in 1998, he lost his
final appeal in 2002. Sadly, Payakan's downward trajectory is a hazard for
indigenous people who become leaders of their people.

The Yanomami, whose history is recounted in chapter 5, are best known
as "the fierce people" because of Chagnon's famous ethnography. Despite
their alleged ferocity, they have become easy targets of disease, invasion,
and exploitation. Although they are often described as the largest uncontacted indigenous group in South America, scholarly research shows
that they have been in indirect contact with the outside world for a very
long time. Overwhelming contact began in the mid- and late 1980s, when
40,000 gold miners (twice the Yanomami's total number in Brazil and Venezuela) invaded their territory. Some 15 percent of the Yanomami may have
died of disease or as a result of conflicts with miners from 1987 to 1992. The
worst single incident of violence was the July 1993 Haximu massacre, when
Brazilian miners killed sixteen Yanomami men, women, and children just
over the Venezuelan border. Because of their continuing vulnerability to
contact diseases and other assaults, the Yanomami's prospects seem less
promising than the Kayapó's.

In sharp contrast to Payakan stands another indigenous leader, Davi Kopenawa, the subject of chapter 6, who has become famous through his international tours. Davi is a shaman who speaks simply but powerfully in prophecies, myths, and oracles. His poetic predictions of doom have had a hypnotic effect on audiences worried about environmental degradation. Supporting Davi are Brazilian and other anthropologists, medical professionals, and activists who lobbied and worked for a Yanomami reserve in northern Brazil for more than twenty years.

One of the most influential anthropologists of the twentieth century, Napoleon Chagnon made his reputation on his work with the Yanomami. Various editions of his book have sold millions of copies since 1968. But in 2000, journalist Patrick Tierney's book, *Darkness in El Dorado*, brought Chagnon's reputation and research into question. Chapter 7 tells the story of the scandal that Tierney's book triggered and its implications for future research on the Yanomami and other indigenous groups.

Many other indigenous groups besides the Kayapó and the Yanomami are struggling to defend their interests and protect their territories. Chapter 8 examines two groups in Brazil's Northeast, the country's poorest region, where Indians encountered Europeans first and have had the longest experience of contact with the outside world. Since the 1980s, they have intensified their efforts to reclaim their identity and their land, leading Brazil's indigenous groups into a new phase of mobilization.

Although similar in many respects, the histories of the Kayapó and Yanomami differ in important ways that may determine their destinies. Both are part of a much larger struggle for cultural and physical survival. The final chapter looks at this struggle in the light of the evolution of indigenous peoples and our species in general.

A final note: Indigenous people continue to seek outside help in defending their cultures, territories, rights, and interests. In association with environmental and human rights organizations, they have taken to the Internet to inform the global public about their struggle to survive. Readers who want to help can find information about indigenous activism and appeals for solidarity in many sites on the World Wide Web.

1 / Setting the Scene

DURING THE PAST TWO DECADES, THE KAYAPÓ AND THE Yanomami have become the most famous of about 200 indigenous groups in Brazil. Painted, befeathered, and armed with stout clubs, the Kayapó have strutted across the world stage, while the Yanomami have been portrayed as once-proud savages reduced to helpless victims of white men's greed. Why and how did these two groups gain the world's attention? To understand, we need to see them in historical, political, and economic context.

Modernization, Military Style

In 1964, a military regime took over Brazil after more than a decade of elected civilian government. Armed with a modernizing, authoritarian, anti-communist ideology, the military tried to transform Brazil from a predominantly rural country dominated by big landowners exporting natural resources into an industrialized, urbanized world power. They partly succeeded. In 1950, 70 percent of Brazil's population lived in the countryside; in 1985, when the military retired to the barracks, 70 percent lived in urban areas. By that time Brazil boasted the world's eighth largest industrial economy (and the developing world's largest international debt). At the beginning of the twenty-first century, Brazil exported steel, airplanes, automobile engines, precision tools, and shoes, as well as the traditional agricultural commodities, coffee and sugar. But social scientists classified almost half its 170 million people as poor or indigent; the richest 10 percent of the population held 45 percent of the country's income, while the poorest 50 percent held less than 2 percent of income (Roque et al. n.d.: 1).

"Despite the economic growth of the past half-century, two-thirds of the population live below the officially defined poverty level of roughly $200 a month. . . . According to a 1995 World Bank study, Brazil has the most unequal distribution of wealth of any country in the world. Brazil remains a rich country full of poor people" (Eakin 1997: 5).

From the 1960s on, Brazil's generals and technocrats were determined to develop the vast interior. In their mind's eye they saw endless soybean fields, thousands of grazing cattle, sugar mills, light industry, burgeoning towns, highways, dams, mines, and tree plantations—a panorama as pros-

Indigenous territories in Brazil, 2002. Courtesy of Instituto Sócioambiental.

perous and civilized as the U.S. Middle West. The reality was very different: interminable, impenetrable rainforests, a handful of unpaved roads, hundreds of unnavigable rivers, a few thousand backwoodsmen and their families clinging to the shores, and a few thousand Indians living in the woods.

After 1964 the military persuaded the World Bank, the Inter-American Development Bank (IDB), and Northern governments, corporations, and banks to support their ambitious development plans. The Brazilian government then offered generous subsidies to domestic and foreign companies to open up the Amazon, created hundreds of state-controlled enterprises, built giant hydroelectric projects and interstate highways in the remotest parts of the country, and sent hundreds of thousands of migrants to settle along the roads. One of the military rulers touted the project as "a land without men for men without land."

The Indigenous Presence

But Brazil's interior was not empty. The Kayapó, the Yanomami, and many other indigenous groups already lived there. The Yanomami had little direct contact with outsiders, but the Kayapó had been dealing and warring with Brazilians for more than a hundred years. When roads reached both groups in the late 1960s, Davi Kopenawa and Paulinho Payakan, both of whom later became internationally famous, went to work on the construction crews. Thus they had their first sustained contact with Brazilians, improved the Portuguese they had learned from missionaries, and picked up the rudiments of Brazilian culture. The roads also brought disease, prostitution, malnutrition, environmental degradation, crime, and a host of other ills to the Indians. They had to learn quickly how to cope, or die.

Many did die. Davi's mother succumbed to disease brought to her village by missionaries. Often, half of "pacified" Indian villages would die in epidemics soon after contact with Brazilians. "Hostile" groups, like the Kayapó, had a better survival rate. Nonetheless, the entire Kayapó population decreased from around 4,000 in 1900 to about 1,500 in 1960. By 2000 their numbers had bounced back up, past 4,000.

Through a series of dramatic struggles with Brazilians, the Kayapó found ways to survive and prosper. The more numerous Yanomami have experienced genocide and also survived, but it remains to be seen if they will manage to preserve their identity and traditional way of life. Many other indigenous groups have not survived, either physically or culturally. Decimated, pushed off their land, or surrounded by impinging outsiders, they migrated to urban slums or faded into the miserable "rural proletariat." But at the beginning of the twenty-first century, some indigenous groups, known as "resurgent Indians," were reclaiming their traditional identity after decades or even centuries of invisibility.

Development for Some

The development of Brazil's interior has been apparently chaotic, with violent conflicts over land; guerrilla warfare; assassinations of peasant leaders by hired gunmen; large-scale devastation of virgin forests by settlers, loggers, and miners; uncontrolled urban growth; and outbreaks of contagious diseases.

One of the most famous examples of developmental disaster is the Polonoroeste Project, funded by the World Bank in the early 1980s, when hundreds of thousands of migrants went to the frontier state of Rondônia and cut or burned three-quarters of its forests. After cultivating crops that exhausted the soil along the highways, they moved deeper into the forests, repeating the same disastrous pattern of slashing and burning. This kind of swidden agriculture may work on a small scale, but not when thousands of people do it on hundreds of thousands of acres of deforested soil unsuited to cultivation.

Across the Amazon, ranching, mining, and logging have had massively destructive effects. Both the Kayapó and the Yanomami have confronted thousands of wildcat gold miners (garimpeiros) who have invaded their territories. As many as 300,000 garimpeiros are said to be wandering through the Amazon region, living and working in miserable conditions. They pan for gold, blasting out riverbanks with high-pressure hoses and separating out the gold with highly toxic mercury. The consequences include deforestation, erosion, flooding, violence, malaria and other diseases, and mercury contamination of soil, water, air, and the food chain (MacMillan 1995).

Logging, mining, and ranching destroy biodiversity, ruin the land for traditional uses, and cause conflicts inside indigenous groups, as some leaders sell off resources while others resist such deal making. These conflicts divide groups at the very moment when they need to unite if they are to protect themselves and their way of life from outside threats to their cultural and physical integrity.

Though apparently chaotic, this kind of "development" does have an internal logic. In the short term, the few who take big risks to invest capital can reap big rewards. Those with economic, political, and social power have a tremendous advantage over the powerless. Force, impunity, fraud, and corruption flourish. Long-term consequences seem irrelevant, though eventually the crash must come. In a larger sense, it seems as if nothing ever changes: The rich win, the poor lose, at a terrible cost in resources and lives. This "boom-bust cycle" has endured throughout Brazil's 500-year history. It explains the coexistence of elaborate mansions and wretched hovels on the same frontier streets, in towns where 10 percent or less of the population has electricity, drinkable water, or sewage pipes.

The military wanted to break the boom-bust cycle and establish permanent development in the interior by building infrastructure, settling thousands on the land, cultivating vast areas, and establishing urban centers. Unlike the U.S. midwestern prairie, however, much of the Amazon's soil is not fertile enough to feed millions. The costs of bringing electricity and natural gas to its cities are high. Severe environmental damage and disappointing outcomes have made investing in ambitious mega-projects very risky in the long term.

Nevertheless, Brazil's military has held onto the mega-project model of development. In a 2002 poll by the World Wildlife Fund, military respondents insisted that mineral extraction and hydroelectric power were the principal economic resources of the Amazon region. The other elite respondents—businessmen, scientists, lawmakers, and journalists—saw the forests as the most important Amazon resource. The poll came out after publication of scientific studies showing that in 2000, destruction of Amazon forests had jumped to the highest level in five years (Bugge 2001).

International Intervention

Mega-project development requires large infusions of outside capital. The nationalistic military had an ambivalent relationship with international backers, who wanted a certain amount of control over the way their loans were spent. For example, in the early 1980s the Inter-American Development Bank placed conditions on an Amazon road-building project that included protection of indigenous groups living near the highway. When the military failed to comply, the IDB withdrew its funding under pressure from environmental organizations that were monitoring the project. Meanwhile, international human rights organizations kept denouncing military repression, which included torture, arbitrary imprisonment, extrajudicial executions, and disappearances in the cities and the countryside.

After the dictatorship ended and as Brazil struggled to pay the interest on its enormous foreign debt, international organizations effectively pressured the World Bank to institute environmental protection policies. International solidarity groups supported Chico Mendes in his crusade to protect Brazil's rainforests and the rubber tappers who lived and worked in them.

Brazilian nationalists inside and outside the government resisted these pressures. As the Cold War waned, they abandoned the military's anti-communist rhetoric to accuse Northern governments and nongovernmental organizations of conspiring, for economic reasons, to prevent Brazil from becoming a world power. There were secret plans, they claimed, for the United Nations to invade the Amazon under cover of protecting the Yanomami Indians from genocide. The foreigners were plotting to set up a puppet Yanomami state on the northern borders. "Internationalization of the Amazon" became the nationalists' rallying cry. A report by the Superior War College in the late 1980s named environmentalists, anthropologists, and missionaries as threats to national security.

When the military left power in 1985, it tried to ensure its control over Amazonia through an ambitious program called *Calha Norte* (northern headwaters), which would "Brazilianize" a 6,500-kilometer-long, 150-kilometer-wide strip along its northern borders with five countries (Rabben 1990). Troops would be based near the border, and migrants would be encouraged to settle there. A few million dollars were secretly budgeted to start up the program; troops were stationed in Yanomami territory. The 1992 demarcation of the Yanomami reserve seems to have forestalled large-scale agricultural development of the remote, mountainous area, but in 1997 the Brazilian and Venezuelan governments signed agreements to build highways and develop hydroelectric projects near the reserve. And in 2002, the Yanomami complained that homesteaders, loggers, and ranchers were invading their territory, as they had invaded so many other indigenous lands.

In the mid-1990s, Asian logging companies started buying Brazilian firms and cutting thousands of acres of forest in the Amazon. Despite government conservation measures, the rate of deforestation in Brazil increased significantly after the 1992 Earth Summit. In the late 1990s it leveled somewhat, but in 2002, Brazilian forests were "disappearing at a rate of more than 6,000 square miles a year" (Rohter 2002b). According to Brazilian sources, about 9,000 square miles of Amazonian rainforest were destroyed in 2001; this figure may not include losses resulting from selective logging (*Estado de São Paulo* 2002). Forest burning in the Amazon (to clear land for export crop production or pastures) has led to explosive growth in Brazil's carbon emissions, making the country "one of the 10 top polluters in the world" (Rohter 2002b). About 15 percent of the Amazon forest has been cut or burned in the past thirty years.

As a result of many years of pressure and criticism by international environmental and human-rights organizations allied with local activists, the World Bank and other multilateral development institutions now hesitate to directly lend Brazil the billions of dollars necessary to bring mega-projects to fruition. The Brazilian government also seeks investment from corporations and private banks and makes agreements with neighboring countries to build projects that have been on the drawing board for decades. Some of these projects may never materialize. Both international and local groups that defend the interests of Indians, other "traditional populations," and the environment keep mobilizing to prevent them from proceeding. But others go ahead and cause tremendous devastation.

The same pattern is followed again and again, as state or federal agencies or private companies seek to push through projects without doing the required environmental and social impact studies (or in spite of their findings). Grassroots groups and nongovernmental organizations then challenge the plans in the courts. An example occurred in 2002, when the federal environmental protection agency, IBAMA, issued a license for construction of the Urucu–Porto Velho natural gas and oil pipeline. According to environmental and community groups, IBAMA failed to take into consideration an isolated indigenous group and concerns of local communities and organizations. . . . The gas pipeline and its access road will run over 500 kilometers from Porto Velho to the center of the state of Amazonas. They will have an enormous impact upon an area of tropical rainforest that until now has been one of the most isolated and inaccessible regions of the central Amazon. . . .

Environmentalists and grassroots groups from the region are deeply concerned that the license fails to incorporate issues raised in public hearings in the affected area. . . . one isolated indigenous group and other traditional forest communities could be displaced or eliminated; ranchers and settlers moving into the region by the road would clear much of the forest; and environmental impact analysis failed to analyze feasible alternatives for transporting gas to Porto Velho that would not necessitate construction of a road.

Brazilian organizations including the Amazon Working Group (GTA), the Coordination of Indigenous Organizations of the Brazilian Amazon (COIAB), the Pastoral Land Commission (CPT), Friends of the Earth and others are calling for emails and faxes to the President of Brazil to oppose its licensing. (Amazon Alliance 2002)

Indians in the Way

Over the years, the Kayapó and the Yanomami have played central roles in the fight to stop what Brazilian officials used to call "the march of progress." These indigenous groups have provided a model of resistance to others. As far back as the 1970s, Kayapó warriors patrolled the borders of their territory with shortwave radios and did not hesitate to attack (and sometimes kill) invaders. When the Brazilian military tried to dump nuclear waste on Kayapó territory in the mid-1980s, the Indians reacted strongly and made national headlines; the military backed down.

In a series of highly publicized struggles involving "ritualized warfare" with federal officials, violent actions against nonindigenous invaders, and strategic alliances with sympathetic outsiders, the Kayapó became nationally and internationally known as determined, fearless, intimidating defenders of their own interests. Over the years they have acquired considerable economic and political clout, so that the Brazilian government could not ignore their wishes as it planned the development of their region. Few other indigenous groups have managed to play such a forceful and effective role, though many also face invasion, destruction of their habitat, health problems caused by contact, lack of access to social services, and other serious problems.

Preoccupied by intervillage disputes, the Yanomami were no match for invading hordes of gold miners armed with guns, airplanes, and killer diseases in the late 1980s. They have survived attempted genocide with the help of concerned outsiders, from Brazilian anthropologists to local environmental and human rights groups in New Jersey, Switzerland, Japan, and many other places. Their defenders struggle to keep the Yanomami in the world spotlight and find support from international donors for projects to protect their health and educate their children.

Despite all the pressure from outsiders, however, the Brazilian government failed to stop garimpeiros from re-entering Yanomami and other indigenous territories in numbers large enough to pose a threat to the Indians. In 1997, the Pro-Yanomami Commission (CCPY), a nongovernmental organization, estimated that 3,000 miners were working in the Yanomami reserve. Allegedly, more miners entered the reserve during the year, after reading newspaper reports that the Congress was about to pass legislation opening indigenous areas to mineral exploration (*Folha de Boa Vista* 1997). The $6 million that the Brazilian Congress had appropriated to expel the miners in 1996 were not used until November 1997 (CCPY 1997). Almost 400 Federal Police, army, air force, FUNAI, and IBAMA agents expelled only a few hundred miners and temporarily blocked thirty airstrips inside the Yanomami reserve. By 2002, after repeated government expulsion operations, the number of garimpeiros had slipped to fewer than 1,000. But if the world price of gold goes up, Yanomami territory again will be vulnerable to large-scale intrusions.

Meanwhile, the Brazilian government has to cope with strong pressure from the "Amazon bloc," Congress members from the Amazon states who defend the kind of development that makes Indians disappear. Responding to political pressure, in 1996 the justice minister promulgated new regulations making it possible for state governments and private interests to challenge the demarcation of indigenous reserves, even when signed by the president—as long as the demarcation had not been registered at the local land office.[1] More than 1,000 challenges were filed at FUNAI, the federal Indian protection agency, and not one was upheld. Later, however, the justice minister used the decree to question eight controversial demarcations or to reduce the size of some indigenous territories. Five years later, Decree 1775/96 remained on the books, and the former justice minister who had introduced it, now a Supreme Court judge, was using it to reduce the size of indigenous territories and put demarcations in doubt.

Indigenous advocates believe this decree was a response to demands from the Amazon bloc to roll back demarcations that threatened powerful regional interests' development plans. In 1997, a Brazilian Congress member claimed that the reduction of the Raposa/Serra do Sol reserve was part of a deal between the justice minister and Amazon bloc Congress members, in exchange for votes to change the Constitution to allow the reelection of Brazil's president (SEJUP 1997b).

International and Brazilian indigenous organizations protested loudly against Decree 1775/96. Amnesty International expressed concern that the decree was putting the safety of many indigenous communities at risk. After the European Parliament passed a resolution criticizing the decree, the justice minister traveled to Europe (especially to Germany, which has funded demarcation of scores of Brazilian indigenous reserves) to explain the policy. Reaction from the U.S. government was muted, but the U.S. Congressional Human Rights Caucus sent a letter questioning the decree to Brazil's president. Around the country, tension between Indians and outsiders remained high. Struggles over indigenous land continued and led to violence in every region of Brazil.

Other indigenous groups besides the Kayapó and Yanomami have moved to center stage since the 1990s. Crises have erupted among the Guarani-Kaiowá of Mato Grosso do Sul, the Pataxó of Bahia, the Krikati of Maranhão, the Nambikwara of Rondônia, all of whom feel threatened by the slowdown and uncertainty caused by Decree 1775/96. All have experienced violence by outsiders greedy for their land and resources.

In Brazil's Northeast, where the first contact between indigenous peoples and Europeans took place in 1500, Indians have long been invisible. Although respected anthropologists had declared them "extinct," they began to reassert themselves in the 1980s and 1990s, traveling to Brasilia to make claims for their traditional territories. In the late 1990s, these forgotten Indians achieved national and international visibility as their leaders were killed defending their land rights. Despite these losses, northeastern indigenous groups have continued to organize associations, campaigns, and other initiatives to reassert their identity and protect their territories.

In contrast, two of the Kayapó's three reserves are securely demarcated and cannot be challenged; the Yanomami reserve is also securely demarcated (though not safe from invasion, depredation, and congressional attempts to roll back the demarcation).[2] Although their problems in defending and developing their land may seem less dramatic and therefore gain less attention than they used to, the Kayapó and Yanomami find them no less pressing. Other indigenous groups have adopted the strategies these two groups use to survive.

Indigenous organizations are proliferating in Brazil as Indians acquire greater knowledge of how the society works. They range from local tribal associations to national solidarity organizations. For years Kayapó leaders from widely separated villages have been meeting whenever necessary to plan strategy, and some Kayapó communities have set up associations for sustainable development. Yanomami leaders from across their vast territory began meeting relatively recently. They rely on the assistance of CCPY, a group of Brazilian anthropologists and advocates, and the leadership of Davi Kopenawa, who is preparing others to follow his example. In these and other ways indigenous people are taking on the task of protecting their interests vis-à-vis the larger society. Because of their relatively small numbers and their lack of political and economic power, they will continue to need the support of sympathetic and concerned outsiders from Brazil and beyond.

The Kayapó and the Yanomami may not be "typical," but they have come to stand for Brazilian Indians and other threatened indigenous groups around the world. To understand what they have accomplished, what problems they confront, and what kind of help they seek, we will look more closely at their histories, the contrasting stories of two men who have represented them, their allies and enemies, and, finally, their prospects — and our own.

2 / In Search of the Other

BRAZIL'S 500-YEAR HISTORY BEGINS WITH AN ENCOUNTER on a beach, far from the homelands of the Kayapó and the Yanomami. In April 1500, Portuguese mariners landed on Brazil's northeastern coast and met a group of eighteen to twenty men on the shore. In a letter to the king of Portugal, Pero Vaz de Caminha described them as "reddish brown, with good faces and noses, well made. They go naked, with no covering, and they make no effort either to conceal or display their shameful parts; and they go about this with as much innocence as they have in showing their faces" (Caminha 1974: 7).[1]

Vaz de Caminha provided a detailed description of the Indians' decorations, hairstyles, and manners. Most significantly, "One of them laid eyes on the captain's gold chain, and began pointing to the earth and then to the chain, as if to tell us that there was gold in the earth. He also saw a silver candlestick and likewise pointed to the earth and then to the candlestick, as if they also had silver." The Portuguese saw what they wanted to see in the Indians' behavior.

Their first conclusion was that the Indians would easily be converted to Christianity "because these people are good and of good simplicity. . . . and He who brought us here, I believe, did not do so for no reason." Soon after this encounter, the Portuguese planted a cross on the shore and named the newfound land "The Island of the True Cross."

Later, the colony was renamed "Brasil," after the red dyewood that became its first principal export commodity. Gold and silver would not be discovered in quantity for another 200 years. Most of the Indians died before they could be converted, and the Portuguese did not take long to change their mind about their character. To the hard-bitten adventurers

Tupinambá family, from Jean de Léry, History of a Voyage to the Land of Brazil, Otherwise Called America, *Janet Whatley, editor/translator. Copyright © 1990 The Regents of the University of California.*

who plunged into Brazil's uncharted interior, Indians were "good" for slavery, death, or rape.

Early European encounters with indigenous people raised serious questions. Were the Indians descended from Adam? Were they really human beings?[2] Pope Paul III declared they were human in 1537, opening America to evangelization. Which of Noah's sons was their ancestor, then? Were they, like the sons of Ham, destined for slavery? European invaders operated on this assumption.

Portugal, France, Spain, and the Netherlands fought for control of Brazil, and they often used rival indigenous groups to fight their battles. In the 1550s, the French established a colony at what is now Rio de Janeiro and invited Huguenot missionaries to live and minister there. Jean de Léry, a Calvinist preacher, spent about two years in "Antarctic France" with the Indians before returning to Europe.

Léry's Ethnography

Léry later survived the horrors of religious war in France, which included Protestants and Catholics tearing one another's hearts out and eating them. Almost twenty years after his stay in Brazil, he published *History of a Voyage to the Land of Brazil, Otherwise Called America*. His account made the allegedly cannibalistic Indians seem charming, compared to the savage Europeans. It became one of the most important sources of information about Brazilian indigenous people, along with chronicles by the French Abbé Thévet and the German mercenary Hans Staden. Even twentieth-century anthropologists like Claude Lévi-Strauss cited Léry.

In rich and shocking detail, Léry described Tupinambá Indians ritually killing, cooking, and eating their enemies, but he was most concerned to portray them as human beings with both good and bad qualities. He frequently used the Indians for moralizing purposes, contrasting their virtues with the evils of Europeans, or fulminating against their lack of true religion. He also took pains to describe their physical characteristics, food, customs, and religion and to correct errors about them that were circulating in Europe. His scrupulous account can be seen as an early example of ethnography, in contrast to popular, fanciful tales of the marvels, monsters, and Arcadian innocence of the "brave new world."

The Tupinambá, he says, live long because they don't worry about the "things of this world." They don't "drink of those murky, pestilential springs, from which flow so many streams of mistrust, avarice, litigation, and squabbles, of envy and ambition, which eat away our bones, suck out our marrow, waste our bodies, and consume our spirits" (Léry 1990: 57).

He admired the Indians because they were valorous, generous, and virtuous:

> I have observed among them that just as they love those who are gay, joyful, and liberal, on the contrary they so hate those who are taciturn, stingy, and melancholy, that I can assure any who are sly, malicious, gloomy, niggardly, or who munch their bread alone in a corner, that they will never be welcome among our Tupinambá; for by their nature they detest such manner of folk. (ibid., 99)

Léry professed to miss the Indians, and he clearly liked them: "Even now it seems to me that I have them before my eyes, and I will forever have the idea and image of them in my mind" (ibid., 67).

Recounting a prebattle ritual, he says, "They sang so beautifully that I stood there transported with delight. Whenever I remember it, my heart trembles, and it seems their voices are still in my ears" (ibid., 144). An admirer of martial valor, he reports, "I have never taken so much pleasure . . . as I delighted then in seeing those savages do battle" (ibid., 118).

On the other hand, Léry condemned the Tupinambá for not accepting Christianity. "When men do not recognize their Creator, it is a result of their own wickedness," he says sternly. In his eyes, the Indians were responsible for their own salvation or damnation, and he even called them "a people accursed and abandoned by God." But he persisted in believing the Indians were "teachable."

While condemning polygamy, he admired co-wives' lack of jealousy. He praised their willingness to nurse their babies, instead of sending them to wet nurses as French women did.

Léry often used the Indians to censure French failings. He mentions the generosity of Indian hosts and adds, "The hypocritical welcomes of those over here who use only slippery speech for consolation of the afflicted is a far cry from the humanity of these people, whom nonetheless we call 'barbarians'" (ibid., 168).

In recent years anthropologists have argued over the reliability of Léry's and others' accounts of ritual cannibalism among the Tupinambá and other Brazilian indigenous groups; some have questioned the very existence of cannibalism in the New World. Considering Léry's scrupulousness, however, it seems unlikely that he invented his account, which Thévet and Staden independently confirmed. Twentieth-century anthropologists described other indigenous customs reported by the chroniclers that (unlike cannibalism) have survived until recent times among some groups. One example is the "welcome of tears," which anthropologist Charles Wagley used as the title of his 1973 book about the Tapirapé Indians. Other surviving customs include gift giving and reciprocity, oratorical duels, manioc processing, belief in spirits, revenge killing, shamanism, and body painting. Even his annoyed observation that women "would be after us incessantly, pestering us" for beads and other presents rings true. Examples also can be found in the work of Napoleon Chagnon and other contemporary anthropologists.

Montaigne's Morals

Léry's work served European writers and moralists well. Michel Montaigne, the sixteenth-century inventor of the essay as a literary form, wrote "On Cannibals" a few years after Léry's *History* appeared. Although he does not mention his sources, his account of the Tupi-speaking Indians of Brazil owes much to Léry:

> They spend the whole day dancing. Their young men go hunting after wild beasts with bows and arrows. Some of their women employ themselves in the meantime with the warming of their drink, which is their principal duty. In the morning, before they begin to eat, one of their old men preaches to the whole barnful, walking from one end to the other, and repeating the same phrase many times, until he has completed the round—for the buildings are quite a hundred yards long. He enjoins only two things upon them: valor against the enemy and love for their wives. (Montaigne 1984: 111)

Like Léry, Montaigne tries to draw moral lessons from Indian cannibalism, to the disadvantage and discomfiture of Europeans:

I am not so anxious that we should note the horrible savagery of these acts as concerned that, whilst judging their faults so correctly, we should be so blind to our own. I consider it more barbarous to eat a man alive than to eat him dead; to tear by rack and torture a body still full of feeling, to roast it by degrees, and then give it to be trampled and eaten by dogs and swine — a practice which we have not only read about but seen within recent memory, not between ancient enemies, but between neighbors and fellow-citizens and, what is worse, under the cloak of piety and religion — than to roast and eat a man after he is dead. . . . We are justified therefore in calling these people barbarians by reference to the laws of reason, but not in comparison with ourselves, who surpass them in every kind of barbarity. (ibid., 113)

Montaigne had the rare experience of meeting three Tupi warriors who had been taken to France to be shown to the king. He reports asking them their opinions of the place. One replied that he couldn't understand how some people there could be so rich and some so poor. "They found it strange that . . . they did not take the others by the throat or set fire to their houses" (ibid., 119). That was still to come.

Rousseau and the Noble Savage

One of the theoreticians whose work would be used to justify the cataclysm of revolution was the eighteenth-century philosopher Jean-Jacques Rousseau. Like Montaigne, he probably read Léry and the other chroniclers and used them as sources for his essays. In *Emile*, his criticism of French mothering and condemnation of swaddling echo Léry, as does his characterization of "savage man" in "A Discourse on the Origin of Inequality." Like many social critics before and since, Rousseau used the savage as a foil to decadent European society.

Rousseau believed that humans were better off before the advent of metallurgy and agriculture. Private property resulted in rivalry and competition that he thought had not existed earlier. "The newborn state of society thus gave rise to a horrible state of war." Once inequality was established as the basis of social life, rules, laws, and rulers emerged to lessen and govern conflict. While "the savage . . . breathes only peace and liberty" and "desires only to live and be free from labor," civilized man "goes on in drudgery to his last moment, and even seeks death to put himself in a position to live, or renounces life to acquire immortality" (Rousseau 1950: 270).

This characterization of the savage bears little resemblance to Léry's Tupinambá, who lived to kill and eat their enemies. But Rousseau echoes Léry and Montaigne in his contempt for civilization: "That men are actually wicked, a sad and continual experience of them proves beyond doubt." It is only in "the state of nature" that "man is naturally good" (Montaigne 1984: 273).

Conquest and Contact

It took the development of technology and European domination to lead western social thinkers to conclude that the condition of humanity was improving and would continue to do so. Indigenous people could be seen as noble only as long as they did not obstruct "the march of progress."

By the eighteenth century, much of the world was open to European penetration, exploitation, and colonization. In Brazil, bands of adventurers called *bandeirantes* (standard-bearers) started plunging into the interior in the seventeenth century, hunting slaves and prospecting for precious metals. They defied the Jesuits, who tried to protect indigenous groups by settling them in villages and teaching them "the arts of civilization." For their efforts, the Jesuits were expelled from Brazil in 1759. By that time, however, plantation owners were increasingly using African slaves, and indigenous groups were fleeing deep into the Amazonian wilderness. Many of the peoples who had inhabited coastal areas were wiped out in conflicts with Europeans or by diseases brought by them. The estimated number of indigenous people in Brazil in 1500 varies from 2 to 8 million; 400 years later, perhaps 150,000 remained, most in remote areas. In 1990 their population was estimated at about 350,000, at least half of whom were under the age of eighteen.

But unexpectedly, Brazil's 2000 census showed 700,000 people had identified themselves as Indians. This sudden increase did not result from natural population growth—Indians were reproducing at rates above the national average, but their infant mortality rates also were very high. Rather it shows Brazilians' reevaluation of and new pride in their indigenous ancestry, probably in light of Indians' well-publicized struggle for survival during the previous twenty years.

Throughout the eighteenth century, groups like the Kayapó were in retreat from the triumphant European invaders. Though hidden deep in the mountains, the Yanomami might have been in indirect contact with Europeans in the eighteenth century, via trade networks through which metal tools traveled. In addition, neighboring indigenous groups raided their area for slaves, whom they sold to whites. Portuguese slaving expeditions in far-northern Brazil "reached a peak between about 1737 and 1755" (Ferguson 1995: 79–80). Between 1740 and 1750, 20,000 slaves may have been taken from the upper Orinoco region. Although indigenous slavery was legally abolished in 1755, slavers operated in the Amazon throughout the nineteenth century. The way of life of the Yanomami and other indigenous groups deep in the Amazon has been threatened and affected by outsiders for quite a long time.

In the early nineteenth century, sentiment built for Brazil to declare its independence from Portugal. Even as the Brazilians began redefining themselves as a nation, they continued to import European fashions in clothing, literature, and music. But soon after declaring independence in 1822, elite Brazilians rediscovered their native heritage and glorified their indigenous ancestors. Some changed their names or gave their children indigenous names. The products of this fashion included three romantic novels by José de Alencar (1829–77), *O Guarani*, *Ubirajara*, and *Iracema*. Brazilian composer Carlos Gomes made *O Guarani* into an opera that achieved international success.

Alencar's Ancestors

Iracema is a simple tale, set in the sixteenth century, about a virtuous Indian princess who falls for a Portuguese invader allied with a rival tribe. In his preface, Alencar claims to tell a true story based on oral tradition, and cites Léry and other chroniclers as the sources of ethnographic details.

An archetypal figure, Iracema (an anagram of "America") is doomed to die after she gives birth to the first mixed-race child in the province of Ceará, Alencar's home. She and the other Indian characters speak stilted prose, generally referring to themselves in the third person. Iracema leans against her lover's breast like a timid bird, tears are always trembling on her eyelids, she is perfectly submissive, and she waits alone in her "love nest" for her lover to return from his glorious deeds. Abandoned without explanation, she dies of a broken heart when her lover finally returns. He buries her under a palm tree, and her mixed-race son survives. At the end of the book, the lover's indigenous friend and battle companion is baptized. This is the happy ending Alencar's readers expected.

Iracema is the easily disposable progenitor of a mestizo culture, an allegorical figure rather than a fully formed character. The realities of indigenous peoples' brutal and tragic encounters with Europeans are nowhere to be found in this novel. As the Indians retreated into Brazil's most remote areas, it became easier to romanticize them at a distance. On the frontiers, however, direct interactions between Brazilians and Indians were violent, often marked by mutual incomprehension, hatred, or uneasy ambiguity. This mixed pattern of idealization and contempt has continued until today.

Penetration

Visitors of all kinds have gone to the Amazon for the past 200 years. A tradition of scientific reporting, pioneered by the nineteenth-century biologist Louis Agassiz and others, grew in tandem with travel literature that reflected the prejudices and insights of cosmopolitan outsiders, from Victorian explorer Sir Richard Burton to twentieth-century German novelist and critic Stefan Zwieg. Professional explorers braved the perils of the "Green Hell"; some, like Colonel P. H. Fawcett in the 1920s, were killed by Indians. President Theodore Roosevelt almost died on an Amazon expedition in 1914. A river previously unknown to outsiders bears his name.

Indians continued violently to resist incursions by would-be settlers, prospectors, and other intruders until recent times. Kaingang Indians attacked workers installing telegraph lines in the populous southern state of Rio Grande do Sul in the 1920s. The Kayapó are still feared in their region because of their former practice of raiding their indigenous and non-indigenous neighbors. In response, the Brazilian government developed an ingenious way of making contact with indigenous groups and persuading them to stop attacking outsiders.

Under the leadership of General Cândido Rondon, who claimed indigenous ancestry, the Indian Protection Service (SPI) was founded in 1910. Rondon's credo was "Die but never kill." His agents set out to contact groups by following them into the bush and leaving presents until they emerged for a nonviolent encounter. Sometimes this process took months or even years. Unfortunately, the SPI became corrupt over the years and abandoned Rondon's model; after a series of scandals it was abolished in 1965 and replaced by the National Indian Foundation (FUNAI).

The Brothers Villas Boas

Among Rondon's inheritors were three brothers, Orlando, Claudio and Leonardo Villas Boas, who began their careers as protectors of Indians on a 1945 government expedition, which opened an unexplored area in Mato Grosso. Orlando and Claudio published *March to the West: The Epic of the Roncador-Xingu Expedition* in 1994, when they were in their 80s (Leonardo died young).[3] They write vividly about the Indians of the Gê language group, who include the Kayapó and some of their neighbors. The Txucarramãe (a Kayapó sub-group)

> constitute a powerful nation that has energetically resisted contact with whites. Deep-seated enemies of all the tribes, both neighboring and non-neighboring, [they] keep their territory shut off from any outsider through a permanent state of war. They keep constant vigilance over their habitats and trekking areas. For more than 50 years, they have been subjected to brutal pressure from the invading civilization. There is no one who has not heard of the Kayapó, a nation feared for its haughtiness and rebelliousness, and currently one of the most numerous in our vast territory. (Villas Boas 1994: 560)

It took months for the Villas Boas brothers to "attract" the Txucarramãe by leaving gifts at the Indians' camps. They "suddenly appeared in front of the Juruna village. . . . Yelling and calling insistently, gesturing and shaking their bows, the 'wooden lips' neither showed nor inspired trust."[4] On another occasion, a couple of years later, a group of Txucarramãe appeared "painted with genipapo [a fruit-based dye]. They were very agitated, confused, making sweeping gestures and talking ceaselessly. . . . There were more than 50, mostly young men. Gathered in the hut, restless, nervous, some quite startled, they hid quickly in the bush, scarcely grabbing the presents we had left" (ibid., 562).

At a second meeting, Kremuro, one of the Kayapó leaders, agreed to travel ten days upriver to the Brazilians' camp. On this excursion, the Villas Boas brothers discovered that the Txucarramãe called themselves "Metotire" and "Mencragnotire." The latter are the people of Raoni, a young man at the time, who toured the world thirty years later with Sting.

After this journey and the Indians' return home, the Villas Boas brothers decided to meet the entire group. They took reporters along with them. Kremuro greeted them cordially but said he could not predict what would happen next. More and more Indians—finally about 400—arrived. "Painted black, extremely agitated, they beat their breasts as they talked and didn't stay for a moment in the same place. It was as if they were walking on a hot griddle" (ibid., 564).

A couple of days later, the Indians called for the Brazilians in the middle of the night. "On sleepily going down to the embarkation point, we were surrounded by more than 100 men painted black (a sign that they are angry), agitated, not one showing the comraderie of a few hours before" (ibid., 566). The Indians told them that the women were afraid and insisted they go and reassure them. Leaving the journalists in camp, they went into the forest with the Kayapó, who grabbed each one by the wrist as they walked.

When they arrived at the Indian camp, no women were to be seen. "After being freed and placed in the middle of a circle of more than 200 men, painted black and carrying heavy clubs, we were told to call the women." The fire went out, and the Villas Boas brothers shouted for it to be rekindled. An Indian yelled, "Kill the whites, they're no good." Suddenly an old woman came out of the forest and called for the other women. "The tension broke. Now the men were laughing. They laughed nervously, but they laughed" (ibid., 568).

According to journalist Washington Novaes, the Villas Boas brothers had erred by offering the Kayapó "only presents that interested men: machetes, fishhooks, etc. Indignant, all the women of the village left. The men tried to attract them by preparing food and calling them—they stomped on the food and went away again. Furious, the men blamed Orlando, Claudio and their companions, who escaped only because an old woman took pity on them" (Grupioni ibid., 183).

Years later, the Villas Boas considered the Kayapó "attracted. They've left the state of war and are great friends of ours today."[5] In this story can be seen the Kayapó's mastery of the art of intimidation, which has served them well in their dealings with outsiders.

Orlando and Claudio concluded their account of the Kayapó with a poignant story of the return of a Brazilian captive who had lived with the Indians for fifteen years. Krumare, a Kayapó leader, accompanied the young man back to his home. On leaving, "Krumare hid his tears. In the boat, as soon as he sat down, he covered his face with his hands." Villagers waved goodbye as the boat pulled away, but "Krumare, in the same posture, did not want to look or respond. We tried to divert him. Nothing worked" (ibid., 576).

A few years later, the Villas Boas brothers founded the Xingu Indigenous Park, a large reserve where seventeen indigenous groups still live peacefully and prosperously. Their health is the best of any indigenous groups in Brazil, and an indigenous director administers the park.

Strangely, the brothers devote only two pages of their memoir to their heroic efforts to establish the park. They portray themselves primarily as nationalists, and only incidentally as protectors of indigenous peoples. In view of the massive impingements that now threaten so many Amazonian indigenous groups, the Villas Boas' description of the Roncador-Xingu expedition's results sounds off-key: "Innumerable ranches began to be established in the region. With the villages that became cities, navigation was stimulated. Consolidating the progress, airlines were founded in various places" (ibid., 611).

The Villas Boas brothers were *sertanistas*, professional backwoodsmen, not scholarly researchers. Brazilian and foreign anthropologists seem to have begun doing systematic field research on indigenous groups in the 1930s. Thus Claude Lévi-Strauss traveled from Paris to São Paulo and thence to central Brazil in the late 1930s, teaching at the new University of São Paulo and going on extended expeditions to collect indigenous artifacts and customs. He spent five years in Brazil and then went into U.S. exile during the Second World War. In 1955, back in Paris, he wrote *Tristes*

Tropiques, apparently for a general audience with some knowledge of European literature and philosophy.

The Anthropologist as Existentialist

Widely read, *Tristes Tropiques* (Sad Tropics) influenced many Europeans' and North Americans' understanding of indigenous people. A richly allusive, highly literary mix of memoir, travelogue, and monograph, it contains unforgettably eloquent passages, amusing anecdotes, and profound meditations on nature and culture.

At the same time, it must have made its readers feel that Brazil's Indians were pathetic remnants of once-vital cultures, doomed to disappear or already gone. In contrast to Léry's Tupinambá, "The societies we could study today, in conditions which it would be a great illusion to compare to those of four centuries ago, were enfeebled in body and mutilated in form . . . . This development had come as a monstrous and unintelligible cataclysm" (Lévi-Strauss 1967: 319).

In a melancholy meditation on the anthropologist's role, he says, "The investigator eats his heart out in the exercise of his profession. . . . The only apparent result is that his presence is forgiven by a handful of wretched people who will soon, in any case, be extinct" (ibid., 374). It should be noted, however, that most of the groups he visited are still struggling to follow their traditional customs where he left them more than sixty-five years ago. They may not prosper, but they have survived.

Lévi-Strauss did not conduct ethnographic research according to the modern model, in which the anthropologist spends an extended period (usually at least a year) with one group, learning the language and sharing village life as a "participant-observer." Instead, he aimed "rather to understand the American continent as a whole than to deepen my knowledge of human nature by studying one particular case." He mounted large, colonial-style expeditions that entered areas previously unknown to Europeans. The first anthropologist to travel overland from Cuiabá to the Madeira River, he made the three-month trip with three other researchers, fifteen sertanistas, fifteen mules, and thirty oxen pulling carts loaded with supplies. He would spend a few weeks with each indigenous group they encountered, doing a census, compiling a glossary of the group's language, drawing up genealogies, making an inventory of the group's material culture, and observing daily life. This style of research gave him little opportunity to know the Indians as people. "If this was 'escape,'" he commented dryly, "I was one of escape's bureaucrats."

Lévi-Strauss tended to objectify the Indians. The "indigence of the Nambikwara material culture" discouraged him as a collector of objects. He compares them to ants as they trek across the barren landscape and describes the young girls as "naked (and supple) as worms" (Lévi-Strauss 1967: 278). He seems more comfortable describing kinship systems and marriage rules or the beauties of nature than the people.

Lévi-Strauss's most famous work, which has come to be known as structural anthropology, is highly abstract and theoretical. For him, indigenous people are objects of study, "a pretext for aesthetic contemplation and disinterested meditation" (ibid., 383). In *Tristes Tropiques*, he uses them as a vehicle for a pessimistic evaluation of the anthropological enterprise and the human condition. At the beginning he complains that he pursued experience "to the ends of the earth without managing either to decipher its meaning or to remain on intimate terms with it" (ibid., 46).

In the concluding chapter, he repeats this note of regret and loss. "Did my decision [to stay in Brazil for five years] bespeak a profound incapacity to live on good terms with my own social group? Was I destined, in fact, to live in ever greater isolation from my fellows?" (ibid., 375). This is (perhaps unintentionally) ironic, considering his inability, as a Jew, to return to France during the war. More broadly, he pessimistically declares the impossibility of doing anything to change society: "The man who takes action in his own country cannot hope to understand the world outside; the man who takes all knowledge for his ambition must give up the idea of ever changing anything at home. . . . his place lies with 'the others,' and his role is to understand them. Never can he act in their name. . . . such a position could not but then prejudice his judgment" (ibid., 384).

Other anthropologists have had a more energetic sense of their responsibility and capacity to act on behalf of the vulnerable people they study. While he reduces anthropologists to "mere spectators," Lévi-Strauss also says anthropology's ultimate goal is to reform one's own society. How this change is to be undertaken, he does not say, however. His main concern (quoting here his philosophical ancestor, Rousseau) is "to construct a theoretical model of a society which corresponds to none that can be observed in reality, but will help us to disentangle 'what in the present nature of Man is original, and what is artificial'" (ibid., 391).

He concludes stoically, "It will eventually become plain that no human society is fundamentally good; but neither is any of them fundamentally bad." Human beings are, however, inherently destructive. "Man has never—save only when he reproduces himself—done other than cheerfully dismantle millions upon millions of structures to reduce their elements to a state in which they can no longer be reintegrated" (ibid., 397).

And yet, writing in the 1950s (when existentialism reigned in France), Lévi-Strauss managed to offer one slim thread to lead us out of "the abyss we are so insanely creating." It is the choice between "appearance and nothing." In choosing, "I take on myself, unreservedly, my condition as a man" (ibid., 398).

But he dances away from grand philosophical conclusions in the final paragraphs of *Tristes Tropiques*, as he wistfully calls for unmediated experience, "beyond thought and beneath society." This seems a long way from an account of the kinship system of the Nambikwara, who lived so simply that they slept on the ground and possessed no pots for him to take back to Paris. What then is this book about? Is its message as evanescent as the sunset he brilliantly describes in an early chapter? Why bother to learn about Indians, after all, if they are doomed to extinction and we to passivity?

Looking for the other, carrying a one-way mirror, we go with Lévi-Strauss to "the ends of the earth." Shadowy figures, the Indians are too far away, or too close, to see clearly. Hovering behind the glass, we finally focus only on ourselves.

Knowing the Other

Since the 1950s, increasing numbers of anthropologists from many countries have gone to Brazil's interior to study indigenous groups. The principal experts on the Yanomami and the Kayapó have been returning to the same groups for more than thirty years, acquiring unequalled knowledge and personal understanding of the people. Despite living in a less accessible region, the Yanomami have hosted more anthropologists and received more attention than the Kayapó. Perhaps this is because the Yanomami have become known as the "largest relatively uncontacted indigenous group in the Western Hemisphere." As scores of indigenous groups have disappeared from the map, anthropologists have felt increasing urgency to study the groups most vulnerable to disease and invasion, while they still preserve the basic elements of their traditional cultures.[6]

Anthropologists studying the Kayapó disagree about how to interpret their culture, but the Yanomami have aroused far more controversy, both inside and outside the profession. For two decades, one U.S. anthropologist, Napoleon Chagnon, had a virtual monopoly on the interpretation of Yanomami culture, though others also had been studying them for years. He published his famous ethnography, *Yanomamö, The Fierce People,* in 1968; almost thirty years later, he estimated, 3 to 4 million U.S. college students had read it in anthropology courses (Alcântara 1995: 8). For a long time his interpretation was accepted as authoritative by many, inside and outside academia. In the early 1980s he fought fiercely with anthropologists who disagreed with him, but these disputes had no impact outside the discipline. Then highly publicized battles over Yanomami culture blew up in the late 1980s, during the massive gold rush that decimated the group.

In 1988 Chagnon published an article in *Science* that purported to explain the Yanomami's propensity for violence as the effect of "reproductive effort." Yanomami men who killed more people had greater access to women and produced more children, he claimed. Brazilian government officials and politicians who supported the gold rush tried to use the article to justify the end of the Yanomami. Soon after its publication in *Science*, a Portuguese translation appeared in one of Brazil's most important newspapers, and Brazilian politicians were still paraphrasing the article years later in interviews and speeches.

Brazilian and French anthropologists who had studied the Yanomami for extended periods tried to protect them from genocide by leading a charge against Chagnon. They published letters challenging his data and analysis in the *Anthropology Newsletter,* one of the official publications of the American Anthropological Association. Chagnon reacted with rage worthy of a Yanomami warrior. Or maybe not—anthropologist Jacques Lizot, who lived with the Yanomami for 20 years, said, "The [fierce] man is calm; he remains silent, but when he does get up from his hammock, it is in order to strike the one who is bothering him, and to strike without uttering a single word" (Lizot 1994: 857). The fight between Chagnon and his critics simmered in anthropological periodicals until it exploded again in 2000, after the publication of Patrick Tierney's exposé, *Darkness in El Dorado*. Chapter 7 tells the story of the scandal that ensued.

Chagnon seems perpetually unaccustomed to being challenged or contradicted. He lashes out, using liberal amounts of sarcasm and hyperbole and accusing his enemies of being motivated by jealousy or ambition. He seems to have no respect for anybody's theory but his own. Experts who have spent more time with the Yanomami than he has are scorned as not knowing what they are talking about. If they charge him with subscribing to a discredited and outmoded form of social Darwinism, he replies that they hate Darwinism or are unscientific. If they challenge the accuracy of his data, he calls them pseudo-scientific. Even scholars who are careful not to criticize him personally arouse his wrath, merely for raising questions about his general approach. And if all else fails, he threatens to sue.

The pyrotechnics exploding around Chagnon have made it difficult to calmly evaluate the validity of his work. Suffice it to say that his image of the fierce Yanomami still dominates the minds of anthropologists and non-anthropologists, and much of the debate over the Yanomami responds to or reacts against it.

How Fierce?

Chagnon has reacted to events and criticism in the succeeding editions of his book (AAA 2002: 34–36). In the second edition, published in 1977, he tried to correct some "misunderstandings and false impressions" by pointing out that the Yanomami did not spend most of their time making war or abusing women. The incidence of warfare varied from village to village, he acknowledged. By the 1983 third edition, he was further qualifying his findings: "This case study does *not* purport to describe all Yanomami villages everywhere or suggest that there is no variation among villages and regions." In 1992, the fourth edition's title omitted "The Fierce People." Perhaps in response to charges that he had not defended the Yanomami during the genocide of the late 1980s, Chagnon said he had published a revised text "to draw attention to the 1987 Brazilian gold rush." But by 1992 the gold rush was old news.

The fifth edition, published in 1997, was issued "to call attention to the rapidly changing political circumstances in the Yanomami area of Venezuela" (Chagnon 1997: ix). However, it does not include an account of Chagnon's own involvement in Venezuelan politics, which led to his being prohibited from entering Yanomami territory. He merely says recent political changes in the country "caused me to become more involved in practical issues, such as health programs, and take more public stands on political matters" (ibid., x).

In the fourth and fifth editions, without acknowledging that he is responding to critics, Chagnon qualifies or backs away from earlier conclusions and shows some changes in attitude. He is now careful to say, "The Yanomami with whom I work" or "the area I work in," instead of generalizing about all the Yanomami (who are divided into four or five linguistic subgroups, spread across a vast area in two countries, and in varying degrees of contact with outsiders). Nevertheless, in the passages remaining from earlier editions, he often slips into generalizations about the entire culture or uses the present tense to describe customs that may have disappeared as a result of contact. For example, in the 1997 edition, he mentions "the recent military activities of . . . a small village" in reference to events that evidently took place a quarter of a century earlier.

Although he says the Yanomami fight mostly over women, he cites plenty of cases in which they fight about witchcraft directed at children or food theft. Ritualistic combats at inter-village feasts often become pitched battles that may have nothing to do with women. He avoids discussing infanticide and taboos against sexual activity that may limit the population. In general, he has very little to say about women and their roles.

After the uproar over the *Science* article and the attempted genocide of 1987–91, plus the political conflicts in which he was involved in Venezuela, Chagnon apparently felt he had to deal more with the effects of the outside world on the Indians. He proclaimed in the fourth edition that he had decided to become an applied anthropologist, since those already acting on behalf of the Yanomami were "doing it all wrong" (Chagnon 1992: 244). He excused himself for not speaking out in defense of the Yanomami during the gold rush by saying, "It took me some time [after a 1985 visit] to marshal the data necessary to demonstrate the problems" (ibid., 287). Yet other anthropologists were denouncing the genocide at the same time he published the *Science* article. In 1992 he finally was ready to acknowledge, "It is patently obvious, however, that there is much suffering and sickness among the [gold rush] survivors, particularly malaria and respiratory infections" brought in by miners (ibid., 291).

As part of his conversion to applied anthropology, Chagnon announced in the fourth edition that he had founded the Yanomamö Survival Fund and was involved in another organization called American Friends of Venezuelan Indians. "Now I want to make sure that [the Yanomami] and their children get a fair shake in the inevitable changes that are occurring. . . . I cannot do that except by becoming an advocate of their right to a decent future. . . . The rest of my useful career will be devoted to them" (ibid., 292).

Chagnon then makes an eloquent plea for citizen action:

> What you and I do now might make a big difference. . . . If the Yanomami go down, so also might many other native peoples, along with the biospheres they have been keeping intact. The Yanomami are a symbol for all tribal peoples and their habitats everywhere— perhaps the ultimate test case of whether ordinary concerned people can stay a destructive process whose course is inexorable if you and I do nothing about it. (ibid., 294)

In the fifth edition, he omits most of this proclamation and merely says he wants "to do what I can to help them. . . . I do so by becoming an advocate of their rights and their chances" (Chagnon 1997: 259).

Chagnon has repeatedly criticized other anthropologists, missionaries and nongovernmental organizations for "competing among themselves to see if they can get the title of sole representative of the Indians in the outside world" and has charged them with transforming the Yanomami into a commodity. "Whoever manages to establish himself as the exclusive owner of the Yanomami cause will be in the money," he told *Veja* magazine in 1995 (Alcântara 1995: 8). This is a common canard in Brazil. But nobody acquainted with the anthropologists, missionaries and NGOs who actually defend the Yanomami has seen them getting rich in the process; quite the contrary. Chagnon has become far more prosperous from his book royalties. It seems just that he invest some of his profits in the people to whom he owes his success.

The American Friends of Venezuelan Indians went out of existence in 1997. According to its lawyer, it "never got off the ground because of political turmoil in Venezuela." A 1997 letter to the Yanomamö Survival Fund was "Returned to Sender, Not Deliverable."[7] It is not unusual for such nonprofit organizations to fail. They often do not manage to raise sufficient funds to operate, or their projects are unviable, or they cannot obtain the cooperation of people on the ground. Without these vehicles to help the Yanomami, how will Chagnon fulfill his repeated pledges to devote himself to their welfare?

The Yanomami require considerable assistance, especially in the areas of health and education, to ensure their future survival as a people. With the halting cooperation of the Brazilian government and modest international funding, a consortium of nonprofit and religious organizations is trying to provide health care and schooling to them. They could use all the help they can get.

Other Versions of the Yanomami

Meanwhile, the long intellectual dispute over Yanomami violence continues. In 1995, Brian Ferguson, an ethno-historian who specializes in the anthropology of war but has no Yanomami field experience, published *Yanomami Warfare*. After surveying the extant literature on the Yanomami, he proposed a theory to explain the ebb and flow of violence over hundreds of years and across their vast territory.

European slavers invaded southern Venezuela and northern Brazil in the seventeenth and eighteenth centuries. With them came western goods, especially metal tools that the indigenous groups of the region prized. Although most of the slavers withdrew in the early nineteenth century (and the Yanomami may have retreated deeper into the mountains), the tools continued to circulate throughout the Yanomami's extensive trading network. In the late nineteenth century, a renewed supply of trade goods entered the area during a short-lived rubber boom.

Ferguson relates waves of direct and indirect contact in the twentieth century to increases and decreases in the level of violence among the Yanomami. Contact led to epidemics and higher death rates. The Yanomami believed these deaths were caused by witchcraft by enemy villages. Conflicts ensued within and between villages. When outsiders withdrew (as they did periodically, sometimes for long periods), the scarcity of trade goods could also cause conflicts.

Ferguson believes increasing polygamy among the Yanomami is a recent phenomenon. For him, the acquisition of women is a side effect, not a cause, of violence. The principal cause is competition for coveted trade goods.

According to the literature Ferguson surveyed, the Yanomami never have been "truly isolated." Their situation always has been affected by events outside. When they found out that neighboring indigenous groups had obtained trade goods, the Yanomami raided them or even abased themselves to them, begging or working in exchange for tools. Such relationships could continue for years. Ferguson paints a very different picture of the Yanomami from Chagnon, who calls them "sovereign and in complete control of their own destiny until only a few years ago" (Chagnon 1992: 1).

When more goods enter the Yanomami universe, Ferguson says, war decreases or stops. But then come genocide and epidemics, which are far more devastating. Some Yanomami have settled at missions, which give some protection from predatory outsiders. But when the Indians become sedentary, the game supply in the area decreases as a result of over-hunting, and so do food sharing and solidarity. Theft becomes a problem; interpersonal violence increases. In recent years this situation, which Chagnon and others have documented, has resulted from invasions by gold miners on both sides of the Brazil-Venezuela border.

Yanomami warfare, Ferguson concludes, "is the result of a major change in access to western manufactures" (1995: 195).

But even according to Chagnon's statistics, three-quarters of Yanomami deaths are due to disease, not internal violence. The greatest threat to their survival comes from outside, not from their belligerence to one another.

Ferguson also questions Chagnon's contention that most Yanomami conflicts are over women. In the long term, he says, only a minority of recorded fights concerned women. Most were related to "demographic disruption" caused by deaths resulting from disease. Men with more trade goods (not, as Chagnon contends, men with more killings) had greater access to women.

Unlike Chagnon, Ferguson explains Yanomami violence as a historical, not a biological, phenomenon. Their patterns of warfare have nothing to do with "our evolutionary past," he insists, but with the events of the past 300 years or so.[8]

All kinds of outsiders have affected the Yanomami. For example, Ferguson says, Chagnon's behavior in the field was "highly disruptive to the Yanomami" in the 1960s. Like other visitors, Chagnon distributed metal tools as presents, and his method of distribution may have created competition within and between villages that led to conflict.[9] From the 1970s on, more serious disruptions occurred after some missionaries gave away or exchanged guns and ammunition for work. In addition to less deadly clubs, arrows, or blows, the Yanomami have been reported to use firearms in their internecine conflicts.

Ferguson states flatly, "At present, there simply are no data that substantiate the claim that aggressive behavior is associated with reproductive success among the Yanomami" (ibid., 362). Nonetheless, he sees the Yanomami not as passive victims but as "aggressively pursuing their own interests." They have "shaped a political milieu in response to the intrusive white presence, which itself is largely beyond their control" (ibid., 367).

For Ferguson, who has studied war for more than a decade, it "is not a natural state of affairs for human societies . . . not the normal condition, leaving peace the state that needs to be explained. . . . War is not self-perpetuating. The costs are too high. But war can be self-reinforcing" (ibid., 370). Although Chagnon and his rival, Jacques Lizot, seem to agree that warfare is endemic among all primitive peoples, Ferguson says this idea is "empirically unsupportable."

There are many problems with Ferguson's argument.[10] In focusing on inter-village warfare, he largely neglects interpersonal violence, such as wife beating. The Yanomami seem ready to fight over almost anything; both scarcity and plenty seem to trigger violence. In some areas but not others, depending on who is doing the reporting and when, violence is endemic or almost nonexistent. Neither the literature he quotes nor Ferguson himself is consistent. An adequate assessment of his work requires a reviewer who is both an expert on the Yanomami and an evenhanded judge.

Ferguson's great accomplishment is his scrupulous examination of all the available source material and his careful attempt to build an explanatory framework. Even Chagnon praises his "noteworthy command of the anthropological literature. . . . He certainly has done his homework and is to be congratulated for the thoroughness of his efforts at researching the published sources in several languages" (Chagnon 1996: 671). He has not managed to construct the definitive explanation, however. The argument over the reasons for Yanomami violence will continue as long as we insist on seeing "something of all of us in the Yanomami, and something of them in all of us" (Chagnon 1992: xvii).

Ever since Europeans first encountered indigenous people on the beaches of America, both the invaders and the conquered have been trying to figure out who and what the other is. In the outsiders' squinting eyes, the Indians have been enemies of Christ, souls to save, subhuman brutes, unsatisfactory slaves, noble savages, passive victims, proud and virtuous warriors, vestiges of the Stone Age, saviors of the environment, or unfit to survive. At least some of the Indians saw Europeans as "subhumans, peripheral and unintelligible" (Albert 1995: 5).

The great challenge for anthropologists has been to try to see others as they see themselves and then to portray them as people. This is a tremendously difficult undertaking. All of our common history stands between us and gets in the way of understanding. Our overblown sense of ourselves also blocks our view. Even the best-intended attempts at understanding may be misused by somebody else. From time to time, however, observers break through their self-created obstacles and show the shape of the other without too much distortion. This may happen only sporadically, unpredictably, in a few paragraphs scattered in a 400-page volume.

In the works of Léry, Montaigne, Lévi-Strauss, Ferguson, and others, that shock of recognition keeps coming: No, the other is not myself, but someone else for whom I, too, am the other. We are, after all, members of the same paradoxical species; but despite our brilliance, we still do not fully comprehend one another. The effort to understand continues, while children die, forests fall, and mercury pollutes the waters.

3 / The People from Between the Waters

IN THE EARLY HISTORY OF BRAZIL, THE KAYAPÓ WERE known by the Portuguese as "the most treacherous of all the heathen" (Hemming 1978: 405). Numbering in the thousands, they occupied a large area between the Tocantins and Araguaia Rivers. They planted sweet potatoes, manioc, corn, bananas, and tobacco and spent several months of the year trekking, hunting, and gathering in forests and savannahs, and raiding their indigenous neighbors.

When the Kayapó encountered white prospectors, slavers, and other intruders in their territories, they gave no quarter, since "none was given to them" (Hemming 1978: 405). As late as the 1950s, they were known as "the terror of the civilized" (Verswijver 1978). The Portuguese used other indigenous groups, the Kayapó's traditional enemies, to mount punitive expeditions against them over the centuries.[1] Another, much larger, Gê-language group, the Southern Kayapó, was apparently wiped out in these conflicts, but the Northern Kayapó, the ancestors of today's Kayapó communities, survived.

According to Dennis Werner, an anthropologist who studied the Kayapó's subsistence pattern during the 1970s, their traditional way of life was "a stable one, which took advantage of the resources of a varied habitat. Although population density was low, this mixed strategy probably supported a larger population more reliably than would have been possible either by hunting and gathering alone or by greater dependence on agriculture" (Werner et al. 1982: 214).

By the early nineteenth century, the Kayapó were retreating west of the Araguaia River. During the nineteenth century they came into contact with settlers and missionaries, not always with violent results. Their first

Kayapó leaders visit Tucuruí Dam, 1988. Photo by Vincent Carelli, Centro de Trabalho Indigenista, São Paulo.

recorded peaceful contact with whites occurred in 1859, when a group of Kayapó visited a missionary post, where they remained until 1882. Until the present, they have had an ambivalent relationship with the outsiders who have encountered them.

At the end of the nineteenth century, most of the Northern Kayapó (about 4,000 people) lived in two large villages in the Xingu region and roamed among campsites in a 200-kilometer radius. They were renowned for their ferocity, not only to whites, but to one another and other indigenous groups. Kayapó villages often split, as a result of conflicts between men's age-sets or moieties (men's houses) that divided villages in two. According to anthropologist Terence Turner, who has studied the Kayapó since the early 1960s, these conflicts expressed "the fundamental tension at the heart of traditional Kayapó social organization, which the structure of Kayapó institutions simultaneously generated and sought . . . to contain" (Turner 1991a: 17).

During the course of the nineteenth century, Kayapó men began to obtain firearms, either by trading with or raiding settlers and other indigenous groups. They used these weapons in their internal disputes, as well as in conflicts with outsiders. Numbers of Kayapó killed in internal fights were usually low, but since the villages that split off were small, the killings had a great impact.

From the two main villages existing at the end of the nineteenth century, at least sixteen communities have formed as a result of these conflicts. A few small Kayapó groups are still "isolated," uncontacted by whites and rarely seen by other Kayapó.

Throughout the twentieth century the Kayapó had a mixed relationship with their nonindigenous neighbors, who included missionaries, rubber tappers and other extractivists, ranchers, and squatters. On the one hand, Werner et al. (1979: 305) observed, they "participate in cash exchange on regional markets, selling forest products, artisanry, labor or other goods." On the other hand, until the 1950s they frequently raided white settlements to obtain firearms, ammunition, cloth, beads, hammocks, metal pots, and other goods. These attacks were sometimes deadly.

Internal conflicts have continued—over women, ritual duties, and other local issues. Over time the moiety system (which seems to have triggered splits) declined. The new villages had populations ranging from twenty-five to a few hundred, and only one men's house per community. As the Kayapó came into more regular contact with whites, they often were decimated by contagious diseases such as influenza and malaria. According to Turner (1991a: 42), one group lost 50 percent of its population of 240 in a single year, 1958. In general, however, the Kayapó's fearsome reputation and behavior served them well. They and other warlike peoples "survived in greater numbers and in better health" than more pacific indigenous groups (Schmink and Wood 1992: 261).

In the mid-1930s the Kayapó first encountered Brazilian government agents from the SPI, the Indian protection agency, which became renowned for its ineffectuality and corruption. The SPI moved Kayapó villages to get them away from Brazilian settlements, diseases, and goods, and the Kayapó continued to fight among themselves and to move away from one another. The period from the 1930s to the 1970s must have been a tragic time for them, with villages wracked by conflict and disease. Unlike 100 other indigenous groups in the twentieth century, however, the Kayapó were not wiped out by the disastrous effects of contact with Brazilian society.

Part of the reason may be luck, but the decisive leadership of some Kayapó men and women also has been important in ensuring their survival as a culture. They took advantage of the presence or proximity of outsiders to attend school, learn Portuguese, and gain some experience of nonindigenous people and culture. Later they used this knowledge to become politically influential inside Kayapó society (Turner 1992a: 319).

In the 1950s, Raoni (also called Rob-ni or Rop-ni) first appeared on the scene as an intermediary between the Villas Boas brothers and the Mekragnoti (who had split into three communities after breaking away from Gorotire around 1905). As we have seen, the Villas Boas brothers played a vital role in protecting dozens of Central Brazilian indigenous groups from extinction, by founding the Xingu Indigenous Park and by acting as peacemakers among indigenous groups and between them and the Brazilians.

Raoni is not the only important chief among the Kayapó — each village usually has three to six influential men who dominate local politics — but he has acquired local, national, and international prominence over the past forty years. He became a leader not through kinship ties but because of his skills as an orator inside the village and as a diplomat to the Brazilians (Verswijver 1978: 56). Turner, who has known Raoni for many years, says he "is generally recognized as the dominant leader and personality of the community, and indeed has become a nationally famous spokesman for indigenous rights, a role duly recognized by his compatriots in Kapot [his home village]" (Turner 1991a: 37).

A Kayapó community became part of the newly founded Xingu Park in 1961, moving to an area near its northern border. Ten years later, when the population had reached more than 200, the Brazilian army and interior ministry "secretly rerouted the construction of one of the main roads of the new Trans-Amazonian highway system, BR-080, so as to cut off the northern 20 percent of the area of the Xingu Park"—exactly the area where the Kayapó lived (Turner 1978: 18). The Villas Boas brothers, then administering the park, wanted the Kayapó to move forty kilometers south to escape what would surely be deadly contact with the highway construction crews and the settlers who would use and live along the road. Raoni led a faction supporting this move, while a more militant group split off and went in the opposite direction.

A few Kayapó staged a daring raid on the road head, terrorizing the crew, capturing a motorboat, and sinking a tug. The "war" faction lost out, but years later young Kayapó warriors were using the captured boat to patrol their territory along the Xingu River. "The Kayapó have been quite effective in their role as a border patrol of the northern part of the Park, as at least a dozen trespassers have learned at the cost of their lives over the past ten years (many others have been either turned away or expelled by less extreme but nonetheless forceful measures)" (ibid., 1978: 19).

By 1984 the Brazilian government had returned the "stolen" area in the northern part of the park to the Mekragnoti. In 1992, Tu'ire, Payakan's relative, told a conference at the University of Pennsylvania, "When whites come illegally into our territory, first we cut their arms with piranha teeth and kick them out. If they come back again, then we get really rough." Turner estimates that between 1970 and 1990, the Kayapó killed some thirty intruders, "and many others were driven off by armed attacks" (ibid., 1978: 19).

In the late 1970s, the Kayapó were known throughout Brazil as formidable opponents. They used shortwave radio to warn one another of incursions, and warriors patrolled their territory, expelling intruders with calculated brutality. Nevertheless, invasions increased as the federal government kept delaying demarcation. In 1981, "16 Kayapó chiefs came together for an unprecedented ten-day meeting. Some of the participants in that historic gathering reportedly had not seen one another for nearly 40 years. The urgent need to protect their territory brought the Kayapó together" (Schmink and Wood 1992: 263).

The Front Lines of Contact

Attention focused on Gorotire, near where gold had been discovered in the late 1970s. The village first became important in the 1950s, when Kayapó from elsewhere moved there to be near the missionary health post. But the Kayapó kept fighting among themselves, and immigrants to Gorotire were sometimes killed or driven away.

In the early 1980s Gorotire became the center of gold mining in the Kayapó Indigenous Area. After many conflicts with thousands of Brazilian prospectors, the Gorotire made a deal with the federal government, whereby they would allow the prospectors to mine gold in exchange for demarcation of their territory and a percentage of the mining proceeds. Payakan, who later toured the world defending Kayapó interests, played a key role in the conflicts and in the subsequent negotiations with the government.

The Gorotire monitored mining operations, doing complete body searches of all those leaving the area, to prevent smuggling. They also monitored all transactions between prospectors and gold buyers. By plane they regularly escorted the proceeds to the bank in Redenção. Paid employees in an office in the city attended to the needs of visiting Gorotire.

CEDI, a Brazilian NGO, reported in the late 1980s:

> During the dry season, they usually arrive in small or full-sized trucks from their fleet of twelve vehicles, driven by hired drivers. During the rainy season, they use their small plane and pay for innumerable air taxi rides. A large part of the funds pays for lodging and supermarket purchases. But there are also large outlays for employees' salaries, air shipping and gas for vehicles and for the village generator, which consumes 40,000 liters of diesel per month. (CEDI 1991: 311)

This kind of contact with Brazilian society strongly affected the Kayapó, directly and indirectly, materially and psychologically. The Kayapó's notorious ferocity became a symbolic weapon, which they used to intimidate outsiders as well as one another. At the same time, they were becoming increasingly dependent on the outside world.

Kinds of Conflict

In recounting the history of the Kayapó people, Turner focused on internal conflict because it was prevalent among them for centuries. Their acquisition of firearms in the nineteenth century had dramatic effects: A high level of both internal and external conflict "militarized" Kayapó society and created an "arms race" among them, "with gun-less groups suffering devastating attacks by groups already possessing guns" (Turner 1991a: 48).

By the 1940s, "raiding for some groups had become a regular means of acquiring a wide variety of Brazilian commodities" (Turner 1991a: 48). The Kayapó had become dependent on their enemies, the whites, for goods they wanted but had no way of producing themselves. Citing oral histories,

Verswijver estimated that the Mekragnoti carried out ninety-two raids between 1905 and the 1950s (Turner 1992a: 329).

Outcry from settlers led the federal government to send pacification missions to contact the Kayapó. These expeditions carried yet more goods that the Kayapó wanted, from fishhooks to cooking pots. By the time the groups were "pacified" in the 1950s, Turner observed, "warfare with the Brazilians had come to mean dependency on Brazilian society for commodities, and peace was seen primarily as a continuation of war by other means" (ibid., 330). The Kayapó seem to have made a pragmatic, tactical decision to reduce raiding and confine outright warfare to the expulsion of people they defined as trespassers. In Turner's words, they had "learned to need" the whites' goods and wanted to obtain more as easily as possible, and so over time they substituted various kinds of trade arrangements for warfare.

From 1900 to the 1950s, charismatic war leaders intensified their power within Kayapó communities. The old balance between groups inside the society was broken, perhaps permanently. Leaders and their followers "could justify their activities and dramatize their importance as the suppliers of the essential means of communal survival" (Turner 1991a: 64). Their power base was independent of the traditional social structure. Men's houses became "mutually independent military organizations" separate from the community as a whole (ibid., 60).

Chiefs derived their power from their ability to withdraw with their followers and start or join another village. Raoni, Tut Pombo, and Payakan all demonstrated their leadership in this way. Traditionally carried out in association with rituals like the New Corn Ceremony, treks became "vehicles for the expression of tension and opposition between rival groups within a single community" (ibid., 62). They all too easily turned into raiding parties. Instead of being months-long expeditions, treks became short forays, losing some of their ritual content. Since the 1950s, treks have remained short. This change may have altered dietary patterns, making the Kayapó more dependent on outside food products that only money could buy.

In recent years relations with the outside world have become ever more important, and as such the focus of political activity. Likewise, "the ownership or control of commodities . . . became, in itself, an increasingly important token and source of status within the community" (ibid., 73). The balance of Kayapó society was altered, with families and households acquiring more importance at the expense of age-sets and other extra-familial institutions. Kayapó society began to lose some of its distinctive, traditional characteristics.

Consumers of Culture

In recent years the Kayapó have compensated for these changes by turning back to ceremonies as a focus of community life and "as the institutional means of expressing the unity of the community in opposition to the encompassing alien society" (ibid., 74). Kayapó of all ages may be found in the villages watching videos that Kayapó filmmakers have produced of recent ceremonies.

Their demands for high-technology consumer goods, and their willingness to sell their natural resources to obtain them, show that the Kayapó are as sophisticated and discerning as other consumers. Like the rest of the modern world, however, Kayapó society has its own "loyal opposition" of critics, moralists, and environmentalists, who call into question the wisdom of modern production and consumption patterns. Raoni, Payakan, and other community leaders have played this role over the years. Furthermore, the Kayapó and their leaders have had to cope with constant challenges to their culture and survival—serious threats from outside that they can neither ignore nor palliate.

International Diplomacy

Charismatic leaders such as Raoni and Payakan transformed venerable patterns of political action by mobilizing their followers for rituals of protest that have provided an alternative to raiding, internal violence, and communal schisms. Instead of trying to obtain much-desired goods through dependency relations with merchants, local authorities, missionaries, or government bureaucrats, they went to the top of the national and international system in defense of their vital interests.

The Kayapó have chosen their allies carefully and worked hard to accomplish their goals. Raoni took on the Herculean task of finding a backer for the demarcation of Mekragnoti territory in the 1980s, when the Brazilian government balked at carrying out its statutory responsibility. He set out to conquer the rock star Sting, on whom he made a powerful impression when they first met in 1987.

In a 1993 interview with filmmaker Geoffrey O'Connor, Sting called Raoni "definitely a leader, he carries himself as a warrior. I took him to huge cities in western Europe—to Paris—he wasn't fazed at all, because he has great self-esteem and understanding of his place in the world." In his talk-show appearances with Sting, Raoni was charismatic, yet patient and good-humored. As Sting described it, "I would sing a song—that was the price—and Raoni would get up and talk—deliver his message, which is a very compelling message. It triggered a groundswell of appreciation of the problem in the rainforest and also how that problem relates to everyone on the planet. It's not something that's somewhere else, it's very connected to everyone. That message has been very successful" (O'Connor 1993).

Although he was defending and advancing Kayapó interests as a diplomat representing a nation, Raoni shrewdly presented himself as an environmentalist to international audiences. In visiting Kayapó territory, however, Sting had the opportunity to see that the issue was more than environmental:

> It's very apparent as you travel towards the rainforest from Brasilia, you fly over what is virtually a red barren desert, which was formerly very lush virgin rainforest, and then you hit the wall of the jungle, which is extraordinarily beautiful, and so the contrast of what it was and what it is is quite a shock. And you meet the people there and you hear their story, and you realize that without their environment they are going to be sucked into the lowest part of Brazilian society, which is basically slavery. (Ibid.)

Sting's 1988 world tour with Raoni was only the beginning of his involvement with the Kayapó. He had promised Raoni that he would ensure the demarcation of the Mekragnoti reserve. After visiting the president of Brazil in a futile quest for official commitment to demarcation (and weathering negative publicity for his efforts inside and outside Brazil), Sting realized he could not carry out his commitment alone. He founded the Rainforest Foundation (RFF) and a Brazilian offshoot, the Fundação Mata Virgem

(FMV), with anthropologists and professional administrators. Then he returned to his musical career.

The foundation's first priority was to demarcate Mekragnoti territory. Three years' collaboration between RFF and FMV resulted in the first privately funded demarcation of a Brazilian indigenous reserve, in 1992. Sting observed, "When the Brazilian government let us demarcate that land, which is the size of Switzerland, I realized that all of that pain and all of that stuff that went down was actually worth it, because it's quite a significant victory, which could possibly be repeated. I don't see why it shouldn't be repeated. We haven't saved that area, we've set up the infrastructure so it can be protected. But it's still a significant victory" (ibid.).

The Rainforest Foundation also supported grassroots development projects among the Kayapó and other indigenous groups in Brazil. Sting raised funds for the foundation's operations by giving yearly benefit concerts at Carnegie Hall; by 2002 he had raised millions of dollars for RFF, some $600,000 of which paid for the Mekragnoti demarcation. In the mid-1990s RFF began to extend its work to some seventeen other countries in South and Central America, Asia, and Africa.

Through direct involvement, Sting came to understand the complexities of "saving the rainforest":

> At first it seemed very simple: Let's stop chopping down the rainforest, let's support these people. But the complexity of the issue when you take in the whole of Brazil and the Indians' needs themselves—vis-à-vis the forest, it's much less simple than I originally thought. . . . It's been a learning process for me, and I've realized a miracle is not going to happen. . . . All we can really hope to do is slow the process down of the destruction of the forest, so that people come to their senses. (Ibid.)

As a witness to the Kayapó's struggle to survive economically, Sting came to an unexpected conclusion: "The real problem is, how do you stop the logging? I think it's better that if there is going to be logging, the Indians control it themselves, because they have a stake in sustainable development, they have a stake in not leaving it as scorched earth. . . . And so—this is quite a different thing—how do you sell the idea of the Indians logging themselves? And yet they are probably the only people who could do it in a responsible way" (ibid.).

With and without Sting, the Kayapó made a spectacular impression on the international public in the late 1980s and early 1990s. But this external political involvement carries on a tradition that goes back at least 100 years.

The Kayapó "have always had an acute recognition of the hierarchical nature of Brazilian society. This is based in part on their own conception of hierarchy as it obtains in their own social structure. Since the very beginning of the contacts with Brazilian society, this has allowed them to formulate very effective strategies aimed at getting the attention of higher-ups" (Fisher 1994: 225).

Since the nineteenth century the Kayapó have maintained trade relations with white settlers, merchants, and landowners. Government pacification efforts in the 1950s effectively ended raiding. Since then, the Kayapó have used other tactics, such as organized but symbolic forms of intimidation, against merchants and landowners to win concessions from the government.

Government's Ambiguous Role

Meanwhile, Brazil was changing. The military government's development model in the 1960s and 1970s was meant to replace traditional extractive economies in the Amazon region. Federal agencies came to towns like Altamira, along with construction firms, mining companies, and logging firms. The new Indian protection agency, FUNAI, stepped in to try to become the Kayapó's intermediary in making deals with private enterprises.

But FUNAI and other federal agencies failed to fulfill their statutory responsibilities to the Indians, while the big companies offered them health care, air transport, goods, and infrastructural improvements in exchange for access to land and resources on the reserves (Fisher 1994: 225). In 1984 the Azzayp logging firm agreed to build a saw mill, three guardhouses, fourteen wood houses, a clinic, two airstrips, a seventy-kilometer-long road, and a fence around fifty *alqueires* of land that were to be cleared for pasture, in exchange for rights to extract mahogany from the Kikretum village region (CEDI 1991: 315). It was Pombo, Raoni's rival, who brokered this lucrative deal, for which he no doubt won as much prestige among his "constituents" as any Chicago alderman.

Over time the focus of power and decision shifted from local economic actors to FUNAI, and the Kayapó began visiting the agency's regional offices. "By their belligerent presence and demands," Fisher noted (1994: 225), "the Kayapó created discomfort among administrators that often resulted in compliance with Kayapó requests." They had discerned that top-level FUNAI officials sometimes shifted resources from one indigenous group to another, "depending on the pressure applied rather than by identification of specific needs" (ibid.).

Their Hour upon the Stage

Thus the Kayapó became important political actors on the state and federal levels. When the Constituent Assembly was drawing up Brazil's new Constitution in 1987–88, the Kayapó went en masse to Brasilia to lobby on behalf of indigenous interests. There they conducted "demonstrations, sit-ins, meetings with leaders in which they asserted themselves in a threatening manner" (ibid., 226). They attracted considerable media attention by wearing war paint, elaborate feather headdresses and beads, and carrying war clubs as they sat watching the proceedings from the congressional visitors' gallery.

In 1988, the young leaders Payakan and Kuben-I clashed with the Brazilian government over hydroelectric development plans and received international attention and support. Through their highly publicized actions in Belém and other rituals of protest, the Kayapó became the most visible and famous indigenous group in Brazil, and the most politically powerful.

The Grande Carajás project and other mega-projects of the 1970s and 1980s marked the internationalization of Amazon development, financed through foreign bank loans, multilateral lending institutions like the World Bank, and transnational corporations. Indigenous people in the Amazon immediately felt the economic, political, and environmental effects of these projects and accompanying large-scale investment in cattle ranching, plantation and export agriculture, and mining. Now the sources of benefits had moved beyond FUNAI to other, more powerful federal agencies, international banks, and intergovernmental bodies. This change "affected the Kayapó's ability to defend themselves and maintain their place within the region" (ibid., 226). As they figured out ways to benefit from selling access to natural resources such as mahogany and gold, the Kayapó became important economic actors. Their formidable abilities to organize and mobilize for political action helped them capitalize on their new economic position to an extent that few other indigenous groups have managed.

The special connections between parastatal enterprises, multinational capital, and government agencies meant that Kayapó rituals of protest aimed at any one of these sectors would have an impact on the others, especially if they could gain media attention. This was as true on the international as on the national or regional level.

With planning decisions coming from Brasilia, the Kayapó no longer gained much by focusing their pressure on local officials or regionally based agencies. Characteristically, they adapted to the changed situation by going to the top of the power structure. Thus the Kayapó have continued traditional war making, raiding, and trekking through their own distinctive brand of international diplomacy, traveling to the global North to gain allies at the highest levels, financial support, and prestige goods to show the folks back home (Raoni's favorite in the 1990s was a baseball cap with a stuffed cloth fish mounted on top). As economic, social, and political conditions keep changing, the Kayapó will keep developing new strategies to defend their interests, their culture, and their resources.

Entrepreneurs and Rentiers

The Kayapó's success as international symbols of environmentalism has been transient, however, especially in light of their propensity for making deals with loggers and miners. "For a Kayapó to be an environmentalist today is in some senses similar to being a warrior in other times" (Fisher 1991: 29). But defending the environment is not an end in itself for the Kayapó. "There is a danger in relying on the Indian image as guardian of the rainforest. This image implies that Indian lifestyles should be given a chance to survive because of specific acts they perform that are beneficial to the environment, rather than basing the defense of indigenous rights on recognition of their rights to self-determination as a nation" (Fisher 1994: 229).

The Kayapó became the most important economic group in their region, as neighboring Brazilians became dependent on the proceeds of logging and mining in the Kayapó reserve. In the late 1990s, around 70 percent of the region's economic activity was related to these two industries. But the Kayapó's success has led to unprecedented problems for the group, their Brazilian neighbors, and the environment (Rabben 1995).

The Downside of Development

In Gorotire, gold mining seemed like a great deal at first. Goods and money rolled into the community, and the benefits were immediate. The health of the people improved, and a teacher came to give the children instruction. People built better houses. Generators provided electricity to every house.

But Gorotire village became dirty as a result of the presence of thousands of miners in the reserve. Mining was environmentally damaging, especially to the rivers and riverbanks where gold was extracted. The incidence of malaria and sexually transmitted diseases increased. Gorotire's residents cut short their traditional hunting and gathering treks and increasingly depended on purchased food. The focus of social life in the village shifted from men's age-sets to families and households. As the outside world massively impinged on the Kayapó, local leaders acquired sufficient knowledge and sophistication to represent their people on regional, national, and even international levels. Young leaders, including Payakan, began spending more time in town, where they acquired a reputation for drinking, conspicuous consumption, and womanizing. Village life was strained by all these changes in the course of a decade.

By the early 1990s, disturbing phenomena, such as stillbirths and congenital birth defects, began to appear in Gorotire. With support from the Japanese Rainforest Foundation, Brazilian anthropologist Olimpio Serra assembled an interdisciplinary team to do research on the effects of mercury contamination on Gorotire residents. Mercury in the soil, on river bottoms, in food, and in the air has contaminated vast areas of the Amazon basin as a result of widespread gold mining by hundreds of thousands of prospectors. The study found that the Gorotire Kayapó, their environment, and the miners all showed signs of serious mercury contamination.

With the outsiders also came diseases, from tuberculosis to gonorrhea. One of the Kayapó's most pressing concerns was providing medical care in the villages, instead of flying sick people 100 miles to the nearest town. In 1993 the Rainforest Foundation sent a nurse to several communities to do a health survey. In Kubenkokre (population 480) she found a nurse, paid by FUNAI, who "uses medications to excess. . . . antibiotics [are] used indiscriminately, with no control of the dosage at the time of administration" (Machado 1993: 1). Basic equipment, such as thermometers and stethoscopes, was lacking. The local diet was healthful, and food abundant, but villagers made coffee from polluted river water. All the houses and the clinic had electricity, and some residents watched national news and soccer games on the television in the men's house.

Problems in Pukanu village included "precarious" medical and dental care, poorly trained health workers, excessive use of medications, poor record keeping, and excessive expenditure on hospital care in town. These conditions are typical of those in many indigenous areas.

A year later, a physician made a follow-up visit to several Kayapó communities (Tanaka 1994). She found 53 abnormal Pap test results among 120 tests, and many cases of sexually transmitted diseases among women, whose husbands had apparently infected them. In Pukanu (population 250), thirty-six residents had malaria, probably as a result of their proximity to garimpeiros. The community cistern was contaminated.

The doctor noted that the Kayapó put "unbearable" pressure on the nurse in Kubenkokre to send patients to the hospital in town. The nurse, who was paid by a logging company, knuckled under because she feared losing her job.

Loyal Opposition

Not all Kayapó leaders wanted to keep making deals that brought disease to their communities, fouled the environment, and allowed outsiders to deplete their patrimony. Raoni and some others represented an important sector of Kayapó public opinion, which saw breakneck development by outsiders as a threat to traditional culture. They also represented those who did not benefit from mining and logging, the proceeds of which were unequally distributed in the community. This sector of the Kayapó saw preservation of the traditional means of subsistence as more desirable than transitory gains that could have devastating long-term consequences, to people as well as to nature, the basis of their subsistence.

In 1993 a delegation of Kayapó leaders went to Brasilia to lobby for permission to sell mahogany that logging companies had illegally cut. They also sought a continuation of federal government responsibility for their welfare (known as *tutela*, "tutelage," in Brazilian law).

Also in 1993, the attorney general's office, an independent federal agency, filed suit to remove all nonindigenous miners and loggers from the Kayapó Indigenous Area, on the grounds that they were depredating the environment and compromising the health of the Indians. Among the evidence was the interdisiplinary team's report on mercury contamination. The federal district court of Brasilia ordered the expulsion in February 1994. FUNAI had the responsibility to carry out the order, but the agency, whose budget had been cut by 90 percent in recent years, said it had no resources to do so (CIMI 1994d; FUNAI 1994).

Márcio Santilli, then working for NDI (Indigenous Rights Unit), a nongovernmental legal assistance group, traveled to the Kayapó reserve soon after the court ruling came down. He observed that the situation in Gorotire was "difficult; food is scarcer and few fields have been planted. . . . the health situation is grave, and there is much tuberculosis, malaria and venereal disease . . . the vehicles were broken, and there was no diesel to run the lighting system. The undergrowth had grown, even in the area of the infirmary and the school" (closed for lack of a teacher) (NDI 1994: 3).

The Indians thought the court had banned them, as well as outsiders, from mining or logging. Santilli explained that only nonindigenous miners and loggers had to stop working, and the environmental law prohibited the kind of work that destroys rivers and forests in any area, even on the lands of the whites. If the Indians decided to take over mining and do it differently, without mercury and with other environmental safeguards, the judge (and the law) did not forbid it.

The Kayapó leaders replied, "Someone has to be held responsible for everything that happened during the 12 years that they taught us the wrong way to work. Who will clean up the rivers and the forests that have been damaged? Who will be responsible for health care? Who will indemnify us for the resources and the lives we have lost?"

By September 1994, the Kayapó could wait no longer for an answer. Encouraged by older leaders who were responding to community pressure, warriors forcibly expelled about 2,000 nonindigenous miners still in the reserve. Under community pressure, older leaders supported their initiative. This alliance across generations outflanked the middle generation of leaders, who had tried to act as mediators between the Indians and Brazilian businessmen in Redenção. The miners fled to the city, where they occupied the main square and threatened to attack the FUNAI office and the Kayapó who were there. Eventually a gold buyer and the mayor negotiated an agreement, whereby the miners would return to Gorotire for six months. In exchange, the gold buyer would pay off the Kayapó's outstanding debts in Redenção, which then amounted to some $200,000. Several young leaders who had benefited from earlier mining and logging deals were primarily responsible for these debts, but the community as a whole agreed to the deal. Uneasy coexistence between the Kayapó and outsiders seemed reestablished in Gorotire.

Nonetheless the attorney general's office insisted on enforcing the expulsion order. And ordinary Kayapó, who have seen few benefits from the depredation of their natural patrimony, kept pressuring community leaders to go along with the federal government. In December 1994 the leaders agreed to support the expulsion of all nonindigenous miners from Kayapó territory for at least a year (Turner 1995b).

Open Questions

The issue resurfaced in late 1995, when a group of young leaders demanded that FUNAI pay their debts—which had allegedly swelled to 2 million dollars—in Redenção. They occupied the local FUNAI office until a settlement could be worked out. Payakan, who had lost his environmental credentials by making deals with loggers, seems to have been involved in this action. How the Kayapó would finance their future development in a sustainable way, without selling off their patrimony, remained unsettled.

Meanwhile, leaders still living on the reserve were organizing associations, which had the legal capacity to seek funding for economic development projects from outside sources. One started an ecotourism project, another an extractive-product project to provide alternatives to mining and logging. The local leaders operate in a traditional way, forming and managing groups of followers, but they seek to integrate the reserve into the local, regional, and national economies.

The Kayapó "have modified many aspects of their village life, social organization, and surroundings in the process of surviving more than 200 years of colonial and post-colonial onslaughts" (Fisher 1994: 229). They do not live in perfect harmony with pristine nature; indigenous peoples, like other human beings, have always affected their environments, sometimes positively, sometimes negatively. Like the rest of us, they must continually make choices about their relationship to nature, which is never static or simple.

Meanwhile, in Gorotire . . .

On a visit to Gorotire in September 1997, I found some of the same problems Santilli had reported three years before. The generator still sat idle for lack of diesel fuel. The village was untidy, the river polluted. Villagers depended increasingly on food trucked in from Redenção. Corroding batteries littered the ground where children played. The hospital was abandoned, its screens torn, its bathroom filthy. A nurse had left a couple of months earlier and had not been replaced. There were no drugs in the infirmary. Someone had sabotaged the village water supply, and the water storage towers were empty.

With a Brazilian engineer the village paid to fix such problems, I climbed a nearby hill to the reservoir, a lovely, secluded pool near the summit. Someone had removed the filter cap from the main pipe feeding water to the village, and twigs, leaves, and branches had blocked the pipe. The engineer and a couple of helpers took about an hour to locate the blockages and clear them. They replaced the filter (which the saboteur had considerately left a few feet from the pipe), and we descended to the plain.

Back at the village, water was still not flowing to the school, which the county government administers. The engineer started digging holes to see where the problem might be. Over the loudspeaker, the headman's wife asked for help from the men of the village, but only one responded to her plea. The others were out hunting turtles for an upcoming festival or did not choose to help. The engineer finally found the place where a pipe had to be replaced. School was cancelled so the two teachers could help him with the work.

The headman paid the engineer for his services out of the money he received from loggers who were extracting mahogany from the reserve. Although the Brazilian government announced with great fanfare in 1996 that mahogany exports would be banned for two years, this proclamation did not seem to slow logging on indigenous land, where most of the mahogany is located. The Brazilian government has since placed and renewed a moratorium on mahogany exports, but smuggling of tropical hardwoods out of indigenous reserves continues. In September 2002, IBAMA agents seized almost 2,000 mahogany logs, with an estimated value of about $7 million, on the Xingu River downstream from the Kayapó reserve (*O Liberal* 2002).

After the Kayapó expelled the miners in 1995, the headman observed, the situation worsened in Gorotire, because FUNAI did nothing for the village, and the people gained nothing from the few miners who remained illegally in the reserve. He hoped to obtain government approval for a project to train the Kayapó to mine gold without using mercury or devastating the environment. But FUNAI obstructed the project. In Brasilia the talk was about the latest bill to give mining companies—not Indians—freer access to indigenous lands. The results of granting such access, either through neglect or design, have already been seen in Yanomami territory and in Gorotire: pollution, destruction, disease, violence, and death.

In Gorotire, the largest Kayapó village and the one most affected by contact with Brazilian society, the Kayapó are still searching for ways to sustainably develop their territory and equitably distribute the benefits of civilization. A two-class system, with a small elite that benefited from development and a majority that did not, seemed to be evolving in imitation of the Brazilian system surrounding it, and the Kayapó did not like it.

Some of the more remote Kayapó villages, especially those west of the Xingu River, have managed to escape or prevent depredation by refusing to make deals with loggers and miners. They are perennially interested in developing ecotourism or sustainable extraction of nuts, fruit, and other forest products.

When the Brazilian government revived the Belo Monte hydroelectric project, which would flood part of Kayapó territory and the city of Altamira, in the late 1990s, environmental and grassroots organizations mounted campaigns to prevent its realization. This time, the Indians were not in the forefront of those protests. In late 2002, the government announced it would postpone the multibillion-dollar project, but pressures are likely to mount in the future for its construction. The Kayapó will have to respond, one way or another, to this revived threat to their existence.

During most of the 1990s, Kayapó politics were dominated by the issue of logging. Most villages gave concessions to Brazilian loggers to cut mahogany in their vicinities. In at least two cases, village leaders sold concessions to land they did not control. Armed confrontations between loggers and Indians ensued, and war between villages was only "narrowly averted" (Turner 2002). Like mining in the 1980s, logging was leading to disunity and conflict among the Kayapó.

Meanwhile, Raoni was trying to find another way to bring revenue to the Kayapó. With a Belgian entrepreneur, he went to Europe to seek funding for a "Xingu Institute" that would develop and manage sustainable projects. But the entrepreneur did not pass along the funds he collected, and Raoni's prestige suffered. It seemed that his method of celebrity fundraising, which had been so spectacularly successful in the 1980s and 1990s, might no longer work.

Meanwhile, the Brazilian government and IBAMA, pressured by Greenpeace and other international environmental groups, made greater efforts to stop the illegal mahogany trade. When Turner visited Kayapó territory in September 2002, the Kayapó told him, "Logging is finished." Conflict among villages eased when the loggers left. Soon after, the Kayapó formed a federation that brought almost all the villages together to decide on development policy.

A new project, to set up a Brazil nut oil–extraction operation in Gorotire, captured the Indians' interest. Equipment was installed and a deal made to sell the oil to businessmen in São Paulo. "Politically and ecologically, the situation has been transformed," Turner believed (personal communication, October 2002). He hoped that other extractive projects, such as collecting and marketing honey from stingless bees, would give the Kayapó diverse and sustainable sources of income.

More than two decades ago, Turner presciently observed:

> Given half a chance, indigenous groups can make a successful and vital adaptation to contact with Brazilian society. The indigenous societies of Amazonia and their cultures are not doomed to disappear: on the contrary, many, like the Kayapó, show strong signs of being on the way to more or less viable forms of accommodation with Brazilian society without losing either their social or political cohesion as internally self-governing communities or the essential elements of their own culture. (Turner 1978: 21)

Actors on regional, national, and world stages, the Kayapó keep facing new challenges in dealing with the outside world and with one another. Since the mid-1980s they have shown themselves to be resourceful and clever participants in Brazilian public affairs, as allies or enemies, depending on how they have defined and redefined their own interests. Their success at transcending internal divisions and protecting their cultural and material patrimony makes them a attractive model for Brazil's other indigenous peoples, who are struggling to survive. But the Kayapó pay a price for this success, and they keep confronting its consequences.

4 / Payakan: A Cautionary Tale

GREAT STRUGGLES BREED STARS: CHARISMATIC CHARACTERS who embody the causes for which they fight. In the age of mass communication, we know their faces, their voices, and their words as if they were our neighbors, instead of remote figures at the other end of the world. At the same time, we want them to be exotic and colorful. Furthermore, we expect them to transcend the circumstances that forced them to fight. They parade like mythological creatures or personifications of virtue on the world stage. But these larger-than-life figures sometimes fail. At those times the public becomes implacable, overturning the pedestal we built and slamming the hapless hero down to our own level, or even below.

The struggles of indigenous peoples for survival (or for something more than mere survival) have made international stars of people drastically different from their audiences. They have had to learn much more about us than we care to know about them. Indigenous activists like Payakan, Raoni, and Davi Kopenawa, who toured the world in the 1980s warning of environmental disasters, had to translate their reality into terms the international public could understand. Seduced by their eloquence and their powerful physical presence, we made extravagant offers of help and then sent them home, sometimes with their pockets full of money, other times empty-handed.

In the meantime, the dangers they denounced continued to threaten their people. On their return to the forest, these leaders had to face local reality. But we were no longer interested; some other heroic figure had taken their place in our imaginations.

Despite our fickleness, indigenous leaders still felt obliged to realize the promises of immediate improvement they had made to their people. These

Paulinho Payakan at Altamira, 1989. Photo by Eduardo Leão, Conselho Indigenista Missionário, Brasília.

promises were ultimately what had sent them to faraway destinations and then brought them back home.

Returning from stardom could be painful and difficult. Often the leaders could satisfy neither the expectations of the outside world nor of their own communities. They were left hanging amidst multiple worlds and multiple demands.

The story of Payakan—defender of the Amazon rainforest, Kayapó ambassador to the First World, dreamer, community organizer, deal maker, profiteer, convicted rapist—includes all these elements. He began as a shooting star and ended as a falling one. Following his trajectory were outside supporters and allies who became too emotionally involved in their ideal of the struggle to back away. Eventually they let him go. To some of them, Payakan seemed like his own worst enemy, but other antagonists were not lacking, either.

Life on the Edge

Payakan was born in 1955 in the village of Kubenkranken, the son of a village leader. Curious, intelligent, and enterprising, he learned Portuguese from the outsiders who came to the village as teachers, missionaries, researchers, and FUNAI officials. As a youth he worked on a road construction crew, where he gained experience in the ways of ordinary Brazilians.

Payakan grew up during a period when increasing numbers of whites were entering Kayapó territory to extract natural resources or seize land for their own uses (cattle ranching, homesteading, and hunting). Famed and feared for their bellicosity, the Kayapó reacted with carefully measured violence. According to Turner, "Perhaps 30 settlers, ranchers and other [invaders] . . . were killed by Kayapó between 1970 and 1990, and many others were driven off by armed attacks" (Turner 1995b: 13).

At the same time, some Kayapó leaders were making deals with loggers and miners in exchange for money and improvements such as roads, houses, and other buildings. The most famous was Tut Pombo, who, Turner says, "became the prototype . . . emulated by several Kayapó leaders of the next generation, who used their command of Portuguese and familiarity with Brazilian ways as a base of political influence" (ibid., 15).

When he was a boy in the 1930s, Pombo (whose names in Kayapó and Portuguese mean "dove") survived a massacre by Brazilians that killed the rest of his family. He was taken to a nearby city and raised in a Brazilian household, where he learned to speak Portuguese. As a young man he returned to Gorotire, and the Indian protection agency named him village "chief" because of his language ability. In 1976 he founded his own village, Kikretum. When gold miners started working near the village without his permission, he raided their camp and expelled them. But later he became the first Kayapó leader to offer concessions to gold miners and mahogany loggers. With the proceeds, he built Brazilian-style houses for the community and bought an airplane, houses, and a hotel in the city of Tucumã, where he lived in high style. He died of natural causes in 1992 (Ricardo 1996: 420–21).

In the late 1970s and early 1980s, as the world price of gold surged up to $850 an ounce, gold was discovered in several parts of the Amazon region. The huge open-pit mine of Serra Pelada, not far from Kayapó territory, attracted tens of thousands of prospectors. The spillover flowed into indigenous areas. Although such mining was illegal, the government condoned it "as a social safety valve, to divert and diffuse the acute social tensions in the region" (Turner 1995b: 14).

Two mining sites opened in 1981 near Gorotire, whose leaders made a deal with mining entrepreneurs to receive a percentage of the profits. The mining company cheated the Kayapó by agreeing to give them 10 percent of the proceeds and then moving the decimal point in the contract from .1 to .001. Not knowing enough arithmetic to perceive the trick, the Kayapó signed the contract. Soon 5,000 miners were mining gold near Gorotire under military supervision.

The Go-Betweens

Payakan understood Brazilian culture well enough to oppose the deal. As FUNAI's "chief of post" at Gorotire, he negotiated a contract slightly more favorable to the Kayapó and deposited the proceeds in a community bank account in the city. Two other young leaders—like Payakan, sons of senior chiefs—took over administration of the deal. They moved the profits to bank accounts in their fathers' names, thus keeping the money under their own control and turning their fathers into figureheads.

Payakan lost prestige as a result of his rivals' maneuvers. FUNAI moved him to its regional office in Belém. "From this vantage point," notes Turner, "he coordinated the confrontation of the Gorotire with the company running the gold mines . . . when its contract with the Gorotire came up for renewal in 1985" (Turner 1995a: 52). On behalf of the Kayapó, FUNAI asked the company for a 10 percent share, but the company balked. Payakan organized (by two-way radio) an attack by 200 warriors from Gorotire and Kikretum, who seized the airstrip and equipment at one of the mine sites and prevented planes from bringing in supplies.

The Kayapó became national news at this point. They demanded that the federal government intervene on their behalf. In exchange for allowing the miners to continue working, the Indians would control mine operations and collect 10 percent of the proceeds—and the government would recognize their rights to their territory by demarcating their reserve.

Astonished by this challenge, the government sent troops, plus a military band that paraded along the airstrip "in a ludicrous and unsuccessful attempt to intimidate the Kayapó" (ibid.). Although the company succeeded in reducing the Kayapó's share to 5 percent, the Indians gained control over both mining and demarcation. It was Payakan who negotiated for them in Belém and Brasília.

Brazil's first civilian government in twenty-one years demarcated a reserve of more than 3 million hectares for the Kayapó. The Indians themselves supervised mining, prevented smuggling, and patrolled their frontiers. "Within a year, invasions effectively ceased" (Turner 1990: 14).

A relatively small number of young, Portuguese-speaking Kayapó leaders, including Payakan, became prominent as a result of the brilliantly coordinated actions of 1985. They imitated Pombo by living in the town of Redenção, where "they acquired cars, trucks, airplanes, Brazilian servants" while the miners extracted millions of dollars in gold every year (Turner 1995b: 16). Thus, Payakan and his age-mates became members of the regional elite. The economy of southern Pará state became dependent on Kayapó resources. A Redenção bank manager conservatively estimated that gross profits from mining and logging on the three Kayapó reserves came to $10 million a year, of which the Indians received about $1.5 million. Suddenly the Kayapó were the richest indigenous group in Brazil. Their political power soared.

In 1986, the federal government tried to dump radioactive waste from the nuclear accident in Goiânia on the Kayapó's western frontier. One hundred warriors flew to Brasília to demonstrate and the dumping plan was abandoned.

In 1987, fifty Kayapó leaders were frequently photographed and interviewed as they attended sessions, gave press conferences, and lobbied at the

Constitutional Convention in Brasília. Several Brazilian NGOs advised and collaborated with them and other indigenous groups to ensure passage of provisions that strengthened indigenous rights.

The Environment Heats Up

The Kayapó came to international attention in 1988, after two hot, dry summers in the Northern hemisphere that fanned concern (if not hysteria) about global warming. Payakan and other leaders got wind of ambitious government plans to build ten dams along major Amazon rivers, including the Xingu. Three of the projects would flood large parts of Kayapó territory.

Payakan and his age-mate Kuben-I, who often competed with him for political and economic power, were invited to an environmental conference in Miami by anthropologist Janet Chernela. On this, their first trip outside Brazil, accompanied by anthropologist Darrell Posey (who studied the Kayapó for many years), they denounced the hydroelectric projects. After the conference they went with Posey and Chernela to Washington, D.C., where they met with officials of the World Bank, which was to finance the dams. At the Bank they obtained detailed information about the project that the Brazilian government was trying to keep from its own citizens.

Soon after their return to Brazil, Payakan, Kuben-I, and Posey were indicted under the Foreigners Law, which forbids aliens from involving themselves in political activities in Brazil. The absurdity of prosecuting indigenous people under this law was immediately obvious. Posey, who lived in Belém and taught at a federal university, was in real trouble, however—despite the fact that he had assisted the Indians while in his own country. During the summer of 1988, he was ostentatiously followed by federal agents and his telephone was tapped. His position at the university became untenable.

Anthropologists, indigenous rights advocates, and human rights organizations around the world leapt to the men's defense. The Brazilian government began to look foolish.

Early in 1989 Payakan and Kuben-I were summoned to Belém for arraignment. They arrived at the courthouse with 500 Kayapó supporters. As Turner (1990: 16) tells it,

Kayapó men and women danced through the streets and massed in the square before the Palace of Justice. . . . . Kayapó orators unrolled the map of the Xingu dam scheme obtained from the World Bank in Washington on an easel erected in the square and explained the entire secret project in Kayapó and Portuguese for the benefit of the many Brazilian onlookers, who included reporters and TV crews.

Photos of Kayapó warriors, painted for battle and carrying war clubs, arrayed against police and troops, appeared on front pages around the world.

Inside the courtroom, Payakan and Kuben-I presented themselves to the judge, who took umbrage at their colorful appearance. He declared that their body paint, feather and bead ornaments, and swimming trunks were not proper attire and showed disrespect for the court. The Indians protested that they were wearing their best ceremonial garb.

Enraged, the judge ruled that an anthropologist would have to be contracted to determine if the Indians were sufficiently acculturated to understand the charges against them. But no anthropologist could be found to take on the assignment. Soon after, the charges against Payakan and Kuben-I were quietly dropped. Posey left Brazil and went on to work on the international issue of intellectual property rights for indigenous peoples.

Spectacle at Altamira

At the time of the arraignment Payakan was already busy with a project that was to bring him and the Kayapó lasting international fame. With the help of CEDI, a Brazilian NGO, he was organizing a pan-indigenous meeting to protest the Xingu dam projects and confront Brazilian officials who were still refusing to release information about the plans. The place was Altamira, a frontier town not far from the northern boundaries of the Kayapó reserve. Payakan invited not only high-ranking Brazilian officials but hundreds of indigenous people, including 500 Kayapó, Brazilian and international NGO representatives, parliamentarians, and journalists— about 1,200 people in all. It was, Turner later said, "an impressive feat of organizational and political coordination" (Turner 1990: 19).

At the meeting site the Kayapó built a model village, as if they were on one of their seasonal treks. They prepared for a traditional ritual, the New Corn Ceremony, which they performed during the five-day meeting. Payakan had no trouble executing or administering his ideas on this occasion, though he did suddenly fall ill with appendicitis. He underwent emergency surgery and showed up, shaky but triumphant, at Altamira a couple of days late. In a moving traditional greeting, the Kayapó burst into tears as he entered the model village.

Despite strong Brazilian opposition to the meeting, it went off without violent incidents—thanks, Turner thought, to Kayapó self-discipline and the massive presence of the international media. Perhaps because the meeting happened only a few weeks after the assassination of Chico Mendes, neither the government nor local landowners and merchants who supported the dam projects had the heart to make trouble. Perhaps they also knew too well the fierce reputation of the Kayapó.

What violence did occur was symbolic. In an incident relayed around the world, Tu'ire, Payakan's kinswoman, strode up to the podium while the director of the regional electric-power authority was explaining the Xingu projects. Deliberately she placed the side of her machete on the director's cheek and made a brief oration in Kayapó as he sat there trembling. It was an electrifying moment.

The meeting became an "international media circus" as famous personalities dropped in. Sting, who had recently raised more than a million dollars for Kayapó demarcation on a worldwide tour with Raoni, came for one day to promote his project. The arrival of Raoni, at that moment perhaps the most famous indigenous person in the world, aroused great excitement among both indigenous participants and journalists.

More important, the Altamira meeting generated "serious political pressure against any international funding of the dam scheme" (Turner 1990: 20). Just two weeks later the World Bank announced that it would not lend the Brazilian government any funds for the Xingu project. The dams remained on the drawing board, though the Brazilian government revived them in the late 1990s.

But even if Payakan had done or would do nothing else, his brilliant work on the Altamira meeting—and its spectacular results—would assure him a place in indigenous history.

Man of the World

During the late 1980s Brazil and the Amazon received unprecedented international attention. As a result, Payakan became a world traveler, meeting with environmentalists, scientists, parliamentarians, indigenous solidarity groups and the public in many countries. The North saw him as a defender of the Amazon rainforest, but Payakan was defending Kayapó interests. The two roles did not necessarily coincide or cohere. Payakan had a keenly pragmatic sense of how to reconcile the differing perspectives and groups to whom he spoke during his travels, however. In a speech at the University of Chicago in 1988, he said,

> The forest is one big thing; it has people, animals and plants. There is no point saving the animals if the forest is burned down; there is no point saving the forest if the people and animals who live in it are killed or driven away. The groups trying to save the races of animals cannot win if the people trying to save the forest lose; the people trying to save the Indians cannot win if either of the others lose; the Indians cannot win without the support of these groups; but the groups cannot win either without the support of the Indians, who know the forest and the animals and can tell what is happening to them. No one of us is strong enough to win alone; together, we can be strong enough to win. (ibid., 18)

With this discourse he helped build coalitions and secure alliances that would benefit the Kayapó and himself. Furthermore, he showed that "the supposedly hapless victims of progress have assumed a leading role" in preserving both the environment and themselves (ibid., 22). Payakan surprised Northerners, accustomed to seeing indigenous peoples as doomed atavists, by demonstrating that the Kayapó had taken their fate into their own hands. Thus, he countered "the hopelessness induced by apocalyptic but often inaccurate news stories of 'genocide' and widespread romantic clichés like the inevitable disappearance of primitive peoples in the path of progress," Turner pointed out. By promoting specific projects such as his "Mebengokre Foundation," Payakan encouraged northern supporters to invest in the Kayapó financially as well as emotionally.

Years later, Payakan made a modest and astute assessment of his travels:

It didn't result in much for the Kayapó, though it helped Brazilian Indians in general. During the period when I was taking the Kaya-pó to the city and traveling outside Brazil, the Kayapó were living well, off mining and logging money. But at the same time I was saying in the name of the Kayapó that my people were fighting on behalf of nature. And later, everybody was against what the Kayapó were doing. That's why I say that my trips outside Brazil and the image I presented of the Kayapó didn't bring results for the Kayapó but rather for Brazilian Indians. (Interview with the author)

The Operator

As a result of his international fame, in the early 1990s Payakan was riding high—perhaps too high for his constituency back in A'ukre, which demanded material gains and improvements in the short term. Other village leaders had already allowed loggers to extract mahogany from forests near the village. Payakan told Turner that although he opposed logging, he had realized it was inevitable and "decided to make deals on the best terms possible for the community" (Turner 1992b: 6). He used the proceeds to build houses and pipe in water from a nearby stream. But he insisted on keeping control, "convinced that only he knew how to make best use of the money" (ibid.). Conflicts with his rivals followed.

One of them told Turner that in 1990 Payakan had made a deal worth about $40 million in timber, for which he received a one-time, 10 percent payment of $392,000. His rival claimed that Payakan was skimming a large monthly sum for himself "without spending a penny on the community." The following year, he forced the rival out of the village so he could continue as sole intermediary to the loggers.

Payakan was not the only Kayapó leader to act in this way. His agemates also made deals with loggers and miners and pocketed much of the proceeds. Beginning in 1990, reports reached the outside world that the Kayapó "were in effect acting as collaborators and profiteers in the destruction of their own forests and rivers" (ibid., 12). In two years they had turned from ecological heroes into villains. International interest and support gradually shifted to other indigenous groups and the upcoming United Nations Conference on Environment and Development (UNCED).

The Road Downhill

In 1991 Payakan's wife, Irekran, went to the doctor in Redenção after suffering a miscarriage. Payakan later charged that the doctor had sterilized her without her knowledge or consent, and he took the highly unusual step (in the Brazilian context) of suing the doctor. Saying that Payakan's status as a Kayapó leader was threatened because he had no male offspring, nonindigenous friends raised funds for an expensive operation to reverse the sterilization. Although the operation was declared successful, Payakan and his wife had no more children. Payakan clearly saw this incident as a deliberate attempt to sabotage him, and his mistrust of whites seemed to increase.

Payakan was not to be seen at the UNCED preparatory conferences in 1991. When he appeared in Brasilia at meetings of the Rainforest Foundation board (of which he was a member), he seemed fretful, even self-pitying. In elaborate fits of pique, he would ritualistically resign from the board at every meeting. Finally the foundation accepted his resignation.

Hundreds of Brazilian Indians attended the 1992 international indigenous conference in Rio, but Payakan did not show up. Just a few weeks before, his serious face had appeared under the headline, "The Man Who Would Save the World," on the cover of a popular U.S. magazine. Nor did he attend the Earth Summit that followed. This was especially puzzling because Payakan had led the struggle to defend indigenous interests in Brazil and beyond since 1988. Almost every month, it seemed, he was traveling to one capital or another, organizing a meeting, giving interviews, leading a delegation. He was one of a few Brazilian Indians whose faces became familiar to international audiences.

So where was Payakan in mid-1992? His absence from the conference seemed to lessen its importance. There was something ominous in other Indians' reluctance to talk about him. Then came the headlines and the elemental shock of scandal: Payakan was accused of raping a young Brazilian woman. News of the rape charge broke as an exclusive story in the weekly news magazine *Veja*, which plastered his glum visage on its cover, above the words, "The Savage," just before the Earth Summit began.

The article was a hatchet job, riddled with inaccuracies and permeated by racist assumptions, clearly aimed at discrediting not only Payakan but the cause of indigenous rights. The source of the "information" in the piece was someone in the office of Pará's governor, who was suing the federal government to repeal the demarcation of the Mekragnoti Kayapó reserve. Surely it was not coincidental that the report appeared a few days before the Earth Summit.

A reporter and cameraman from TV Globo, Brazil's biggest network, went to A'ukre to interview Payakan. On nationwide television he seemed to admit his guilt: "Yes, I did it," he said, looking sheepish, "but I can't remember it because I was drunk." Supporters who rushed to his defense claimed Payakan had never admitted to rape; the footage had been cut to take his words out of context, they said.

Eighteen-year-old Silvia Ferreira, the alleged victim, told a sordid story: After a marathon party at a farmhouse outside Redenção, Payakan and Irekran gave her a ride home in Payakan's car. All three were extremely drunk. Payakan stopped the car, jumped into the back seat and assaulted Silvia with Irekran's assistance. Bloodied and dazed, Silvia finally managed to escape. Two Brazilians, who happened to be nearby, rescued her as Payakan was trying to throttle her.

According to the *Veja* story, several days later Silvia underwent a forensic examination at the local hospital, and Payakan's semen was found on her underwear. Any rape-victim's advocate (or a rape victim who has undergone such an exam) would find this part of the tale hard to believe. A forensic examination for rape is a painstaking procedure with an elaborate protocol, requiring special equipment, and it must be done within forty-eight hours of the crime. In order to determine whose semen is present, a DNA sample must be taken from the alleged perpetrator and tested. There is no indication that Payakan's blood or semen was tested, or that a forensic report was filed. And would a small hospital in a frontier town in the Amazon have the capability to carry out these procedures?

The *Veja* story also claimed that the inside of Payakan's car was stained with Silvia's blood. American journalist Scott Wallace went to Redenção a few weeks later and found the car. It had already been sold without the police examining it for evidence and was completely clean. As a result of this and other discoveries, Wallace doubted that a rape had occurred; in any event, he thought, the legal case against Payakan was weak. More than two years later, a judge threw out the case for lack of evidence. But the charge was later revived and Payakan was finally convicted, almost ten years after the fact.

Rape-victim advocates know from experience—and scientific studies of rape confirm—that most rape victims tell the truth. Silvia Ferreira probably did suffer some kind of violent assault in the back of Payakan's car. Whether or not Payakan's statement was taken out of context, he did admit that something had happened. It is possible that Irekran did most of the attacking. Under Brazilian law, however, she was considered an "unacculturated Indian" with insufficient understanding to be charged.

Turner visited the Kayapó soon after the rape charge was made and reported:

> The Kayapó with whom I spoke in A'ukre, Gorotire and Kuben-kranken accept that Payakan and his wife Irekran did something bad to the girl who accuses them. They think that the couple had drunk too much (Irekran more than Payakan), Payakan was messing around sexually with the girl, and Irekran attacked her, scratching her genital area and other parts of her body. The majority is doubtful whether rape or even intercourse occurred, remaining skeptical about the details. . . . The Kayapó are much more concerned about the reaction of the whites. . . . There was unanimous agreement that white reaction in general, and specifically that of the media, was excessive, far beyond what Payakan's actions deserved. . . . Despite their disapproval of his actions, the Kayapó with whom I spoke were disposed to defend him as a "relative" against the whites, because they saw the accusations . . . as expressions of hostility toward them in general, motivated by the greed of some whites for their lands and resources. (Turner 1992b: 1)

If the original intent of the rape charge was to bring Payakan down, it succeeded. Some Brazilian and international supporters defended him publicly in 1992 and called the charge a sham, while others repeated the rumors of his deals with loggers and his high life in town, as if they proved his guilt. Payakan became a liability to the indigenous cause and an unreliable ally for environmentalists. Funders of sustainable development projects lost interest in financing his initiatives. Within his community, he retained some power and prestige, but significant opposition developed against him in his home village, A'ukre.

After the Fall

A few years after his disappearance from the international scene, in the mid-1990s, Payakan moved restlessly between the Kayapó reserve in central Brazil and the rough frontier town called Redenção ("Redemption"). Many of his supporters on the reserve had moved away from him, and his ideas for developing his community seemed more like illusions than dreams. In the international arena, he was largely forgotten.

A few sympathetic people still tried to help him. Canadian biologist Barbara Zimmerman, who ran an ecological research station near A'ukre, kept him on her payroll. One steamy afternoon in 1995, she was beginning a two-day journey home to Toronto after four months in a Kayapó village. She made a strangely glamorous impression as she waited in the tiny airport of Redenção. Traces of body paint stained her shins, above serviceable Timberlands and just below the hem of a fashionably long cotton dress. She chatted with Payakan as she waited for the small plane that would take her to Brasilia.

A few minutes after her arrival, Márcio Santilli, then the embattled president of FUNAI, checked in. He was on his way back to Brasilia after difficult negotiations with Kayapó warriors who had invaded the FUNAI office in Redenção and taken several hostages. Santilli's mobile face looked miserable, as if he were asking himself, "Why on earth did I take this job?"

Three months later, twenty Xavante warriors armed with clubs stormed his office in Brasilia, forced him into the building's underground garage, and harangued him for an hour, thrusting their forefingers in his face, demanding immediate assistance for their people. All he could tell them was that the Congress had not yet passed FUNAI's appropriation, and the agency had no money to spend on the Xavante or any other indigenous group.[1] Santilli resigned soon after.

Some Kayapó leaders in Redenção also were demanding money, to pay the estimated $2 million debt they had run up in the town while buying everything from cases of Coca-Cola to ship to their villages to the services of local prostitutes. They claimed they had spent most of the money hiring planes to send sick relatives from the reserve to hospitals for emergency medical treatment. They had to do this, they told the media, because FUNAI was not carrying out its statutory responsibilities, which included providing schooling, medical assistance, infrastructure, and environmental protection to fourteen Kayapó communities in three reserves. Therefore, they said, FUNAI should pay the debt.

Santilli flew 600 miles from Brasilia to Redenção to tell the Kayapó warriors that FUNAI auditors would look into the matter. The Indians let the FUNAI workers go but kept the office administrator hostage in a Kayapó village. Three months later, he was still there.

The Kayapó used these highly visible strong-arm tactics time and again against Brazilian federal officials because they worked. As if going to war, they would paint themselves, put on feather and bead decorations, heft their heavy wooden clubs, and shoulder their video cameras. Government officials almost always blinked first. Payakan was often involved in (or behind) these dramatic sorties.

Barbara Zimmerman saw another side of him and the Kayapó during her years in A'ukre. Leaving her husband and three children in Toronto, she would stay in the village for weeks at a time, living as the Kayapó did, during four-month stints in Brazil. "It's tough physically, it's tough in every way," she said.

The Kayapó, she noted, "are really open to any new idea." They are very intelligent, and "if you explain something to them, they understand it" and are eager to try it. One village wanted to start an ecotourism project but didn't know how to manage it. Zimmerman was looking for funding and people, "mature people, with some experience" of Brazil, to operate it. Back in Toronto, she seemed to find fundraising and proposal writing more daunting than weeks in the bush. Funders, she complained, "don't have any idea of what Indians are really like."

No sooner had Zimmerman arrived in A'ukre for the first time in 1992 than she faced a crisis. The village was split by personal rivalries and conflicts centered on Payakan. He had persuaded the Body Shop to set up a pioneering extractive project in A'ukre.² Although this triumph gave him great prestige, his allegedly authoritarian ways stirred up opposition in the village.

Anthropologists who have studied the Kayapó point out that internal divisions are common among them. In the old days, villages split as a result of fights over women or ceremonial practices; now the fights tend to focus on money: Who gets it, who gives it away, who spends it, and on what. Up-and-coming leaders gain prestige by bringing goods back from the outside world and distributing them to the community. They bought shipments of Coca-Cola with money obtained through deals with loggers and miners, who extracted gold and mahogany from Kayapó lands and paid a percentage of the proceeds to Kayapó leaders, including Payakan.

It was said he gave jobs and goods only to his close relatives. Other community members felt left out and resentful. Among many indigenous societies, stinginess is the greatest sin, and accumulation of goods is praiseworthy only in so far as it leads to equitable distribution.

When Zimmerman arrived in A'ukre to direct the new research station in 1992, she faced an angry crowd who complained about Payakan's control over the resources that had come into the village through the Body Shop project. To her the solution seemed obvious: a council of village men and women to oversee the project. But more dramatic developments made the council extraneous; the village split and about half the population moved away. Payakan's control was re-established.

Zimmerman learned how to work with Payakan and the Kayapó through trial and error. "The first year I really screwed up," she recalled, by giving money to the Kayapó leader who ran the local FUNAI post. Community members told her never to do that again. Afterwards she sought written authorization from as many community members as possible for every decision she took on behalf of the village.

Because money was coming into A'ukre, some of the disaffected villagers drifted back over time. Within a year, however, the community split once again. Conflict centered on Payakan. More than half the villagers, who did not believe they were benefiting from the Body Shop project, left, this time apparently for good, and set up another village downriver. Two such splits during a three-year period showed, Zimmerman thought, that Payakan was a particularly problematic figure for his own people.

Brazilians also found him both difficult and compelling. During the 1995 Kayapó takeover of the FUNAI office in Redenção, from behind the scenes he advised the young warriors who carried out the invasion. In the outside world he was fatally compromised by the rape charge. Periodically throughout the 1990s, a local prosecutor would re-indict him, and Payakan would flee to the reserve. Finally, in 2002 he lost his final appeal, but the authorities decided not to send police to A'ukre to apprehend him. He risked arrest and imprisonment if he left, and so he stayed in the village.

Brazilian television reporters went to Redenção to interview him during the 1995 takeover, more than three years after the rape charge was first made. There was still something about Payakan that forced whites and Indians to pay attention.

Physically, he had none of the exotic allure of his older kinsman, Raoni, who also became internationally famous during the 1980s, when he toured the world with Sting. A large, powerful man, Raoni has a commanding presence, reinforced by the prominent wooden lip plate he always wears in public. Raoni seems a true representative of the "Fourth World," an ambassador from another reality. Payakan is smaller, though stocky enough to be physically imposing on occasion. Unprepossessing, he has often been photographed with an unsmiling, almost uneasy, expression.

In contrast, Payakan looked at ease and seemed in good spirits as he sat with Barbara Zimmerman in Redenção airport that day in 1995. Dressed in casual Brazilian style, he chatted and joked with other Kayapó leaders, Santilli, and the mayor of Redenção. After Zimmerman and Santilli left, he went off with his age-mates and the mayor for lunch in town.

Payakan at Home

Arranging an interview with Payakan was not easy. He kept postponing the meeting time or not answering the telephone. His wife would pick up the receiver and start speaking in Kayapó, or another member of the household would come on the line and say Payakan was not there, then turn to him and ask him what to say next. Finally a meeting was set for the next day.

Payakan lived in an ordinary-looking but large stucco house on an unpaved street in Redenção. Like his house, most of the town had the raw, unfinished look of the frontier. When I arrived to interview him, he was standing in front of a camera, giving an interview to a TV reporter on the takeover of the FUNAI office. His manner was assured and friendly, his statement brief but articulate. He clearly had considerable experience at presenting himself as a spokesman for his people.

But he could not give the scheduled interview; apologetically he said he had to go to the FUNAI office to talk to the Kayapó warriors still occupying it. How about later in the afternoon?

At four o'clock, as the light faded slowly from the brilliant blue sky, he greeted visitors at his house. A few Kayapó women and children sat on the courtyard pavement and stared. The house was crudely finished, with little furniture; it looked almost unoccupied. The rooms were large and dark, and there was a sadness about the place. Payakan's office contained a desk, two chairs, a couple of tables, a shortwave radio, a generator, and other equipment.

Payakan was unwelcoming, resistant, almost hostile. He sat behind the desk, fiddling with a pencil. Having talked many times about his early life with journalists from Europe, the U.S., and Japan, he did not want to answer questions about it. There was a long silence.

Almost defiantly he said: "The struggle I've waged has been my own, not for all the Kayapó; it was a struggle that I sought. Nowadays I'm at the disposal of the Kayapó people. If they want me to act, I will. If they don't want me, that's it."

Asked if he would choose to fight the same battles again, he answered no. "It was worth the effort, it was good. I wanted to do it, and I did it. I don't want to do it anymore. . . . I've had enough, I don't have the desire anymore."

Nevertheless, he described himself as "part of a group that has the capacity to lead the people," but he had learned that leading does not mean telling people what to do. And he said he was "someone who observes and analyzes," a surprising self-characterization from a man known, for better or worse, for his actions. After this revelation, the unsmiling face in the news photographs made more sense. Perhaps his face had not expressed unease, but the concentration of someone trying to figure things out and keep on top of them as they happened, in languages and cultures utterly alien from his own.

He blamed whites for the occupation of the FUNAI office:

This crisis isn't the Indian's fault, but the whites'. They taught us wrong, and FUNAI itself didn't bother to guide or teach the Kayapó so they could cope with white society. We've realized that the whites taught us to get money but didn't teach us how to spend or use it. There's still time to teach, and that's why we are preparing ourselves to help our people. Dependence on whites will never help. (Interview with the author, November 1995)

Oddly, this sounded like what Márcio Santilli had said in an interview a few days before, and what he would say three months hence to the angry Xavante who surrounded him in FUNAI's underground garage. Indigenous people have to come up with their own sustainable-development projects, Santilli told them; the era of white paternalism is over.

Between Two Worlds

Despite his declaration of independence, Payakan depended on whites for his subsistence. According to Barbara Zimmerman, "He's nobly trying to put his three girls through school" in Redenção. He paid tuition out of his salaries from FUNAI and Zimmerman's project.

He said: "The important thing is for the Indian to keep being an Indian, to know his culture. If the Indian doesn't maintain his culture, doesn't know it, forgets and goes to the city to live like whites, doesn't want to be an Indian or know about his people, doesn't fight for indigenous rights, then you can say he doesn't care about Indians" (interview with the author). Although he said he was moving slowly back to the reserve to live, he seemed to see his daughters' future in the white world, not in the forest.

Rumors about his fabulous wealth, his cars and airplanes, seem to have been extremely exaggerated. Zimmerman's housekeeper insisted that "he isn't in any kind of need," but the cupboards and refrigerator in his house were almost bare. Payakan's control over large sums of money from loggers or the Body Shop ended sometime after the 1992 rape charge terminated his career as an international celebrity, though he apparently continued making deals with loggers. He seemed to have no success raising funds for the grandiosely named "University of Kayapó Culture," a maloca without walls next to an airstrip in a remote corner of the reserve.

Barbara Zimmerman, who said, "I probably know him as well as anybody can," described Payakan's character as "incredibly complex." Sometimes he seemed "manic," with lots of good ideas, "but he has trouble focusing" and lacked the capacity or training to execute or administer projects. Within his community, however, he was "a powerful character." What happened to the man who had organized the 1989 Altamira meeting and many other actions with considerable administrative skill?

Payakan was a well-known Kayapó leader for more than a decade, and the ups and downs of his career paralleled the indigenous group's adventurous experiments with modernization. Most of the Kayapó have been in "peaceful" contact with Brazilian society since 1950. Nonetheless, they did not hesitate to defend themselves or attack outsiders when necessary.

The Kayapó suffered the devastating consequences of epidemics, invasions, conflicts, and other insults that predatory outsiders inflicted on them. Unlike many other Brazilian indigenous groups, Kayapó culture did not collapse or disappear under the assaults of "civilization." Despite their internal divisions, they have consistently managed to close ranks against external threats to their survival as a people. Moreover, they have taken audacious actions to ensure their vitality and prosperity. For more than a decade Payakan often organized or led these initiatives.

In Retrospect

Payakan portrayed his retreat to A'ukre as a positive development: "Back in '91, when I made my final trip overseas . . . I was already saying then that I wanted to stop traveling. . . . I was already thinking I had nothing more to say. . . . The other thing was that I wasn't taking anything back to my community. I don't want to speak anymore to teach you [whites]. I returned with the assurance that I was bringing back something positive for my community" (interview with the author, November 1995).

His self-assessment of his recent career was tinged with a mixture of resentment and pride. "Many people, including my Indian and non-Indian colleagues, think Payakan got burned, he's finished. No, I don't have to be invited by anybody to struggle. But when I see that nobody else wants to fight, I also don't want to fight. I don't own any Indians. I don't own the forest. I'm one of the people who has responsibility for the forest and nature."

It was difficult to see how Payakan would carry out this self-proclaimed responsibility. He seemed to support recent initiatives to teach sustainable mining and logging techniques to the Kayapó: "In the beginning, I had the idea that the Indian could learn how to extract gold. But neither NGOs nor the government gave this kind of help to the Kayapó. I tried to convince the Indians but I couldn't. But it so happened that the government managed to expel the miners with Kayapó support. Now is the time for the whites to teach the Indians how to manage certain techniques to extract gold without polluting or destroying the environment."

But Payakan did not participate in these initiatives, nor in the establishment of Kayapó community associations. He became marginalized, both in Kayapó society and in the white world. While his age-mates exercised leadership in village and town (one became president of Redenção City Council), he hid in his village.

It might be premature to count Payakan out, however. In his late forties, he is no longer a "young leader," but Kayapó culture still presents opportunities for him to exercise influence, as Raoni has done. As time passes and the Kayapó face new challenges, they may need his formidable organizational skills and his audacity again.

I asked to take a picture of Payakan en famille, and he told me to come back at noon the next day. When I arrived with my camera, I was told he was not at home. Perhaps he did not want to pose as a smiling father or expose his children to the scrutiny of an uncomprehending world. Or perhaps he did not think it would do him any good. The first time I had seen him, at a Washington press conference in 1988, his features had been suffused with uncertainty and mistrust. No matter how far Payakan traveled, it seemed, the phantoms of 500 years of history still pursued him.

5 / Yanomami Apocalypse

THE NEWS PHOTOGRAPH LOOKS AS IF IT CAME FROM THE Vietnam War: A strapping soldier in camouflage gear hoists a small, limp, almost naked body into the back of a cargo plane in the jungle. But the caption says the picture comes from Brazil, not Vietnam. This frail human being is a Yanomami Indian, one of more than 1,500 who died under the assault of "civilization" between 1987 and 1990. News of their fate led the American Anthropological Association to accuse the Brazilian government of complicity in genocide, and thousands of people around the world carried protest banners in front of Brazilian embassies. The international outcry pushed the Brazilian government to change its policies, demarcate a large area on its northern frontier for the Yanomami, and provide millions of dollars' worth of medical care to the Indians.

Yet, more than ten years after the demarcation of their reserve, the Yanomami keep dying of malaria, sexually transmitted diseases, viral infections, and complications of malnutrition, among other maladies. Their traditional way of life is precarious. The end of the world as they know it seems all too close. What has happened—what will happen—to the Yanomami, and why?

According to the Yanomami, Omame, their creator, buried a lethal substance under the ground, from where its deadly smoke could not escape to poison them. "As long as the gold stays in the cold depths of the earth, everything's all right, it isn't dangerous," explains Yanomami leader Davi Kopenawa. From the sky and the forests come supernatural threats and diseases, but helper spirits controlled by shamans keep them at bay. Some of these helper spirits hold up the sky, so it will not collapse as it did once before, at the beginning of the world.

Brazilian Air Force pilot carries Yanomami woman to helicopter, Aemosh village, Roraima, 1990. Photo by Charles Vincent/Instituto Sócioambiental.

The Yanomami have lived in the forests of the northern Amazon for a very long time. Davi told anthropologist Bruce Albert (1991: 171): "Tell them how in the beginning . . . how we were, how we had good health, how we weren't dying so much, we didn't have malaria. Tell how . . . we hunted, how we held feasts, how happy we were."

The Ethnographic Present

Anthropologists who have studied the Yanomami since the mid-1950s tell different tales. Some recount constant conflicts between Yanomami villages, duels with clubs and machetes, ambushes in the forest, wife beating, gang rapes, and other forms of endemic violence. Others say the communities they studied were not particularly violent. Ferguson's book claims that Yanomami warfare has correlated over hundreds of years with intrusions by outsiders and their goods, while other scholars call the Yanomami "the largest relatively isolated indigenous group in the Western Hemisphere." The interpretation of Yanomami culture is still much contested.

Whatever the "true" picture, most observers agree upon a few facts. Because of the remote location of their territory and the geographic obstacles hindering contact, the Yanomami knew little of whites until missionaries began living among them in the 1950s. Scientists do not seem to have identified the Yanomami as one people until the 1960s (Ribeiro 1967, Galvão 1967). They have determined that the Yanomami speak four or five distinct languages that derive from the same linguistic trunk (Gomez 1997b).

Yanomami maintain extensive trading networks and alliances with neighboring villages, but their relations with more distant communities may turn hostile. They tend to identify themselves by village (populated by 40 to 300 individuals), rather than seeing themselves as part of the larger group, which numbers almost 13,000 in Brazil and a similar number in neighboring Venezuela. Nonetheless, their customs are similar across the large area in which they live. They believe that the forest around them teems with spirits—some helpful, some evil—which shamans can harness by going into trance under the influence of a hallucinogenic plant. When someone dies, the death is usually assumed to be caused by spirits mobilized by a hostile village. The Yanomami cremate their dead, pulverize their bones, and mix them into a plantain beverage that they reverently consume.

They live in large *shabonos*, round or oblong thatched shelters that house the whole village. Women gather forest plants and tend gardens, while men clear new gardens and hunt. Storytelling is a great art and a form of entertainment, as is political oratory. The Yanomami have a rich "oral literature." The shaman and the village headman are important figures, but neither can tell anybody what to do.

When the fertility of the gardens wanes, the supply of game decreases, and tempers flare, Yanomami communities divide and groups go their separate ways, starting new villages and dispersing the population. They keep in touch via vast webs of trails through the forest, visiting other villages frequently. Spaces that look empty on the map "are in reality completely used by the Yanomami" (Distrito Sanitário Yanomami 1991: 14).

The problem with this description is that it is in the present tense, as if Yanomami culture had survived intact the deadly assaults of the past forty years. Davi sadly observed, "We used to call the spirits to heal us. Today the Yanomami don't even build their big malocas, they just live in little huts in the forest, under plastic sheeting. They don't even plant gardens, they don't hunt anymore, because they're sick all the time. That's how it is" (Albert 1991: 171).

It would be a mistake, however, to see the Yanomami of fifty years ago as living in a timeless Eden (or a Hobbesian dystopia where life was nasty, brutish, and short). For at least a hundred years, perhaps much longer, Ferguson says, the Yanomami have had access to machetes, cooking pots, and other items from the outside world, via trading networks with other Yanomami villages and neighboring indigenous groups such as the Maiongong and the Yekuana. It is incorrect to call them "Stone Age Indians."

When whites began arriving in numbers in their territory in the 1950s, the Yanomami wanted their wonderful goods: A steel tool is many more times efficient than a stone ax. Visiting anthropologists and missionaries complained that the Yanomami would mercilessly importune them, only to give the objects away after a short time. "To be stingy is to be antisocial, to deny the inviolable reciprocity that governs relations between people. To breach such reciprocity was to trigger sorcery accusations, or bad feelings, to say the least," observed anthropologist Alcida Ramos (1995c: 8), who has studied the Sanumá subgroup of the Yanomami for more than thirty years.

Some missionaries would establish themselves in an area by giving away vast quantities of trade goods. Their attempts to convert the Yanomami to Christianity mostly failed. Sometimes they brought deadly contagious diseases, such as measles and tuberculosis, into the Yanomami world; but they have also provided life-saving medical treatment and education in the Portuguese language.

Anthropologists also have complicated the lives of the Yanomami. Some arrived in Yanomami villages with stocks of gifts, and their presence inevitably affected the tenor of community life. Some may have inadvertently transmitted diseases and precipitated conflicts. According to Ferguson, little warfare took place among the Yanomami before anthropologists and other outsiders arrived, from the 1930s to the 1950s. When outsiders were present, however, rivalry for goods would increase and so would conflict. When they left, the constant flow of goods they had provided stopped, and villages went to war. By that time, the outside world had intruded massively, in a far more destructive way.

The Invasion of Civilization

Large numbers of whites arrived in Yanomami territory in 1973, when the Brazilian government decided to build a highway across the northern Amazon. Construction crews brought contagious diseases such as influenza, measles, and tuberculosis to Yanomami territory. Since the Indians had no immunity to these illnesses, many died. A perverse relationship of dependency and hostility, "mistrust and seduction," grew up between the Brazilian workers and the Indians (Medeiros 1995: 85).

In areas near the highway, Yanomami culture was devastated. Game fled, and the Indians begged for food instead of planting gardens. Pressure intensified on the Yanomami to abandon their traditional ways and assimilate into Brazilian society as the poorest of the poor. Yanomami living near the highway wanted Brazilian goods to prove that they, too, were "civilized," not "wild Indians" (Saffirio & Hames 1983: 19).

Ironically, only 250 kilometers of the proposed 1,500-kilometer highway were completed, 200 in Yanomami territory. Work was abandoned because of lack of funds in 1976. The Northern Perimetral Highway is a road to nowhere that brought disease, social degradation, and conflict to the Indians (Ramos 1995c). It also brought Brazilians and other outsiders in increasing numbers.

Along with freebooting prospectors, squatters, prostitutes, and other poor refugees from the impoverished northeastern region and Brazil's big cities came people of another sort: anthropologists, journalists, missionaries, physicians, and young adventurers looking for a cause. In the early and mid-1970s several went to the Catrimani mission post, not far from the highway. Among them were John Saffirio, a Catholic missionary priest who became an anthropologist to understand the Yanomami better; Alcida Ramos and Kenneth Taylor, a Brazilian-British couple who passed through on their way to do anthropological research on the Sanumá; Bruce Albert, a French graduate student in anthropology; and Claudia Andujar, a Swiss photographer on a Guggenheim fellowship. Ramos, Taylor, Albert, and Andujar became the nucleus of a group of outsiders who decided to dedicate themselves to defending the interests of the Yanomami.

In 1975 the Brazilian government conducted a satellite survey of Amazonian natural resources called RADAM, which found impressive deposits of gold, uranium, cassiterite (the basis of tin), and other strategic minerals in Yanomami territory. Also in 1975, Kenneth Taylor, then a professor at the University of Brasilia, drafted a plan to protect the health of the Indians who lived near the highway. It was never fully implemented, and "less than a year after it began, the project was cancelled due to the military's antipathy to a foreigner operating along the frontier" (Ramos 1992: 53).

Then the prospectors arrived. In 1976, 500 miners were deep in Yanomami territory, looking for cassiterite. The military government expelled them after an international outcry at the dire results of their presence. The government also expelled Taylor, Ramos, and Andujar, presumably because it did not want them monitoring exactly what was going on in Yanomami territory. The governor of Roraima (then a federal territory) was quoted as saying, "An area as rich as this one can't afford the luxury of preserving a half-dozen Indian tribes and holding back development" (CEDI 1991: 164).

Claudia Andujar tried to return to Yanomami territory for three years. In 1978, she and some of the other "veterans" of Catrimani formed the Commission for the Creation of a Yanomami Park. They presented to the federal government a project to demarcate a large reserve—about 7 million hectares. The military regime had its own idea about the proper dimensions of a Yanomami reserve. After the RADAM surveys showed where the minerals were, the military drew up a plan to create a number of "islands" where the Yanomami would live. Around them, prospectors would have free access to the mineral-rich areas. This scheme did not take into account the Yanomami's traditional way of life or the web of trading networks and trails that ramified throughout their territory. Indeed, it reduced the reserve's extent by 70 percent. Also unaccounted for was the persistence of the prospectors, who, the government expected, would open up remote areas so that modern mining operations could move in afterwards.

More than twenty-five years later, the big mining companies have yet to establish themselves, while the garimpeiros keep invading Yanomami territory and the lands of other indigenous groups throughout the Amazon region.[1]

Ramos observed, "The vast majority of these people were either underemployed or unemployed, smallholders who had lost their lands, or urban workers who had lost their jobs. Victims of the country's grossly unequal land and income distribution, these migratory human masses have been pushed off into Indian lands by the shock waves created by underdevelopment" (1995c: 276).

Between 1970 and 1980, gold's international price increased 17 times, reaching $850 per ounce in late 1980. In 1981, 2,000 miners invaded Yanomami territory to look for gold. Outbreaks of disease and violent conflicts between miners and Yanomami resulted. The Brazilian government's sporadic and feeble attempts to deal with the situation had little effect on the larger pattern, which has repeated again and again, from the mid-1970s to the present.

Parts of the Brazilian government worked against or contradicted the policies of other parts at various times. For example, in the mid-1980s FUNAI signed contracts allowing mining companies to explore for minerals in indigenous areas, including Yanomami territory. These agreements triggered garimpeiro invasions, epidemics, conflicts, and other deadly consequences, so that the Federal Police, the army, the air force, and other agencies had to go in and expel the miners. During certain government development projects, various federal agencies encouraged or even subsidized invasions of indigenous lands—by landless peasants, garimpeiros, loggers, and others—that the federal courts eventually declared illegal. The same sad history keeps repeating, with increasingly deadly results, as more Indians die with each invasion.

After twenty-five years, the Brazilian government cannot claim ignorance of the inevitable outcome of uncontrolled entry into Yanomami territory. Some observers have wondered if the government has a more sinister goal, the "Final Solution to the Yanomami Problem." Alcida Ramos bitterly called epidemics "efficient instruments for creating empty lands for white occupation" (Ramos 1995c: 275).

In 1983, anthropologists John Saffirio and Raymond Hames (1983: 19), both students of Napoleon Chagnon, commented, "As long as the Yanomami do not have full control over their aboriginal territory, from which their life derives, then they will not have the choice of staying as they are or becoming Brazilians."

The military had headed and controlled FUNAI since its founding in the mid-1960s, at the beginning of the military dictatorship. Anthropologists and indigenists deemed too sympathetic to Indians were periodically purged from the agency. But in 1984, as the 21-year dictatorship approached its end, pro-Indian factions inside FUNAI asserted themselves by asking Claudia Andujar to advise them on Yanomami demarcation. Andujar had traveled throughout Yanomami territory in 1981 and knew its true extent better than anyone else. She stayed at the house of Alcida Ramos, recently returned to Brazil after several years' exile in Britain and still considered "suspect." Ramos wrote an anthropological justification for demarcating the largest possible area for the Yanomami: more than nine million hectares (about 58,000 square miles), spanning the states of Roraima and Amazonas. No "islands," no mining areas. CCPY's proposal became the official basis for demarcating Yanomami territory.

Demarcation is a rather torturous, time-consuming, and polemical process requiring anthropological field research, geographic surveys, and a series of legal procedures that usually take years. Once accomplished, demarcation guarantees indigenous people "preferential use and control" of the land they live on, but the land remains the property of the federal government. According to Brazil's 1988 Constitution, Congress is supposed to determine subsoil rights on a case-by-case basis. Before 1988, various federal agencies could sign mining and logging agreements with private companies "on behalf of" indigenous groups.   Despite a constitutional provision mandating demarcation of all indigenous territories by 1993, only 260 of Brazil's 575 indigenous areas had been demarcated by mid-2000 (Instituto Sociôambiental 2000). Chronically underfunded, FUNAI never seems to have sufficient resources to carry out this or other responsibilities.

In February 1985 a ragtag gang of forty to sixty garimpeiros led by José Altino Machado, a mining entrepreneur, invaded Yanomami territory, beseiging the FUNAI post at Surucucus for five days. Machado wanted to mine cassiterite in the area, but FUNAI had signed an exclusive contract with a big mining company. The Federal Police finally expelled and arrested Machado and his "troops." The significance of this event went unremarked at the time, but it came at a crucial moment: the end of the military dictatorship and the beginning of an indirectly elected civilian government. Machado would keep appearing—in Yanomami territory, in Brasilia at congressional hearings, even at the 1992 Earth Summit in Rio de Janeiro—as the Roraima garimpeiros' principal spokesman.

In 1986, before the military's Calha Norte project became public, the Brazilian air force enlarged an airstrip at Paapiu, in the heart of Yanomami territory. "Declaring the strip to be a national security area, they had the Indian communal house within it destroyed and went away" (Ramos 1995c: 276). Ramos believes this action was in preparation for Calha Norte colonization efforts. The Paapiu airstrip would soon become the main entryway for tens of thousands of invaders.

In the wake of the Calha Norte leak, the military launched a public-relations campaign to defend their development plans for the Amazon. Reviving the national-security ideology they had used to legitimate military rule, they claimed in interviews and articles that Calha Norte was necessary to defend Brazilian sovereignty from an alleged conspiracy to "internationalize" the Amazon. They claimed the Yanomami and other indigenous groups living near the border were pawns of "ultra-leftists," multinational corporations, Catholic bishops, the CIA, and others who wanted the Amazon's riches for themselves. These "outside agitators" were encouraging the Yanomami to set up an independent state straddling the Brazilian–Venezuelan border. Foreign forces were just waiting for an opportunity to sweep across the border. Demarcation of a Yanomami reserve was, therefore, a threat to national security. To neutralize this threat, the military said it needed to set up military posts all along the northern frontier and "Brazilianize" the region by encouraging colonization of its "empty spaces" by "civilized" people.

Nonetheless, Senator Severo Gomes, of São Paulo state, publicly proposed the formation of a nine-million-hectare Yanomami Park, which would cover 36 percent of Roraima's territory. Gomes became an important ally in the Yanomami's struggle for survival.

As the military disseminated its vision of Amazon development and candidates campaigned to participate in the convention that would draft Brazil's eighth Constitution, something ominous was happening in Roraima. In May 1987 Davi Kopenawa sent a letter to President José Sarney, alerting him to a massive garimpeiro invasion of Yanomami lands. A month later Sarney replied that he was aware of the problem and the government was working on it.

The following account, which summarizes the deadly, convoluted history of the Roraima gold rush of 1987–90, was compiled by CEDI (Ecumenical Information and Documentation Center), a Brazilian nongovernmental organization.[2] It shows how genocide happened with the complicity of the

Brazilian government, and how international pressure helped end it. Most of the information comes from Brazilian press reports.

Anatomy of a Genocide

In June 1987, Federal Police prohibit food shipments to garimpeiros inside Yanomami territory, but the Garimpeiros' Association obtains an injunction permitting the shipments.

In August, four Yanomami are killed in a conflict with garimpeiros near Paapiu. Garimpeiros plant a news story saying eight garimpeiros were killed; Federal Police investigate and say the report is false. FUNAI requests that Federal Police forcibly expel all anthropologists, missionaries, and medical personnel from Yanomami territory. Federal Police carry out the expulsions.

Claiming that the armed forces and Roraima business interests support them, in September the garimpeiros refuse to leave Yanomami territory. By December about 2,500 garimpeiros are working in Yanomami territory. A month later, an estimated 10,000 garimpeiros are extracting thirty kilograms of gold daily in the territory.

After news of the gold rush reaches the outside world, 197 Italian parliamentarians call for emergency aid for the Yanomami in February 1988. Six Brazilian senators (including future President Fernando Henrique Cardoso) denounce the genocide of the Yanomami in an April letter to President Sarney. The United Nations Environment Program informs the Brazilian government that it has awarded the Global 500 Award to Yanomami activist Davi Kopenawa. The Brazilian government does not release this information until August.

By August, one Indian per day is dying of malaria or disease resulting from contaminated water in Roraima, but FUNAI President Romero Jucá says most Yanomami deaths are due to old age, not disease. Jucá will be indicted for malfeasance, but never tried. Years later, his bill authorizing mining in indigenous territories will move through Congress as indigenous supporters try to stop it.

The next month FUNAI proposes a Yanomami reserve divided into nineteen "islands," reversing its earlier support for a 9.4-million hectare reserve. President Sarney names Romero Jucá governor of the newly created state of Roraima. Indians denounce to the attorney general twenty Yanomami deaths caused by mercury poisoning and disease.

In October 1988, Survival International organizes weekly demonstrations at twenty Brazilian embassies around the world to protest the nineteen-island demarcation plan. These demonstrations will continue for more than three years. Nonetheless, Governor Jucá states his support for the garimpeiros and proposes that medical supplies and food be distributed to them. Ex- (and future) Governor of Amazonas Gilberto Mestrinho invests in a mining project inside Yanomami territory.

A federal judge orders that three missionaries be permitted to return to Catrimani mission in November. Within a month, FUNAI asks for a judicial order forbidding the missionaries' return.

In February 1989 the United Nations secretary general receives a petition with 250,000 signatures protesting genocide of the Yanomami. President Sarney ratifies the nineteen-island plan. He then signs decrees creating two national forests in Yanomami territory. "Entry or residence by third parties or the exercise of any activity without prior authorization of FUNAI and IBAMA (the environmental protection agency) is prohibited," the decree declares (CEDI 1991: 172–93).

In April the Venezuelan National Guard expels Brazilian garimpeiros found 100 kilometers inside Venezuelan territory. On April 19, the national Day of the Indian, General Bayma Denys, the head of the National Security Council, declares that expelling garimpeiros from Yanomami territory is "impossible." Later that day, he promises Davi Kopenawa and another indigenous activist that the army and the Federal Police will expel the garimpeiros.

A VIP delegation headed by Senator Severo Gomes visits Yanomami territory in June. Meanwhile, Governor Jucá proposes garimpeiro "reserves," road paving, and other development projects in Yanomami territory, to facilitate mineral exports. By July, 50,000 garimpeiros are estimated to be working in Yanomami territory. At Boa Vista airport, 400 light aircraft going to and from mining areas are making up to 15,000 landings and takeoffs daily. The VIP delegation publishes a report, "Roraima: Warning of Death," and calls for repeal of the nineteen-island demarcation plan. The attorney general's office brings suit in federal court to close illegal airstrips and expel garimpeiros from Yanomami lands. Mining entrepreneur José Altino

Machado visits the Ministry of Mines and Energy with three Yanomami, who say nothing.

Kayapó leader Raoni visits the interior minister in August and asks that garimpeiros be expelled from Yanomami lands. Two other indigenous activists visit Nagasaki, Japan, and ask the Japanese government to cut off aid to Brazil until the garimpeiros are expelled. President Sarney personally promises Raoni that the garimpeiros will be expelled. Garimpeiros kill two Yanomami near a Calha Norte barracks.

Garimpeiros claim in September that Paranapanema, one of Brazil's biggest mining companies, is trying to have them expelled from Surucucus, so that it can begin mining cassiterite there. Demanding the garimpeiros' expulsion, leaders from eight indigenous groups try to see President Sarney, who does not receive them. They dance around the statue of Justice near the presidential palace. The presidential guard surrounds the palace to keep the Indians away. Sarney later says he did not know the Indians were there.

In October, Governor Jucá says he has signed an agreement with the National Department of Mineral Research, transferring responsibility for mining to the Roraima state government. This seems to be illegal under Brazil's new Constitution. A federal judge orders the closing of 9 million hectares of Yanomami territory to outsiders and the expulsion of all garimpeiros in the area. IBAMA, the environmental protection agency, announces that it is studying the establishment of small "industrial units" for timber and mineral exploration in the Roraima National Forest, inside Yanomami territory. FUNAI says it has no resources to expel garimpeiros; state and federal security forces will have to do it.

Garimpeiros attack Yanomami in November, killing three to five; Yanomami wound three garimpeiros in retaliation. Garimpeiros close a nearby airstrip so that Federal Police and FUNAI cannot investigate. Elton Rohnelt, owner of Gold Amazon mining company, future Congress member, and "a businessman who has accumulated a fortune estimated at $20 million during 15 years in the jungle" (CEDI 1991: 186), says he wants to help the Yanomami. "We invaded Indian lands, so we're obligated to preserve them and find a way for them to live," he says. His idea is "to integrate the Indian into the community through work."

More than 120 Yanomami are in the Indian House in Boa Vista, Roraima, and another 200 are in various hospitals, suffering from malaria.

Two weeks later, 214 Indians with malaria are at the Indian House. FUNAI's regional office reports that between January and August, 59 died. FUNAI medical teams are flying the sick out of Yanomami territory in air force helicopters.

As the Yanomami death toll rises in December, a federal judge orders the air force to close illegal airstrips in Yanomami territory. Congress appropriates funds for emergency medical aid to the Yanomami. President Sarney signs a decree expelling the garimpeiros within ninety days and setting up a medical assistance program. On November 15, Fernando Collor de Mello is elected president of Brazil with 52 percent of the vote. His inauguration is scheduled for March 15, 1990.

In January 1990, Federal Police and FUNAI report that eighty-two illegal airstrips are serving 200 mining sites in Yanomami territory. Three-fourths of the gold mined in Roraima is smuggled to Venezuela and Guyana, denying revenue to the Brazilian government. Federal Police prevent small planes from using Boa Vista airport. Four-hundred garimpeiros demonstrate in protest, blaming the bishop of Roraima for the shutdown. Romeo Tuma, director-general of the Federal Police, arrives in Boa Vista to command the expulsion operation. After meeting secretly with garimpeiro leaders, he agrees to the establishment of garimpeiro "reserves" inside Yanomami territory. Justice Minister Saulo Ramos supports the agreement, saying, "No judicial decision can determine the impossible."

The attorney general's office threatens to issue arrest warrants for the president of FUNAI, the director-general of the Federal Police, and the air force minister if they do not carry out the expulsion. Nonetheless, the expulsion operation ends after two days, leaving most of the garimpeiros inside the Yanomami area. Tuma denies having agreed to the garimpeiro "reserves." A flurry of announcements, decrees, injunctions, and counter-orders follows. At the end of January, the justice minister takes full responsibility for implementing the expulsion order.

After visiting Paapiu in February, the justice minister says he saw Yanomami children so malnourished they "looked like Biafrans." He then issues an arrest warrant for French photographers who took pictures of a Yanomami child dying of malaria, which led to an international outcry. The photographers are charged with "failing to give first aid."

The Prince of Wales gives a speech in which he criticizes the Brazilian government for its treatment of the Yanomami. President Sarney decrees two garimpeiro "reserves" inside Yanomami territory. The justice minister says the reserves have been created to prevent the miners from spreading diseases to other parts of the country. The attorney general issues a bill of impeachment against the president, for flouting the garimpeiro expulsion order.

Sarney leaves office in March with impeachment charges pending. A week after his inauguration, President Collor visits Yanomami territory and orders the dynamiting of 110 illegal airstrips. The new governor of Roraima, a Collor appointee, says, "We can't stand with our arms crossed, eyeing a mountain of gold." Severo Gomes visits the new justice minister, Bernardo Cabral, and asks for enforcement of the expulsion order and repeal of the nineteen-island demarcation plan and the garimpeiro "reserves." The order expelling the missionaries from Catrimani is overturned in federal court. In April, President Collor calls for "further study" of Yanomami reserve boundaries.

The next month, a Roraima judge issues orders permitting mining and airstrips in Yanomami territory. FUNAI's regional coordinator in Roraima says in June that dynamiting the airstrips is ineffective, because the garimpeiros quickly rebuild them. A constant stream of Yanomami arrives in Boa Vista for emergency medical treatment. Davi Kopenawa is laid off from his job as a FUNAI interpreter.

The VIP delegation publishes a report in July, saying the situation of the Yanomami has not improved. Dynamiting the airstrips was, in its judgment, "just a show." Five-thousand garimpeiros remain in Yanomami territory. The rivers are contaminated by mercury, and the fish population has plummeted; hunting is poor. At least 1,000 Yanomami have died in two years. In August the foreign minister informs the justice minister that the international community views Brazil as "an agent of genocide."

In September garimpeiros attack a Yanomami village, killing two and wounding one; two garimpeiros are also killed. The attorney general asks for a federal genocide investigation in this case. The president of FUNAI sends a demarcation order, repealing the nineteen-island plan and establishing a 9.4 million-hectare Yanomami reserve, to President Collor in October. He signs it.

At the end of 1990 the justice ministry runs out of funds for the expul-

sion operation on December 17. Garimpeiros are said to be on their way
back to Yanomami territory.

Consequences of Genocide

It is possible that 15 to 20 percent of the Yanomami in Brazil died during the
three-year gold rush. In Surucucus and Paapiu, the centers of garimpeiro
activity, 65 percent of the indigenous population was infected with malaria,
most with the deadly falciparum strain. Before the garimpeiro invasion,
malaria had been rare; afterwards, it became endemic. Thirty-five percent
of the Yanomami were malnourished, and 76 percent were anemic; 13 percent of children lost one or both of their parents. Some of the orphans were
sent to Brazilian households in Boa Vista, where they probably became
domestic servants. This dispersion, plus the abandonment of villages where
mortality was high, devastated Yanomami culture and disaggregated Yanomami society in many areas. "In the last 15 years, the Yanomami have gone
from being an exotic and fierce people to becoming a symbol of indigenous
peoples on the verge of extinction" (Ramos 1995c: 281).

The difference between this process and previous decimations of indigenous groups is the extent of its documentation. Despite the remoteness of
the region, the Yanomami died in plain view, and each excruciating step
along the path to genocide was recorded. Millions of people around the
world watched. Many protested. Everyone involved in trying to save the
Yanomami seems to agree that international outcry and pressure did make
a positive difference. But the international public has a short attention span.
More horrible human catastrophes soon replaced the Yanomami as subjects
of international concern.

The terrible effects of the gold rush did not end, even when most of the
garimpeiros left Yanomami territory (usually for other indigenous areas).
In March 1991 Alcida Ramos visited the Sanumá for the first time in many
years and found the group in a pitiable state. Although the Sanumá lived
far from the centers of garimpeiro activity, malaria had spread to their region, and 71 percent of the population was infected. One of the side-effects
of malaria is anemia. The visiting medical team "instead of getting a drop
of red blood for the microscope slide, drew a diluted pinkish liquid" (ibid.,
295).

Everywhere Ramos went, people were ill. Entire communities had dispersed, not because their members had died, but because they did not have the strength to collect or store food. Ramos made a difficult and dangerous journey to Boa Vista, over "countless rapids and waterfalls," because the Brazilian Air Force helicopter usually available for such trips was "out of service." She could not find a doctor to return to the Sanumá with her, only a "health attendant." Back in Yanomami territory with three colleagues, a week's walk from Surucucus, she heard that the air force had suddenly withdrawn its support for the Yanomami health program; there would be no more helicopters. "We were stranded in the middle of nowhere for more than 10 days, during which I had ample opportunity to be infected by malaria," whose effects she felt after she returned home.

As the military withdrew from the health program, garimpeiros began entering Yanomami lands. Ramos and her colleagues had no idea who would find them first. Finally the National Health Foundation (FNS), the federal agency sponsoring the program, hired a small helicopter to take them to Surucucus. Five people and 180 kilograms of equipment made a frightening half-hour trip in the overloaded helicopter. Ramos was furious at the capricious attitude of the FNS and the military: "It is one thing to be aware of the global and irrevocable process of Western domination that engulfs all indigenous peoples. It is another thing to observe the sordid details of the here and now—the cynicism, the murder, or the neglect—that go into the making of this domination" (Ramos 1995c: 312).

The International Response

The American Anthropological Association (AAA) sent Terence Turner to Brazil in early 1991 to investigate the situation of the Yanomami. Turner was the chairman of a special AAA commission whose members included Alcida Ramos and Bruce Albert; Claudia Andujar and Davi Kopenawa were consultants. The commission's report lambasted the Brazilian government for its "attempts . . . to avoid its responsibilities to protect the welfare, lands, resources, and social integration of its indigenous nations" (AAA 1991: 1). In considerable detail, the report documented the government's sins of omission and commission and the devastating effects of the gold rush on the Indians' health and culture. Yanomami territory had become "a death camp for its own people," the commission charged.

Turner published an op-ed piece based on the report in *The New York Times* during President Collor's state visit to the United States in June 1991. At the same time, commission member Steve Schwartzman, of the Environmental Defense Fund, persuaded eight U.S. senators to send a letter to the Brazilian government expressing their concern about the Yanomami. The AAA also sent the commission's report to international nongovernmental organizations, scientific associations, the Inter-American Commission on Human Rights, and multilateral funding institutions such as the World Bank. These actions triggered critical U.S. media coverage of Brazil. At about this time, anthropologist Gail Goodwin Gomez, who studies Yanomami linguistics, sent information about their situation to the U.N. Human Rights Office. U.N. Secretary General Perez de Cuellar then expressed his concern about the Yanomami in a private chat with Collor. The day after his return home, Collor fired the president of FUNAI and named a new commission, more likely to favor the Yanomami, to restudy reserve boundaries. This is a classic example of the power of international pressure, strategically applied.

Demarcation and After

President Collor announced the demarcation of a 9.4-million-hectare Yanomami reserve on November 15, 1991, one of Brazil's most important national holidays. Many seemed to think that the Yanomami's problems had been resolved. Few garimpeiros remained in the area at the time; but by mid-1992, when the Earth Summit convened in Rio de Janeiro, some 11,000 garimpeiros were said to be working in the reserve. The expulsion operation was reactivated, and by September 1993, only 600 remained, most in Venezuela.

At the 1992 Earth Summit in Rio de Janeiro, Collor gloried in his new reputation as a protector of indigenous peoples. As a result of the demarcation and several environmental initiatives by his government, Brazil won promises of more than a billion dollars in loans and other international aid. But six months later Collor was out of office, the first president of any country in the Americas to be successfully impeached, for corruption. Collor maintained his ouster had been a coup by retrograde elements of Brazilian society, threatened by his "modernizing" measures. His vice president, Itamar Franco, became president in January 1993. Franco was notable for his erratic, unpredictable behavior and his nationalistic prickliness.

CCPY published disturbing reports throughout 1993 of epidemics and conflicts between Yanomami and garimpeiros. But the world's attention seemed to be elsewhere until mid-1993, when three spectacular incidents of savage violence highlighted the deep crisis of Brazilian society. On July 23, 1993, eight street-children were killed in front of the Candelária Church in downtown Rio de Janeiro. About a month later, on August 29, hooded police invaded the slum of Vigário Geral, on the outskirts of Rio, in the middle of the night and randomly killed twenty-one unarmed men, women, and children, some while they slept. In between, news came of the massacre of sixteen Yanomami men, women, and children by garimpeiros. Though announced in mid-August, it probably happened in June and July, in two stages. Because of the remoteness of the location, it took weeks for the news to reach Brazil's capital. Gail Goodwin Gomez, who was doing research in Yanomami territory at the time, faxed a message about the massacre to the U.N. Human Rights Office in New York.

The justice minister announced the Yanomami killings on nationwide television and then went to the reserve to investigate, an indication that the Brazilian government took the incident very seriously. So nervous was the government about international repercussions that the foreign ministry denied a Canadian and a U.S. diplomat access to the area, despite the justice minister's invitation.

During the following days, the estimated number of victims kept rising, from sixteen to forty to seventy-three, to possibly more than 100; it seemed as if the justice minister and the president of FUNAI were competing to give the most horrific accounting. Meanwhile, the head of the Federal Police, whose responsibility is to investigate crimes committed in indigenous reserves, publicly expressed doubts that a massacre had happened. There was, he insisted, no direct physical evidence — no bodies, only a few burnt bone fragments and a burnt-out village. Yanomami cremation rituals leave almost no traces; afterwards, they never mention the names of the dead again.

Politicians from Roraima and other Amazon states echoed the police chief's skepticism. The army read satellite signals to determine exactly where the massacre had occurred, and discovered that it had happened just inside Venezuelan territory. The story faded into the back pages of Brazil's and the world's newspapers.

About two weeks after the justice minister's announcement, Brazil's biggest television network reported what seemed like an authoritative version of events. Reporters and cameramen followed Bruce Albert across Roraima to the neighboring state of Amazonas. There he met with a group of Yanomami who had fled the scene of the massacre about a month earlier and walked almost 200 kilometers through the jungle. As the cameras rolled, Albert called names from an official list of presumed victims. One after anther, sixty-some Yanomami refugees raised their hands, indicating that they were very much alive (Albert 1996).

Story of the Massacre

After interviewing the survivors, Albert published a long and harrowing article detailing the terrible events of June and July that had culminated in the massacre at Haximu. Though it had occurred in Venezuela, there was no doubt that Brazilian miners had planned and carried it out. The motive was escalating tension between the miners and Yanomami villagers who were dependent on them for food and goods.

Albert observed: "The Indians turn from being a threat to being an annoyance with their incessant demands for the goods that they are accustomed to receiving. . . . If gifts and promises do not get rid of them, then the solution is to intimidate or even exterminate them" (1996: 203). According to testimony gathered from Indian and Brazilian witnesses, fifteen garimpeiros, four ringleaders, and four hired gunmen set out to kill all the inhabitants of two shabonos, some eighty-five people, in a series of attacks.

Most of the victims died at Haximu. "After a few very long minutes, the miners stop shooting and enter the shelters in order to finish off anyone still living. Machete blows kill not only the injured but also the few who had not been hit; they mutilate and dismember the bodies that are already riddled with buckshot and bullets" (ibid., 206). This attack caused the deaths of four adults and eight children or adolescents.

The survivors "will never forget that the whites are capable of cutting up women and children, just like 'people-eating spirits.'" They consider the garimpeiros inhuman, "not even fit to be enemies" (Albert 1996: 206).

While fleeing to the other end of Yanomami territory, the Indians quickly conducted the customary funeral rituals. "The belongings of the dead have to be disposed of, the personal names obliterated, and their ashes either buried or ingested" until all traces are gone. Otherwise, the ghosts of the dead would "wander between two worlds, haunting the living with interminable melancholy even worse than death" (ibid., 206).

Thus the Indians destroyed most of the material evidence of what had been done to them. But according to Aurelio Rios, then assistant attorney general for indigenous affairs, enough remained at the crime scenes to show that the massacre really had occurred. Some twenty garimpeiros were arrested in the weeks following the massacre; all but two, thought to be the ringleaders, were quickly released. "But once media attention turned elsewhere, a local judge quietly released them [and] the two immediately disappeared. . . ." (Brooke 1995b: 1). At the end of 1996, the federal court delivered a precedent-setting verdict of genocide against five defendants, all but two of whom were still at large. Brazil's Supreme Court turned down the two jailed defendants' final appeal in 2000. But the others remained at large. If this case follows the pattern of other indigenous massacres, all those responsible will never be brought to justice.

The Nationalist Reaction

Opponents of indigenous rights claimed that the massacre was the invention of the international press, the Catholic Church, or the NGOs that supported Yanomami demarcation. The governor of Roraima called the killings a "pseudo-massacre" and equated the Yanomami funeral ritual with cannibalism. True to his nationalist principles, President Franco commented, "It's not whether people died or not that matters, but the fact that we have to keep an eye on Amazonia" (CCPY 1993: 2).

For the Brazilian government, "keeping an eye on Amazonia" meant pushing through a project that the military had long advocated: installation of a sophisticated radar surveillance system that would cover the entire region. The armed forces also proposed that they be given additional funding to revive the moribund Calha Norte program, intended to "Brazilianize" the frontier with military outposts and agricultural settlements.

Another result of the furor over the massacre was the creation of a new "Amazon Ministry," with Rubens Ricúpero, then Brazilian ambassador to the United States, at its head. By mid-September 1993, Ricúpero had taken over the Environmental Secretariat as well, to create a new Ministry of the Environment and the Amazon.

The military's reaction to the massacre was ominously complacent. The commander of the Jungle Infantry Brigade, João Paulo Saboya Burnier, was quoted in August (Martins 1993):

> The Yanomami tribes should, in our opinion, be acculturated gradually, with respect to their characteristics. They should be oriented to emerge from indigence. . . . Without a doubt, this will take away the Indians' cultural identity, as happened with your ancestors and mine. . . . The danger isn't the occurrence of a confrontation between Indians and Brazilian citizens.

The army minister, General Zenildo de Lucena, said in an interview (Cubel 1993) after the massacre:

> Who knows if the Yanomami, after they're acculturated—on the frontier with Venezuela and with relatives on the other side—who knows what they'll want later on? This is a half-crazy idea, but we have to worry about it. There is no Yanomami nation. They're tribes. We can't keep them isolated from the world. . . . We'd have a zoo if we kept these Indians for research in the future. We can't leave the Indians without the benefits of civilization. I believe it has to be something progressive, done scientifically. . . . One solution is the humanization of points on the frontier. . . . It would be a kind of colonization.

Clearly, the military had not surrendered its determination to decide the development of the Amazon region—and if that meant the disappearance of the Yanomami as a people, so be it.

Aligned with the military were members of the Amazon bloc in Congress, who kept introducing bills to repeal the Yanomami demarcation or drastically reduce the size of the reserve. These efforts continued for years, long after FUNAI's president insisted in late 1995 that the demarcation was a fait accompli.

Elton Rohnelt, the fabulously wealthy mine owner, federal deputy from Roraima, and assistant leader of the government party in the Chamber of Deputies, led the forces against Yanomami demarcation. In an interview with the author in late 1995, he said:

> I know the Yanomami, because I lived with them. They don't travel much. They're not healthy, they're weak, they can't walk far. They don't have proteins, they're not protected. They die at age 30, 33 at the most. Their biochemical makeup has no protection. Their diet is horrible. Their lives are short. What's most important—to protect their culture? They don't have a culture, they're primitive Indians, they have subcultures that they acquire from other tribes. They don't have a rich culture, they're poor in culture—either let them end their lives at 30 or 35, or try to help them attain civilization. Are we whites being selfish, when in the first world we try to lengthen our life spans, spending millions of dollars—aren't we being selfish when we let them live to 35, because we want to keep them the way they are?
>
> This is a hypocrisy on the part of the world, those who don't know about the problem—the NGOs especially. Of the NGOs in Brazil, if five percent are serious, that's a lot. Ninety-five percent are there to get money from abroad and set up campaigns, invent stories, to get dollars from abroad.
>
> The hypocrisy is in the world's wanting the Yanomami to stay the way they are, with no help from FUNAI, which doesn't have resources, with no other form of assistance, letting them die of hunger and malaria. There are some international health organizations there trying to work, but that isn't enough. . . .
>
> We don't want the Yanomami area transformed into a zoological garden of men and animals. We want the Yanomami in a reserve

with legitimate, good assistance, so they can survive.

I don't see any action by the NGOs, the Brazilian government, FUNAI or anybody to solve the problem of the Yanomami, who keep on dying.

The problem, he continued, is that too much land was given to them; it should be decreased. "Talk, talk, talk doesn't resolve anything." Here his tone became harsh.

When asked for his suggestions, he snorted slightly and said:

Revise the criteria for demarcation, everything's included in that: all the necessary studies to re-study the Yanomami problem and see if it's important to have nine million hectares or not. . . . For example, I think all the Yanomami should stay on the Pico da Neblina [Brazil's highest mountain], in upper Amazonas, a place where there's much more game and it's already a national park. They should stay there rather than in Roraima. I don't see why they should stay in Roraima. In Roraima there's no game for them, nothing.

The fact that the Yanomami have lived in Roraima since time immemorial and have first rights to their territory according to the Brazilian Constitution apparently means nothing to Rohnelt and his allies. Their rhetoric provides the backing for continuing attacks on the Yanomami and other indigenous groups who get in the way of Brazilian economic and military activities in the Amazon region.

"Genocide by Omission"

The massacre of 1993 was one incident among dozens of killings of Indians in Roraima since the mid-1980s. The only difference between it and the others was its magnitude. Many more Yanomami have died of contact diseases spread by miners than in violent confrontations with them. As long as garimpeiros continue to enter Yanomami territory, the Indians will suffer the consequences of their presence. Hundreds still come in every year. At the end of 1995, for example, the Federal Police and FUNAI announced yet another multimillion-dollar operation to remove 4,000 garimpeiros from Yanomami lands. A year later, the Federal Police had yet to arrive, and the $6 million appropriation had apparently been spent elsewhere (CCPY 1997: 1). Five years later, hundreds of garimpeiros still remained inside Yanomami territory.

Even when garimpeiros are no longer present, the diseases they brought in have remained or even spread to remoter areas. It took millions of dollars and years of work by hundreds of health professionals under the auspices of the Federal Health Foundation and the nongovernmental Urihi project to bring down astronomically high rates of mortality among the Yanomami. From 1999 to 2002, Urihi managed to reduce Yanomami mortality rates by 50 percent.

Getting health care to the Yanomami is not easy. Urihi points out:

The dispersion of the Yanomami in a territory of more than 9 million hectares of tropical forest creates difficulties for health teams. The mountainous terrain is an additional obstacle, and few communities can be visited by river. However, transportation to regions that Urihi assists is carried out by small airplanes to bases with lodging for staff and a health post. From these installations, the teams make monthly trips on foot to all the communities. Some villages are many days' walk from these bases, necessitating use of a helicopter so that they can be visited regularly and in emergencies. In addition, the Yanomami are divided into social groups that are politically antagonistic to one another, often obstructing teams' direct movement between groups of communities. For these reasons, health activities in the Yanomami area depend on complex logistical planning and a support infrastructure composed of landing strips and health posts located in all the regions. (CCPY 2001b: 7)

Unlike some other indigenous groups in Brazil, the Yanomami are small, delicately built, with a physique that belies their reputation for internecine violence and feuding. To outside invaders, they look vulnerable. Few have guns or ammunition and so are easy targets for armed garimpeiros. Entire villages languish in the grip of malaria, tuberculosis, river blindness, and other vicious diseases. Their ability to defend themselves against unscrupulous and violent intruders is thus severely limited by illness, hunger, and lack of weapons or protection.

The Yanomami live scattered across international boundaries. Thus they have become pawns in a political struggle, between the Brazilian military and its civilian opponents, to define "national security." The military and their allies in Congress and the private sector play the nationalist card every time the Yanomami become the objects of international concern. A British journalist summarized the nationalist argument soon after the reserve was demarcated:

> It's all the fault of the Catholic Church, whose priests, agents of foreign powers, are secretly stacking up vast troves of gold and diamonds. It's all the fault of the multinationals, who want to encourage an independent Yanomami nation which they can go into and rape of its minerals without trouble.
>
> It's all the fault of the CIA, which wants to destabilize Brazil to stop it joining the ranks of the superpowers. It's all the fault of foreign bankers who want to stop Brazil exploiting its mineral riches to keep the noose of debt around the country's neck.
>
> Such are the views expressed publicly not by a crackpot minority but by senior politicians, generals, and business leaders. (Pisani 1991)

This orchestrated response to international expressions of humanitarian concern—plus indigenous people's geographic and psychological remoteness from most Brazilians, racist sentiments, and unacknowledged guilt—has dampened public sympathy for the Yanomami. This has translated into a general lack of political support for the protection of indigenous rights or demarcated territories. Diffusely anti-indigenous rhetoric, especially in areas where Indians are visible, dominates public discourse on these questions, and defenders of indigenous groups must struggle to be heard. With the exception of Davi Kopenawa, almost no Yanomami speak for themselves on television or in newspapers; they usually appear only as anonymous, voiceless victims.

How Can the Yanomami Defend Themselves?

The Yanomami define themselves as members of villages, allied with or against other villages, rather than as members of a single people or nation. Claudia Andujar estimates 200-some Yanomami villages in Brazil, spread across a vast territory, divided by four or five distinct languages. Consequently they have not yet managed to unite against the overwhelming external forces threatening their survival. Few Yanomami speak or understand Portuguese, and only a few dozen have acquired schooling. Most of those that do speak Portuguese, such as Davi Kopenawa, learned it at mission schools, usually in villages located near highways or Brazilian settlements. Villages in remote areas have little opportunity to come to grips with the outside world. The number of potential leaders capable of dealing with, or even understanding, Brazilian society is very small.

In 1983, Saffirio and Hames noted (1983: 5), "The major stumbling block they have in making . . . decisions is their gross ignorance of the long-term consequences of whatever decision they do make." Twelve years later, Rohnelt commented, "The poor things don't even know what's happening to them" (interview with the author, November 1995).

Teaching the Yanomami how to defend themselves against the onslaught of civilization is an urgent task. At the request of local Yanomami leaders, CCPY has established village schools where students learn to read, write, and count in their local language as well as in Portuguese. Urihi has moved ahead by training Yanomami who have attended such schools to be microscopy technicians. Twenty are now working with the health project. Urihi plans to train them to be community health agents who will provide basic health education to Yanomami villagers.

Scores of Yanomami are also training to teach in the reserve's schools. In the process, they are learning how to function in and deal with Brazilian society—how to use money, be wise consumers, produce goods for sale, keep written records. In one course attended by seventy-six teachers in 2002,

> as the teachers were increasing their understanding of commercial relations in an interethnic situation, they were also surveying the principal problems that affect the demarcated territory. They em-

phasized the presence of garimpeiros, the threat of mining companies' entry, ranches impinging on the reserve's borders, the army's
presence in the Auaris and Surucucus regions, construction of roads
and cities near Lower Marauiá. (CCPY 2002)

As they trained to be more effective teachers, the Yanomami also were
learning to be leaders inside and beyond their communities.

Also in 2002, CCPY staff and advisers from Brazilian universities and
international environmental and development groups were helping plan
sustainable development and recuperation projects in areas where mining
had devastated the environment.

These efforts, though promising, are part of a protracted process. It
remains to be seen if CCPY, Urihi, anthropologists, doctors, missionaries,
and others who have already devoted decades to helping the Yanomami
will succeed in these initiatives. The majority of the Yanomami, who live
in Venezuela or in remote parts of Brazil, are still suffering from endemic
diseases and the long-term effects of outside impingement.

With the encouragement of neighboring indigenous groups, who have
been in contact longer with Brazilian society and know more about coping with it, the Yanomami have begun to respond more assertively to the
outside world. Over the past few years, hundreds of Yanomami leaders have
met to discuss their situation and make alliances with neighboring indigenous groups and organizations in Roraima and Venezuela.[3]

At one such meeting in 2001, 136 leaders from 12 villages issued a com-
muniqué to the president of Brazil, the justice minister, the president of
FUNAI, the attorney general, the environmental protection agency, the
congressional human rights commission, and the regional FUNAI office.
The letter bluntly said:

We sent a strong statement, we have already sent many documents
and you whites do not want to listen.

Because we defend the land, we are sending a new document.

The chiefs and the women spoke very loudly because all of us defend
our forest, and we say we are very angry.

Thus we chiefs [say] we do not want in our land garimpeiros, ranchers, loggers and soldiers.

We are saying again that we do not want ranchers; that is how we chiefs think, a strong and true statement. We forest dwellers do not want the ranchers, they are cutting and burning our forest, planting grass and bringing in cattle, and we are very worried because they say they want to kill the Yanomami.

We defend our land from the border at the 30th Parallel, for this reason we do not want ranchers in the subdivision. . . . the rancher Paludo already entered, as well as Miguel, Raimundo, Douglas, Margarida, Paulo, Tereza, Abram, Timbó and Zizero.

They are living in our area and we are very worried.

You whites expel them soon. (CIR 2001)

Other intruders into Yanomami territory included hundreds of soldiers living at bases near Brazil's international borders with Guyana and Venezuela. In an attempt to revive the Calha Norte project, the armed forces set up the outposts inside indigenous reserves, to keep armed conflicts in other countries from spilling into Brazil. The indigenous inhabitants were not consulted. In late 2002, a *New York Times* article drew international attention to the fact that soldiers were fathering children on Yanomami girls and women, spreading venereal disease, and otherwise disrupting village life near the outposts. Brazil's defense minister, who already had called the demarcation of Yanomami territory "a big mistake," denied that the soldiers were causing any problems: "A relationship that lasts two or three years is not sexual abuse. It is natural that these relationships occur. . . . To block them is to impede the fruit of human nature" (Rohter 2002c).

But in an indignant note to the press, CIR replied, "These acts of aggression and violence cannot be considered natural facts. They amount to the violation of human rights that must be investigated and those responsible punished." And a local leader worried, "The soldiers say they are here to protect us, but they have brought diseases and taken over our land without asking us. Soon there will be more, and then what will we do? Where will we go?" The Yanomami fear that if they become racially mixed, they could lose "the benefits and protections provided to indigenous peoples. For that reason, the mixed-race children here are regarded not just as a source of shame but also as a threat" (ibid.).

So the Yanomami and other indigenous groups in Roraima joined to sue the government, asking for dismantling of two army bases on the grounds that their construction without indigenous consent was unconstitutional. Their struggle to control their traditional territories continues as they face grave new threats to their physical and cultural integrity.

The Yanomami will need as many allies as they can muster in their coming confrontations with "the whites." Continuing international pressure; assistance from Brazilian groups; indigenous mobilization on the regional, national, and international levels; infusions of financial aid—all are necessary. In the past, outside attention has waxed and waned, according to the vagaries of news gatherers. The Yanomami need constant allies—people willing to help them confront long-term issues such as education, medical care, political organization, and sustainable economic development. Without this kind of coordinated, ongoing work, the Yanomami could lose their cultural identity and distinctiveness, as have hundreds of other indigenous groups during 500 years of Brazilian history.

The next challenges facing the Yanomami are even greater than seasonal invasions of garimpeiros and outbreaks of deadly diseases. The Brazilian and Venezuelan governments have carried out bilateral agreements to jointly develop their frontier regions. Ongoing projects include paving a road from the Brazilian border all the way to Caracas, installing electrical lines to transmit power from a Venezuelan dam to Boa Vista, and, most ambitious of all, linking the Amazon and Orinoco Rivers via a canal. In every case where similar development projects have been carried out, indigenous peoples have suffered catastrophically.

Davi Kopenawa warns (Albert 1991: 170):

Not only the Yanomami will die—all of us will die together. When the smoke fills the breast of the sky, it will also die, just like the Yanomami. . . . The sky will be torn apart. The Yanomami shamans who have died are many, and they will want to take revenge. . . .

they'll want to cut the sky into pieces so that it will collapse on top of the earth. They'll also make the sun fall, and when it falls, everything will become dark. When the stars and the moon fall, the sky will be dark. We want to tell all this to the whites, but they don't listen. . . .

The Yanomami have to keep finding ways to make the world hear.

6 / Davi

A WIDELY SHOWN DOCUMENTARY FILM ABOUT THE YANOMAMI, "Warriors of the Amazon" (CSL Films 1996), stirred feelings of fascination and sympathy, revulsion and shame in many viewers. In some scenes the Indians seemed beautiful and fragile, threatened human beings whose vulnerability cried out for help. In others, they seemed as frighteningly unpredictable and menacing as members of an unknown species. They were the ultimate other: mysterious, unknowable, remote.

I was reminded of Napoleon Chagnon's books and films, which had done so much to influence, if not determine, my views of the Yanomami. Like thousands of other college students, I first read his book, *Yanomamö: The Fierce People*, at the impressionable age of nineteen or twenty. Years later, many of its descriptions of Yanomami violence seemed repulsive, as much for Chagnon's gusto in the telling as for the violence itself:

> One of the young men took the wife of another because she was allegedly being mistreated by the husband. This resulted in a brutal club fight that involved almost every man in the village. . . . When the husband's rival speared his opponent, the headman went into a rage and speared him in turn, running his own sharpened club completely through the young man's body. He died when they tried to remove the weapon. The wife was then given back to her legitimate husband, who punished her by cutting both her ears off with his machete. (Chagnon 1983: pp.172–73)

Anthropology students (and some of their instructors) still cringe at one of Chagnon's films, about Yanomami drug taking. They watch green mucus

Davi Kopenawa Yanomami at the United Nations. Photo by Claudia Andujar.

pouring from the nostrils of Yanomami warriors dancing and chanting under the influence of a hallucinogenic powder. All the scholarly explanations (and the sight of Chagnon himself, befeathered and painted, prancing about in a drug-induced trance) cannot eclipse that image.

Jacques Lizot's austere, scrupulous accounts of Yanomami daily life, stripped of explanation, also do not seem to show Yanomami culture in a positive light. Other anthropologists avoid the problems created by Chagnon's emphasis on violence by writing dryly abstract analyses. It is their personal stories of their fieldwork experiences that stir empathetic responses in the reader.

Yet some of the anthropologists who studied the Yanomami have fallen in love with them. Photographer Claudia Andujar took thousands of pictures of their delicate beauty and then dedicated her life to trying to save them from extinction. Was this devotion the mere obverse of revulsion? Or had Andujar and the anthropologists attained a higher level of understanding by spending years in the forest with the Yanomami?

The rainforest is a magical place; perhaps its enchantment created an aura around the slight, painted, combative bodies of the Yanomami for those who visited them. But for many Northerners, Chagnon's portrayal seems indelible.

In "Warriors of the Amazon," when Yanomami talk to the camera, they seem like anyone else: people with motives, explanations, rationales. But when they visit the former enemy village—rushing in, shaking bunches of six-foot-long arrows, hurling bloodcurdling cries like spears, and pantomiming assault on their hosts, who sit silent, unmoving, on the ground—they seem so startlingly strange as to be incomprehensible.

In an early scene in the film, a visiting shaman undertakes a cure. Finding the sickness he once sent to torment his enemy in his enemy's knee, he sucks it out with gusto. He jumps up and spits a silvery thread of mucus into his hand, then holds up the dripping trophy. In an interview to a Brazilian news magazine, Chagnon remarked, "Real Indians get dirty, smell bad, take hallucinogens, belch after they eat, covet and sometimes steal their neighbors' wives and make war. They're normal human beings" (Alcântara 1995: 7). If the Yanomami were just like us, however, Chagnon would have had few readers. Their radical differentness challenges our definitions not only of normality but of humanness. Anthropology students are assigned to read about the Yanomami to prod them into rethinking those definitions.

While Northerners thousands of miles away create idealized images of indigenous people, Brazilians on the frontier have no scruples about expressing frankly derogatory views of Indians. After the Haximu massacre, the governor of Roraima snorted, "In truth, what the Indians do is cook the limbs of the body and eat them like bananas" (Brooke 1993b: A4). This was his description of the Yanomami funeral ritual, in which they cremate the dead, pulverize their bones, mix them into a plantain gruel, and drink it.

A foreign journalist noted, "The term 'Indian' is used as a term of abuse in Brazil. It implies dirty, lazy, ignorant." The bishop of Roraima commented, "Brazil has always wanted to dominate and integrate the Indian, to denigrate, to humiliate" (Pisani 1991: 26).

People far from Brazil and its 500-year history are more likely to think of the Yanomami as threatened and vulnerable human beings. Horrified by the terrible story of Yanomami genocide in the 1980s, thousands protested in front of Brazilian consulates and embassies around the world for years.

They welcomed Davi Kopenawa to their countries and thrilled to his eloquent, apocalyptic prophecies.

The Ambassador

Davi has many faces. He seems innocent and sophisticated, profound and simple, tormented and serene. After the Yanomami massacre of 1993 he painted his face black and participated in a war dance. A photograph shows him holding arrows, looking over his shoulder at the camera, wearing an expression of unvarnished hatred, as if he were thinking: "You white bastards, you killed my people; why should I say another word to you, ever?"

Another Davi, calm ambassador from the Fourth World to the First, weaves eloquent words for audiences across the world. Then he goes home to share the fate of his people. As a shaman, he is respected as a leader by the Yanomami. Seeking nothing for himself, he goes to the outside world and returns with goods for all. He lives as everyone else does in the village.

It is almost too easy to present Davi as an avatar of virtue. In a bitter essay called "The Hyperreal Indian," anthropologist Alcida Ramos, who has done much to help the Yanomami, says whites insist on putting Indians into a noble straitjacket. The acceptable Indian hero, she says, is "dependent, suffering, a victim of the system, innocent of bourgeois evils, honorable in his actions and intentions, and preferably exotic" (Ramos 1994: 163). But Davi is something more than this: a leader and man of action, as well as a poet and prophet.

Davi's quiet concentration, dignity, and firmness make him an attractive personality. He bears no apparent resemblance to Chagnon's picture of the fierce Yanomami. Each time I meet him, I feel that in any culture, he would be considered a good man. It is hard to say what this goodness consists of, but it is a recognizable quality, almost an aura. Davi presents a comprehensible, sympathetic image of the Yanomami to the world.

Davi has much greater success outside Brazil, where he is an exotic visitor and prophetic visionary, than inside the country, where he is just another Indian, an obstacle to "progress." In Brazil (and many other places) Indians are not even seen as persons. During 500 years of competing with Indians for land and resources, Brazilians have shown undisguised, sometimes murderous, contempt for them. Davi, however, has managed to move through the looking glass of culture and become something other than the other.

He is a short, stocky, but not heavy man with a broad, placid face. His habitual expression is serious, attentive. Claudia Andujar, who may know him better than any other white person except Bruce Albert, says he is "very clever, very independent, very curious" (interview with the author, 1995). She first met him in the mid-1970s, when he was in his twenties, working for FUNAI as an interpreter. He was one of a handful of bilingual Yanomami.

They met in a village where, as a result of diseases brought in by road construction crews, 50 percent of the population had died. When she heard about the village, Andujar, who was working as a nurse's aide at Catrimani mission, sent a message to FUNAI, asking for emergency help. FUNAI took a month to send assistance. In the meantime, she and her companions decided to walk (a five-day journey) to the village. They stayed, doing what little they could, until a FUNAI helicopter arrived; among the passengers was Davi, working as an interpreter. Years later, when they met again, Davi reminded her of their first encounter. He had not forgotten her effort to help his people. "Then somehow we started to work together. . . . we became friends" (interview with the author, 1995).

The End of Isolation

Davi was born in 1955 in an isolated village in the Toototobi region of Yanomami territory. As a child he learned to read the Bible in Portuguese from New Tribes fundamentalist missionaries. He left the village in 1967, after his mother died of measles brought in, Bruce Albert says, by the missionaries.

As Claudia Andujar tells the story:

The New Tribes [Mission] wanted to make out of him a pastor. That's how he started to learn how to read and write.

Then he got very sick, he had to be taken to Manaus. He had tuberculosis. Then he had his first contact with the city and was invited to

work with FUNAI. So he had already various influences. Somehow
in all these groups, people must have felt that he had a very good
head, no? and tried to attract him to become a leader or an important person, but in a partisan way.

I know that at a certain point he wasn't sure if he should become an
evangelical pastor or not. And then suddenly he turned against it.
He decided that what they were doing was something that didn't go
along with his upbringing. . . .

Then he went and worked with FUNAI. . . . Suddenly he saw the
penetration of the road builders and his people getting sick. . . .
Through the indigenist movement he met other indigenous leaders
who were fighting for a similar cause, and this identified him with
the problems of his own people. Afterwards he definitely was an
engaged person, who started to fight for his people in a global way.
(Interview with the author, 1995)

In the late 1970s Davi worked at Demini as an interpreter for FUNAI. There
he married the daughter of a village leader and shaman, who taught him
the rudiments of religious practice. Appointed head of the FUNAI post, he
became a liaison between the Yanomami and the Brazilians, a distributor of
trade goods, and a political leader, with no conflict, Bruce Albert says, between his traditional and modern roles. Albert calls him an "intercultural
mediator par excellence" (interview with the author, 1997).

Andujar and other activists working with Brazil's indigenous movement needed spokespeople to make the issues real to international audiences. People like Davi were—and are—rare. He has witnessed his people's
decimation and can communicate its enormity to people worlds away. More
than that, he has the capacity to enlist their support. For these skills he won
the United Nations Global 500 Award in 1989.

Others with similar talents and backgrounds, like Paulinho Payakan,
have been damaged or brought down by their international prominence.
"We never wanted him to be a VIP," Andujar says of Davi. She maintains
he has remained unaffected by his experiences in the North. Andujar is
partly responsible for this, it seems. An ageless, statuesque woman with an

evocative alto voice, she travels with him. "He often says I'm very strict. We have a very curious relationship, we joke together, we respect each other" (interview with the author, 1995). She attributes the success of their working relationship to his personality and his understanding of the need to abide by the rules of the outside world as long as he is in it.

According to Bruce Albert, Davi experienced a tumultuous childhood and much emotional turmoil. For a while he wanted to be white but could not manage it. Under the influence of his father-in-law, an important shaman, he became calmer and more self-confident. His wife insisted that the family live in her village, not at the FUNAI post where Davi was in charge. Their children are fully integrated into village life.

At home, Davi is an activist as well as a visionary. He wants bilingual education—reading, writing, and counting— for Yanomami children, even as they continue to live in traditional ways. Providing teachers and educational materials to more than 200 villages spread over 9.4 million hectares is a daunting task. It is one of the main priorities of CCPY, but finding the funds and personnel has been a continual challenge.

The Organizer

In 1993 Davi tried to turn a dream into reality by supervising the construction of an airstrip inside Yanomami territory for health-care teams to use (Zacquini 1993). First he traveled the world seeking financial support for his project. Back in the village, he rounded up Indians to do the work and paid them with trade goods. Soon, half the people working on the strip or living by it had contracted malaria.

Instead of hunting and gathering in the vicinity of the strip, the workers walked forty minutes to four hours to obtain food provided by CCPY, slowing the work considerably. When neighboring Yanomami came to visit the construction site, tools went missing. (Metal tools are prime trading goods that travel along networks stretching for hundreds of miles throughout Yanomami territory.) Davi kept bringing presents to the workers, but they were "never enough."

Carlo Zacquini, a priest who has worked for many years with the Yanomami, reported that one worker "did not come back in January for the second round of work, as he had promised earlier. The reason he gave was always the same: the need to organize and to take part in festivities. One of these, in Novo Demini, ended in a fight and, as a result, most of the men were unable to work for several weeks" (ibid., 2). For the Yanomami men, feasts were important political and social events that demanded their presence and took priority over Davi's project.

Then an ant invasion, probably caused by the human invaders' disturbance of their habitat, made work difficult and drove the medical team out of their hut.

At first Davi had insisted that the Yanomami could do the work of building the airstrip themselves. Eventually work stopped completely, and Davi had to ask CCPY for help. The Indians did build a clinic, but Davi did not accomplish all he had dreamed of. Given the difficulties of life in the rainforest, his capacity to conceive and coordinate such a project is impressive enough.

Davi is most effective as a defender of his people. Perhaps influenced by his early training in evangelical Christianity, he has developed a powerful mythological discourse that synthesizes Western and Yanomami concepts to express the fears and beliefs of both Yanomami and Northern audiences. He speaks "to defend the forest and keep my people from disappearing." He told Albert he came to understand his duty in a shamanic trance, when he had a vision of the forest being destroyed.

Davi finds the Northern idea of "preserving" or "protecting" bits of "nature" ridiculous, however. "What you whites call 'the environment' is what remains of what you destroyed" (Albert 1995: 20). He recognizes that some whites, like Chico Mendes, are enlightened enough to be educable in Yanomami teachings, and he feels his mission is to overcome white ignorance. In his "Letter to All the Peoples of the Earth" (Yanomami 1989), he concluded, "I, Davi Yanomami, want to help the whites learn with us to make the world a better place."

The Prophet

To this end, Davi carefully translates Yanomami concepts into Portuguese terms acceptable and comprehensible to Northern audiences. But he believes whites are deaf and blind to the spiritual meaning of his words. He told Albert that whites think they are so intelligent because they mistake words for reality. It is the Yanomami who understand the true nature of reality.

The Yanomami traditionally viewed other peoples, and especially whites, as "subhumans, peripheral and unintelligible" (Albert 1995: 5). They still regard whites as little better than cannibals, because they kill Yanomami children. In Davi's mythological vision, the principal evil spirit, Xawara, embodied in smoke and pollution, is "white, and all the details of his macabre expeditions are linked to his whiteness: he has hired guns to capture his victims, he cuts their throats with a machete, he skins them to make hammocks, he fries them in big ovens, he throws their entrails to his hunting dogs, he grills their bodies and keeps them in wooden boxes or vacuum-sealed cans" (Albert 1995: 14–15).

Xawara "kills and eats our children. . . . he's hungry for human meat." Mercury fumes from the gold extraction process are the form of Xawara that the Yanomami know and fear. But smoke (from forest burning and industrial pollution) contaminates not only the forest but the world beyond, even threatening the sky and, thus, the equilibrium of all life on earth.

> As long as the gold stays in the cold depths of the earth, everything's all right, it isn't dangerous. When the whites take the gold out of the ground, they burn it, they put it on the fire as if it were flour. This makes smoke come out of it. That's how the Xawara that is gold smoke is created. Then this smoke epidemic spreads through the forest, where the Yanomami live, but also through the land of the whites, everywhere. . . . When this smoke arrives at the breast of the sky, the sky begins to get very sick, it also is affected by Xawara. The land gets sick, too. . . . There's also smoke from the factories. You think that God can drive away this smoke, but he can't. He too will end up dying, even though he's a supernatural being. . . . (ibid., 16)

For Davi it is imperative to protect not only the forest but the shamans and their traditional knowledge. They are the ones who mobilize the guardian spirits that keep the heavens from falling down. But "the Creator has already left this world and gone far away and will not create any more Yanomami." And without the Yanomami, the earth is doomed.

At the opening ceremony of the International Year of Indigenous

Peoples at the United Nations in December 1992, Davi told the General Assembly: "The leaders of the rich, industrialized world think that they are the owners of the world. But the shamans are the ones who have true knowledge. They are the real first world. And if their knowledge is destroyed, then the white people too will die. It will be the end of the world. This is what we want to avoid" (Brazil Network Jan.-Mar. 1993: 6–7). Like any prophet, he has no hesitation about "speaking truth to power."

As time passed and Yanomami continued to die of contagious diseases or in violent confrontations with invaders, Davi's vision became more vividly threatening:

> We try to put an end to the Xawara, but it's very resistant. It's wrinkled and elastic, like rubber. The spirits can't cut it with their weapons, and it grabs them when they attack it.

> The whites don't think, "The sky will collapse," they don't say to themselves, "The Xawara is devouring us." So she's eating a bunch of children, she does away with them, eats them without stopping, kills them and grills them as if they were monkeys that she'd hunted. She piles up a bunch of grilled children. . . .[1] Xawara is very hungry for human meat, doesn't want to hunt fish, only Yanomami meat. . . . When the smoke fills the breast of the sky, it will also die, just like the Yanomami. When it gets sick, continuous thunder will be heard. The thunder will get sick and it will bellow in anger without stopping, as a result of the heat. The sky will be torn apart. [The spirits will] cut the sky into pieces, so that it will collapse on top of the earth. They'll also make the sun fall, and when it falls, everything will become dark. When the stars and the moon fall, the sky will be dark.[2] (Albert 1991: 71)

Western depictions of similar intensity can be found in the fresco of hell in the baptistery of Florence Cathedral, or in Revelation:

> And he opened the bottomless pit; and there arose a smoke out of the pit, as the smoke of a great furnace; and the sun and the air were darkened by reason of the smoke of the pit. (9:2) There fell a great

star from heaven, burning as it were a lamp, and it fell upon the third part of the rivers, and upon the fountains of waters; (8:10) . . . and the third part of the sun was smitten, and the third part of the moon, and the third part of the stars; so as the third part of them was darkened, and the day shone not for a third part of it, and the night likewise. (8:12)

Davi's apocalyptic vision is no literary conceit, however; it expresses his realistic fears for the future of his people: "If the garimpeiros keep going through our forest, if they don't go back home, the Yanomami will die, they'll really be finished. There won't be anybody left to cure us. The whites that cure us, doctors and nurses, are few. . . . Only a small number of us will survive. Many people have already died, and I don't want to let everybody else die" (Albert 1991: 71).

In a desperate race against time, disease, and neglect, Davi harnessed the eloquent oral and religious traditions of the Yanomami to their sense of natural superiority and made a powerful, poetic vehicle out of his prophecies. On his journeys he has acquired a unique breadth of knowledge:

I also see white people suffering in the city, hunger, everything expensive, homelessness, lack of food, everyone is suffering. . . . Our custom is better than that of the whites, because we preserve the rivers, floodplains, lakes, mountains, the hunting, the fish, the fruits. . . . The mining activity taking place on our lands is not only illegal, it is also harmful to the miners themselves. Many of them are held like slaves. Like us, they also are victims of the greed of the handful of men who control the gold trade. (Yanomami 1989: 68)

Davi is the only Yanomami leader who has managed to gain the attention of the international public. Few others have learned enough Portuguese to communicate with Brazilians; schools are few in the far-flung Yanomami villages.[3] Most Yanomami still have only indirect contact with outsiders. Some adult Yanomami who have learned Portuguese over the past generation have thrown in their lot with prospectors and loggers, but others have begun to emerge as defenders of their communities and resources.

Davi is trying to pass along his knowledge of the outside world and his sense of mission to other Yanomami, and he takes them along on his trips whenever possible. Even with the help of sympathetic and devoted allies like Claudia Andujar and Bruce Albert, however, Davi's crusade may not be sufficient to save his people's traditional way of life, even though the health and education projects he originated have improved their chances for survival.

Feuds between villages, structural in their culture, are still the focus of many Yanomami lives. But it seems inescapable: To survive physically and culturally, the Yanomami must stop expending their energies on internal conflict, redefine themselves as one people, and unite to defend their lives and lands from outside impingement.

Davi plays a prominent role in organizing meetings of village leaders from across the Yanomami's vast territory to join in common endeavors. His commitment to education comes from his recognition that his leadership alone is not enough. A new generation of leaders, conversant with the outside world, must continue the task of mobilizing the Yanomami. Education takes years, however, and the Yanomami are struggling with urgent problems—malaria, river blindness, deadly childhood diseases, and invasions—that could destroy their culture before the new generation of leaders emerges. It will take decades of efforts by Davi and his allies and successors to ensure that his words will not be lost in the smoke of Xawara.

7 / Savage Anthropology

You have to work calmly. You have to work the way nature works. You see how nature works. It rains a little. The rain stops. The world clears. This is how you have to work, you anthropologists of the United States.

— Davi Kopenawa

THE YANOMAMI HAD LONG SINCE DISAPPEARED FROM THE headlines when *Darkness in El Dorado*, Patrick Tierney's muckraking study, "How Scientists and Journalists Devastated the Amazon," burst on the scene in autumn 2000. Tierney's book purported to expose the misbehavior of well-known scholars whose reputations seemed well established, if not unassailable. Tierney's primary villains were anthropologists Napoleon Chagnon and Jacques Lizot and geneticist James Neel. The victims were the Yanomami, used and abused by ambitious careerists who invaded their shabonos, drew their blood, incited them to violence, seduced their children, colluded in their genocide, and otherwise took advantage of them from the mid-1960s on.

The "uncorrected proofs" (actually paperback advance copies meant to promote the book before publication) deeply dismayed the anthropologists who received them in late summer 2000. Many of Tierney's stories were not new to the first readers, some of whom had been criticizing Chagnon for years. But collected between two covers, buttressed by nearly sixty pages of notes and an extensive bibliography, and aimed at the general public, they devastated the image anthropologists cultivate of their discipline. Added to Tierney's sordid charges and overheated language was a sensational allegation most readers had not heard before. Tierney implied that James Neel,

"Shamans Holding Up the Cracking Sky," by Koromani Yanomami, 1974.

a renowned and respected geneticist who had recently died, and Chagnon, who was his assistant at the time, deliberately precipitated a fatal measles epidemic while conducting research among the Yanomami in 1968.

Scandal Explodes

Alarmed by the implications of Tierney's findings (gathered during eleven years of research in Brazil, Venezuela, and the United States), two longtime antagonists of Chagnon sounded a tocsin to the American Anthropological Association. Professors Terence Turner and Leslie Sponsel sent a confidential memo to the association's executives, summarizing the book's most incendiary allegations and warning that the impending scandal could damage the profession of anthropology. Someone leaked the memo to Chagnon's and Neel's friends and the media, causing a storm of controversy even before the book appeared.

Both Chagnon and Neel had powerful allies in the scientific establishment. They wasted no time in savaging the book and hurling counter-charges at Sponsel and Turner. Tierney was forced to revise his chapter on the 1968 measles epidemic and the book's publication was delayed a couple of months. After the book came out, the battle continued in the review columns of major newspapers and magazines, as well as in academic journals and at professional meetings. Some anthropology professors started assigning Tierney's book along with Chagnon's to their classes.

Two special sessions at the American Anthropological Association's annual meeting in November 2000 dealt with Tierney's charges. About 1,000 people attended each session. Tierney attended the first one but said little—he was outnumbered by a phalanx of opponents, who castigated him for sensationalism, exaggeration, or outright falsification. One of the most poignant statements came from a letter by a missionary who had worked with the Yanomami in 1968. The missionary sorrowfully admitted that his infant child had carried measles into Yanomami territory and thus precipitated the fatal epidemic described in Tierney's book.

Under considerable pressure from anthropologists and scientists of other disciplines—especially Neel's defenders—the association appointed a committee to determine if further action should be taken. In February 2001 the panel recommended creation of a five-member task force to inquire into Tierney's principal allegations. The task force had a delicate task; it had to act impartially and could not be seen as conducting either a witch-hunt or a whitewash. Because the American Anthropological Association does not accredit or issue credentials to its members, it says it cannot investigate, censure, or expel anyone for ethical misconduct. The task force said all it could do was "provide a forum" for exchanges about anthropologists' work with and effects on the Yanomami.

Anthropologist John Peters, who has studied the Yanomami, averred, "Anthropologists are on their own. . . . There were and are no professional bodies that placed . . . control upon any of the anthropologists, medical researchers or cameramen mentioned in the Tierney book" (Borofsky 2001: 18).

The task force's work was marked by ill-concealed dissension among its members. One—an associate of Chagnon, appointed late to ensure "balance"—resigned because of an apparent conflict of interest. A preliminary report was posted on the association's website while two task force members were still interviewing Yanomami in Venezuela; it had to be withdrawn because the two protested they had not approved it and took strong exception to its contents.

The task force's final report was posted on the AAA website in May 2002. More than 300 pages long, it was a hodgepodge of opinions, interviews, meditations on ethics, recommendations, and even the members' résumés. In the meantime, thousands of pages of comments, articles, and other materials related to the controversy had appeared on a website set up by a University of Connecticut graduate student. A professor at Hawaii Pacific University sponsored an electronic "forum" of polemics by experts on the Yanomami, Chagnon partisans, and Chagnon opponents. It would later appear as a book. And some of the major actors in the controversy organized an international conference, featuring Yanomami and other indigenous representatives, anthropologists, and Tierney. The meeting took place at Cornell University a few weeks before the task force's report appeared. All these will provide food for thought and the subjects of dissertations for a long time.

Scientific Sins

Perhaps because it was the weakest part of Tierney's book, the chapter on the 1968 measles epidemic received the most attention in the reviews, articles, and reports that grew out of (and fed) the controversy. It was all too easy to refute his contention that Neel and Chagnon had deliberately induced the measles epidemic by administering the Edmonston B vaccine to 1,000 Indians. Epidemiologists quickly pointed out that no measles vaccine could cause measles (though that particular vaccine could lead to side effects almost as severe as the disease itself).

The ground shifted to the question of Neel's intentions in vaccinating the Yanomami: Did he inoculate them for humanitarian reasons or as part of his research? Was it ethical for him to continue collecting blood, feces, urine, and other samples, instead of stopping his research to treat the Indians during a raging outbreak of a disease that would kill large numbers during many months? Scholars with sharply opposed views went to his papers and field notes, kept at the American Philosophical Society, and unsurprisingly came up with differing interpretations of Neel's actions and motives.

Most seriously, the task force decided that the 1968 expedition had not obtained the Yanomami's informed consent to take blood and other samples, even according to the standards of the times. A major report detailing these standards had been written for the World Health Organization a few years before the expedition—by none other than James Neel. As the expedition's advance man, Chagnon told the Indians the knowledge gained from the samples "would help treat them more effectively if they became ill" (Borofsky 2001: 84). Such treatment never came, and the Yanomami have remembered this with bitterness and resentment that cast a shadow over their relationships with other researchers.

Chagnon's partisans reacted to his opponents by accusing them of being "anti-science" because they disagreed with his sociobiological interpretations of Yanomami violence. One of the fiercest, Kim Hill, charged that Chagnon's critics "attempted to discredit Chagnon and Neel ONLY BE-CAUSE of theoretical disagreements with the type of work they were doing. Chagnon enemies . . . are displeased with the questions he asks and the results of his scientific research" (ibid., 26).

As Terence Turner repeatedly pointed out, these partisans had little to say about the specific charges against Chagnon for unethical actions *after* 1968; instead they accused his accusers of ideological intent. Although the AAA task force disagreed with Tierney's interpretation of the 1968 measles vaccinations, they did conclude that many of his other allegations could be substantiated.

Chagnon under Attack

What were these charges? For years, Chagnon's opponents had accused him of presenting a distorted or untruthful picture of the Yanomami as "the fierce people." Political enemies of indigenous people used his portrayal to justify invading Yanomami territory, stealing their natural resources, taking away their land rights, failing to prevent or colluding in genocidal attacks, and failing to provide emergency medical assistance. The task force found that Chagnon not only "made insufficient effort to undo this damage," but also compounded it by attacking Davi Kopenawa and NGOs that tried to protect the Yanomami during the attempted genocide described in chapter 5. (AAA 2002: I: 31).

Tierney's other charges against Chagnon included ethically dubious field research methods over many years—such as bribing children to provide taboo information and "the playing off of enemies against one another . . . especially in a context where conflict is dangerous and easily precipitated" (AAA 2002: II: 85). Chagnon persistently took photographs without the Yanomami's consent, although he knew they objected to being photographed. The task force also found Chagnon had improperly involved himself in conflicts between villages (ibid., II: 88). They did not undertake to determine if he had actually *caused* conflicts by his gift giving, as Brian Ferguson and others have alleged.

Some anthropologists denied these were serious charges—one said, "Chagnon was accused of capital murder, and it appears that he's now been convicted of a parking violation" (Gregor and Gross 2002: 1). But others saw such actions as betraying the discipline's humanistic ethos in the name of science: "Something was seriously amiss in the relation between these confident and determined soi-disant 'scientists' with their cameras, their vials, their syringes and their notebooks and the beset and puzzled, put-upon 'natives' to whom they looked for facts to fill them with—something in their encounter was deeply, and mutually, misconceived" (Geertz 2001: 20).

According to the Yanomami who gave their testimonies in Venezuela, Brazil, and the United States, Chagnon's alleged violations of professional ethics had profoundly negative consequences for them. Their recorded comments are scathing. Davi Kopenawa told task force member Janet Chernela in June 2001 that Chagnon had

> brought pans, knives, machetes, axes. And so he arrived ready, ready to trick the Yanomami. This is how the story goes. I was small at the time . . . about nine. I remember. . . . An anthropologist should really help, as a friend. He shouldn't deceive. He should defend [the Indian] when he is sick and defend the land as well. . . . If a Yanomami gets a cold, he can die. But he didn't help with this. . . . He wrote a book. When people made a feast and afterward a fight happened, the anthropologist took a lot of photos and he also taped it. . . . He wanted to show that he was brave. If the Yanomami could beat him, he could beat them. This is what the people in Toototobi told us. (AAA 2002: II: 31)

Julio Wichato, an elderly Yanomami nurse in Venezuela, told Chernela:

> He took me to Siapa. . . . There was a *very* large shabono. [Chagnon
> said,] "Let's go down there." The helicopter was *big*—it blew out
> houses within 20 meters! So people came out with bows and arrows
> to shoot the helicopter. Chagnon said to go back down. The pilot
> said no and went up again. Then Chagnon wanted to go back. . . . he
> ruined the shabono. . . . This is what he was like, Chagnon. (ibid.,
> II: 48)

Chagnon's partisans insisted these Yanomami did not represent the whole
group (and given their chronic internal conflicts, the truth of this must be
acknowledged). But the Indians' unfavorable comments echoed those of
Brazilian and Venezuelan anthropologists, medical personnel, and many
others who had encountered Chagnon in the field over the years. Davi
summed up what still may be a widespread sentiment among his people:
"I don't like these anthropologists who use the name of the Yanomami on
paper, in books. . . . They are using our name as if we were children. The
name Yanomami has to be respected. It's not like a ball to throw around, to
play with, hitting from one side to another" (ibid., II: 39).

The AAA task force strongly criticized Chagnon on other counts. "Chagnon has never spoken out clearly and unequivocally to attack misuse of his
work by journalists. Instead he has repeatedly used precious opportunities .
. . to attack professional enemies rather than to render clear support to the
Yanomami" (ibid., I: 33). The task force characterized his language in his
1995 interview with *Veja* magazine ("Real Indians get dirty, smell bad, take
hallucinogens, belch after they eat, covet and sometimes steal their neighbors' wives and make war. They're normal human beings") as "inappropri-
ate, vulgar and unhelpful" (ibid., I: 33). They pointed out that on this and
other occasions, he had failed to discredit negative stereotypes that have
had deadly consequences for the Yanomami.

Of his negative characterization of Davi Kopenawa, task force member
Jane Hill said, "To raise questions, in very widely distributed publications,
about the authenticity of a person who has unquestionably become a very
positive symbol of the Yanomami and an important political asset in this
fight, cannot fail to undermine Yanomami interests" (ibid., II: 90).

In response to such charges, Chagnon partisans denied that his pronouncements in Brazil during and after the attempted genocide had had any effect on government policies or legislative initiatives. But Brazilian anthropologist Leda Martins declared that Chagnon's work, published or extensively quoted in Brazilian newspapers and magazines, "has without a doubt significantly influenced the ideas of the general public and has served to give the appearance of a scientific basis to arguments against Yanomami rights in Brazil" (Borofsky 2001: 32). According to Martins, who was working as a journalist for the Brazilian government's Yanomami health project at the time, Chagnon did nothing to oppose the use of his ideas to hurt the Yanomami and joined in attacks on their leaders and supporters. "These are the ethical breaches of Chagnon," she said (ibid., 78).

The task force also criticized Chagnon's involvement in a Venezuelan development scheme called FUNDAFACI (Fundación para la Ayuda de la Familia Campesina y Indígena) in the early 1990s. Tierney described this dubious endeavor at length in *Darkness in El Dorado,* and the task force said his allegations "may be well founded" (AAA 2002, I: 41). With Charles Brewer-Carias, his longtime Venezuelan collaborator, and Cecilia Matos, the mistress of Venezuela's then president, Chagnon tried to set up a giant research project in a federal bio-reserve where some Yanomami lived. The task force found that in Venezuela, "it was widely believed that the foundation was merely a smokescreen behind which Matos concealed corrupt business activities" (ibid., I: 41). Brewer-Carias was notorious in the country for alleged involvement in illegal mining projects. "Brewer-Carias would have been able to pursue his mining interests and Chagnon to advance his anthropological research unhampered by their lack of local support or by professional or governmental controls," the task force found (ibid., I: 43). "Chagnon's involvement with FUNDAFACI was unacceptable on both ethical and professional grounds. . . . The task force believes that a charge of a breach of ethics is proper under the AAA Principles of Professional Responsibility [and] the current Code of Ethics" (ibid., I: 44).

Chagnon's partisans were hard-pressed to defend his involvement in FUNDAFACI. Kim Hill said, "Chagnon simply associated with these characters because they were powerful Venezuelans who could help him gain access to the Yanomami at a time when it was being denied," and implied that Chagnon was unaware of their bad reputations (Borofsky 2001: 24–25).

Chagnon has not disassociated himself from Brewer-Carias, calling him "my Venezuelan co-researcher" and "a life-long friend, well-known in studies of many aspects of the Amazon Basin" in the most recent edition of *Yanomamö*, published several years after the FUNDAFACI episode (Chagnon 1997: 231, n. 81). At last report, Cecilia Matos was a fugitive from Venezuelan justice. Her paramour, President Carlos Pérez, was impeached and kicked out of office for corruption.

Fierce or Not?

Despite the great success of *Yanomamö: The Fierce People*, Chagnon has repeatedly come under attack over the years for his characterization of the Yanomami. The critiques started as early as 1976, and since then, some anthropologists have "argued that Chagnon's characterization was incorrect ethnographically. . ." (AAA 2002, I: 32).

The task force considered the effects of his portrayal on the Yanomami and on students of anthropology. Their report observed, "Many studies took from [Chagnon's] book primarily a strong impression of violence, filth and irrationality. . . . The Yanomami became 'The Fierce People,' famous above all else for warfare and violence, and more complex readings of Chagnon's work received little attention" (ibid.).

The task force acknowledged that Chagnon has revised succeeding editions of the book, "which we take to demonstrate his understanding of their potentially damaging characterization in their original form" (ibid., I: 34). A student would get a somewhat different impression of the Yanomami from the fifth edition than from the first edition. For one thing, Chagnon removed "The Fierce People" from the title after the third edition. In the fourth edition, he admitted, "Government officials in, for example, Brazil might try to justify oppressive policies against them on the argument that they are 'fierce' and, therefore, 'animal-like'" (ibid., I: 36). The task force notes that these changes "appear to directly address the concerns of the Association of Brazilian Anthropologists that the image of fierceness can be used against the Yanomami" (ibid.). The task force also apologized to the Brazilian anthropological association for not paying sufficient attention to its complaint (received by the AAA in 1988 but not published until 1989) about Chagnon's failure to defend the Yanomami during the gold rush.

The task force pointed out that despite loud criticism, Chagnon continued his earlier pattern by attacking missionaries and unnamed Venezuelan
anthropologists, as well as Davi Kopenawa, in his book's fourth edition
(1992).

Chagnon's representations of the Yanomami as a "Stone Age people,"
noble insofar as they are uncontaminated by contact with whites, also came
in for criticism. The task force recommended, "Any use of Chagnon's books
in [an] anthropology course should include . . . a full discussion of these
usages and their implications with [the] goal of critical understanding in
mind" (AAA 2002, I: 39). Jane Hill pointed to his charge that Yanomami
who speak Spanish are "inauthentic." "The challenge of inauthenticity is,
fundamentally, unanthropological," she wrote. "It fails to recognize the
contemporary contexts in which indigenous people must live, and it fails to
grant indigenous speakers their claim to autonomy within these contexts"
(ibid., II: 91).

Finally, the task force noted that despite repeated criticism of his field
methods, Chagnon continued to act in ways others considered improper
or unethical. In Venezuela in 1991, "a Yanomami headman threatened him
with an axe because he believed that Chagnon's photographing babies
caused them to die" (ibid., II: 86). On a 1995 trip to Brazil, he attempted to
obtain Yanomami blood samples without the required government authorization. As a result, he was expelled from their territory.

In his review of *Darkness in El Dorado*, Clifford Geertz portrays Chagnon in a sympathetic, even pitying, light:

> He spent a quarter of a century, in the field and out, desperately
> trying to find evidence for Neel's conjecture, counting, measuring,
> photographing and perhaps stimulating violence, at the expense of
> his own more nuanced, immediate, finely detailed, and above all
> personally observed sense of what the Yanomami—less "the fierce
> people" than the resilient ones—were all about. He became . . . the
> victim of a hypothesis. There is a certain pathos in all this. (Geertz
> 2001: 21)

The task force seems to have concluded that the Yanomami (not Chagnon)
were the principal victims of a hypothesis. The pathos belongs to them.

The Blood Issue

After the publication of Tierney's book, the Yanomami were told that the blood samples extracted during the 1968 Neel expedition were still being stored and used in several laboratories in the United States. The Yanomami believe such human remains should be destroyed, as they destroyed the corpses of the Haximu massacre victims in 1993. Davi Kopenawa and other leaders firmly told interviewers the Neel expedition samples also must be destroyed or returned to them for destruction. Davi told Janet Chernela:

> So now we are asking about this blood that was taken from us without explanation, without saying anything, without the results. We want to know the findings. . . . Our relatives whose blood was taken are now dead. . . . But their blood is in the United States. . . . If it helped cure a disease over there, then they should compensate us. If they don't want to pay, then they should consider returning our blood. . . . My mother gave blood. Now my mother is dead. Her blood is over there. Whatever is of the dead must be destroyed. . . . To keep it in a freezer is not a good thing. (AAA 2002, II: 36)

José Seripino, a Venezuelan Yanomami leader, told Chernela: "You can destroy it. But if you destroy it [in the U.S.], we won't know whether it will be all destroyed. You should send it all to us. . . . It *has* to be destroyed. They are treating us like animals! We are human beings!" (ibid., II: 44).

The Yanomami also were angry because the blood had been taken from them without their informed consent. Davi said, "When the doctor wanted to take blood, Chagnon translated it. But he didn't explain the secret. . . . no one understood the purpose of giving blood. . . ." His uncle agreed to give blood "because he would receive pans" (ibid., II: 35).

Julio Wichato, the Yanomami nurse who has drawn blood from the Yanomami for almost twenty years, had a sophisticated understanding of the ethical problems of the Neel expedition: "The problem is that they studied it and didn't send us the results. If they help us it's different. . . . They can never use this blood. They can never study it. They should send the results or destroy it or send it back. But they cannot study it. Never" (ibid., II: 47).

Anthropologist Kenneth Weiss, the curator of 1,500 Yanomami DNA samples at Pennsylvania State University, told the task force he "is fully willing to return samples or to invite Yanomami to visit his lab and examine the specimens so that they may make practical decisions regarding their return or destruction" (ibid., I: 29). He said he had stopped allowing research on the samples while awaiting the Indians' decision.

Meanwhile, Venezuelan Yanomami leaders discussed the blood at a meeting in late 2001 and "elected to receive compensation in the form of collective health benefits" (ibid., II: 77). The Brazilian attorney general's office also became involved, sending a request for information about the samples to some of the laboratories known to possess them (University of Michigan, Pennsylvania State University, Emory University, University of Illinois, and the National Cancer Institute). In consultation with the Brazilian government, the Pro-Yanomami Commission, and the Indian Law Resource Center in Washington, D.C., the Yanomami were considering suing the laboratories if a settlement could not be reached.

Compensation

The Yanomami interviewed for the task force report expressed far more concern about their health situation than about the blood issue. They regard medical assistance as the best form of compensation for the knowledge they have provided to researchers over the years. And they are keenly aware of what anthropologists, scientists, filmmakers, journalists, and others have gained, both personally and professionally, from them. Davi Kopenawa caustically observed:

> Patrick [Tierney] left the fight to the others! He can let the anthropologists fight with Chagnon, and . . . he's outside, he's free. He's just bringing in the money—he must be laughing at the rest. It's like starting a fight among dogs. . . . Now he should share some of this money with the Yanomami. We Yanomami are here, suffering from malaria, flu, sick all the time. But he's there in good health—just spending the money that he gained in the name of the Yanomami Indians. (ibid., II: 40)

Bruce Albert has proposed going well beyond paying for information with money or goods:

> The knowledge that sociocultural anthropologists gain from indigenous people can be reciprocated . . . by an involvement in advocacy for indigenous rights. . . . anthropologists can make use of this knowledge to benefit the people who transmitted it. . . . they can be asked to engage or collaborate in advocacy activities to create medical programs for the indigenous people with whom they work or serving as ethnographic consultants to make health services more effective and less culturally damaging. (Albert 2001: 87)

And Davi recommends to anthropologists a mutually beneficial way to do their research:

> Work with great care. If a young anthropologist enters here in Brazil or Venezuela, he should work like a friend. . . . He should say, "I am an anthropologist; I would like to learn your language. After, I would like to teach you." Tell us something of the world of the whites. The world of the whites . . . is good, but it is not all good. There are good people and bad people. So, "I am an anthropologist here in the shabono, defending your rights and your land, your culture, your language, don't fight among yourselves, don't kill your own relatives." We already have an enemy among us—it is disease. This enemy kills indeed. (AAA 2002, II: 34)

Other Sins and Sinners

Tierney did not restrict his exposé to Neel and Chagnon. He also charged the French anthropologist Jacques Lizot with seducing or molesting Yanomami boys. The task force reacted to the allegations against Lizot with an essay by Jane Hill on anthropologists' sexual behavior. Hill observed, "Lizot's sexual exploitation of adolescent boys was greatly resented, very repugnant and totally unacceptable to the Yanomami, and left them suspicious of anthropologists in general, who they fear may share Lizot's sexual proclivities" (ibid., II: 101). She expressed bafflement "that Venezuelan authorities permitted [him] to continue over a very long period of time," but pointed out that

> sexual exploitation of the Yanomami that is far more dangerous to them than anything undertaken by Lizot is reported by those who have observed the behavior of soldiers around Brazilian army posts, where young Yanomami women . . . are prostituted in a context that includes epidemic levels of venereal disease including AIDS. (ibid., II: 101)

In a general discussion of anthropologists' sexual behavior in the field, Hill pointed out:

> In most field situations, most of the power in a relationships with a member of a study population will reside with the anthropologist. . . . sexual relations with members of study populations should be undertaken only after the most careful reflection on this point, and with full attention to the dignity and autonomy of the potential partner. (ibid., II: 102)

The essay concludes, "Undertaking a sexual relationship in the field community is almost always ill-advised," and "behavior by any anthropologist reflects on all anthropologists" (ibid., II: 102–3). Some teachers and students who sent comments on the report to the AAA's website wrote that the association should express more strongly an absolute taboo on anthropologists' having sexual relationships with the people they study.

Tierney also reported on the negative effects that resulted from the making of the documentary, "Warriors of the Amazon." He noted that the crew had filmed the death of a Yanomami woman rather than moving her to a medical mission post where her life might have been saved. The task force agreed with Tierney that the film was "profoundly problematic . . . given that Nova/WGBH is obviously marketing it to schoolteachers." The film was "obviously staged," inaccurate, "racializing and dehumanizing" (ibid., II: 104, 106). Although they found Tierney's analysis of this film "clear and revealing," they also pointed out that his interpretation of the unused sound from one of Chagnon's films was "extremely careless." Thus, he "undermines the credibility of his entire critical edifice" (ibid., II: 146).

No wonder the task force regarded Tierney's work "with profound ambivalence, finding the book deeply flawed, but nevertheless highlighting ethical issues that we must confront" (ibid., I: 9). They acknowledged, "All anthropological practice is implicated in what went wrong in research conducted among the Yanomami" (ibid., I: 10).

Making Amends

What, then, could be done to repair more than thirty years' damage to the Yanomami? One of the task force members proposed that the American Anthropological Association pay "reparations" to them. Janet Chernela said the association's sins of omission and commission are "the collective acts of a professional association. . . . It is a mistake to look for personal or individual wrongdoing" (ibid., II: 148–49). She proposed a special program to

> provide the healing that is called for and the return of dignity to a people who appear to have been subject to wrongdoing. A collective act would represent an official apology from the body and a step toward making whole the damages, harm and losses that have been incurred by Yanomami. . . . A properly structured reparations program enacted by the AAA could return or destroy blood samples as well as funnel resources to health or other service programs. (ibid., II: 150)

In fact, the association has tried to help the Yanomami in various ways for more than twenty years. Resolutions calling on the Brazilian government to demarcate territory for the Yanomami go back to 1978. In 1980–81, the AAA and ABA, the Brazilian anthropological association, cosigned a complaint to the Organization of American States regarding Brazilian government policy toward the Yanomami. Similar resolutions followed during the 1980s.

But when ABA's president wrote to the AAA in 1988, warning of the negative effects of Chagnon's *Science* article, the *Anthropology Newsletter* waited several months before publishing it with Chagnon's reply. Another letter supporting Chagnon spoke disparagingly of the ABA complaint, and the newsletter's editor would not allow the Brazilian anthropologists to publish a reply. The Brazilians were frustrated and offended.

In 1990, the AAA participated in international efforts to prevent the genocide of the Brazilian Yanomami. The dramatic results included the expulsion of the gold miners, delivery of emergency medical aid to the Indians, and the demarcation of a huge reserve for the Yanomami in 1992.

The association then created a human rights commission, chaired by Leslie Sponsel, and it continued to pay attention to the situation of the Yanomami. Accusations against Chagnon were aired at a tumultuous session during the association's annual meeting in 1994. In 1996 the AAA's president wrote to Brazil's president to express concern over a new garimpeiro invasion of Yanomami territory. The AAA took no further action until *Darkness in El Dorado* appeared in 2000. Then the task force's inquiry forced the association to revisit controversies that had been percolating for years. Meanwhile, Brazilian anthropologists, "who have been active on the front lines of advocacy for the Yanomami . . . believe that the AAA has been unresponsive to their concerns" (AAA 2002: II: 11). Chernela's proposal should be seen in this context.

But the rest of the task force rejected her suggestion for reparations. On their behalf, Native American anthropologist Joe Watkins wrote, "I . . . feel it important that we *not* try to bear an overwhelming or unearned guilt of our predecessors' sins" and pointed to an "overall debt owed to *all* indigenous populations" (ibid., II: 151–52). He seemed to be saying that the association could not pick and choose one indigenous group to which to make amends. Watkins continued:

> Rather than issuing a formal apology to indigenous populations for real (or perceived) past wrongs, the AAA and all national organizations of any countries must establish and develop a covenant outlining beneficial programs to be entered into between those organizations and the unempowered peoples throughout the world that they study. (ibid., II: 152)

Bruce Albert had another idea. He called for an independent bioethics panel to investigate various issues raised by *Darkness in El Dorado*, including Neel's research in the 1960s and 1970s, disposition of the Yanomami blood samples, and other medical research that included administering dangerous radioisotopes to the Venezuelan Yanomami in the 1960s. Compensation would go to Yanomami health projects as "the only ethically respectable way to redress the damage" (Albert 2001: 56).

Albert also suggested action that Chagnon himself could take: "A concrete commitment from Chagnon to help the Yanomami (for example, in coping with their extremely precarious, and at times tragic, health situation) and to fairly redistribute the economic benefits he gained from them during his long career is still awaited" (ibid., 68). Albert believes the royalties from Chagnon's books and *Darkness in El Dorado* should go to the Yanomami.

Albert pointed to concerns the Yanomami themselves have expressed at recent meetings as areas where anthropologists and other concerned people could help them. The Indians' main preoccupations in recent years have been sexual abuse of Yanomami women by soldiers and other outsiders in the reserve; continuing invasions by ranchers and garimpeiros; and threats of cuts in national health budgets that could lead to denial of much-needed medical assistance. He called for the AAA and ABA to disseminate a joint declaration supporting Yanomami land rights in the face of continuing challenges and threats. He also suggested that North American anthropologists collaborate with Venezuelan scientists to investigate the Yanomami health situation there and set up programs to provide medical aid in Venezuela. But

> reciprocating the knowledge they gain through their research by merely paying their "informants" and hosts (or even by redistributing royalties) does not constitute a sufficient form of reciprocation. . . . the sociocultural anthropologist inevitably becomes a special cultural-political link to the outside world for them. . . . the anthropologist [must] engage in advocacy to support their rights and welfare. (ibid., 97)

Some North American anthropologists have questioned or rejected this kind of "engaged" approach. Daniel Gross and Stuart Plattner, anthropologists who work outside academia, have expressed their concern about the task force's call for "collaborative models, in which anthropological research is . . . inherently advocative in that research is, from its outset, aimed at material, symbolic and political benefits for the research population. . . . All parties are equal partners . . . participating in the development of research design" (AAA 2002: I: 45–46). Gross, Plattner, and many other anthropologists believe such collaboration would take advocacy too far and could compromise the objectivity, accuracy, and acceptability of field research in a number of ways. A thorough discussion of this complex issue is beyond the scope of this book. But it is surely healthy and constructive for anthropologists to pursue this discussion. The task force did a service to the profession by raising the issue in the life-or-death context of a threatened people.

Terence Turner observed, "Amid the barrage of charges and counter-charges, the most important ethical issue, namely what, how and why the Yanomami have suffered from the actions of those who have come to study, document, film, convert, aid, and otherwise impinge upon them over the past 30 years, has tended to get lost" (Borofsky 2001: 40). For those who want to learn from past mistakes, perhaps that is the most important issue. But for the Yanomami, the most important issue is how to survive day by day. The question remains: What is to be done?

8 / Emerging Indians

THE XUCURU PEOPLE OF NORTHEASTERN BRAZIL HAVE COME back from the dead. A few years ago, they were said to be "extinct." Now about 8,500 of them live and struggle to control 70,000 acres in the fertile hills of Pernambuco. After much resistance and the assassinations of several of their leaders, the Brazilian government completed the demarcation of their territory. But the Xucuru must take the initiative to protect their hold on the land from the nonindigenous ranchers, politicians, judges, and homesteaders who covet it.

Even the local Catholic bishop stands against the Xucuru. He backs a project to develop the Indians' land as a Catholic pilgrimage site. The ranchers who refuse to leave Xucuru territory want to turn their farmhouses into resort hotels. The plans call for 5,000 to 10,000 parking spaces, paved roads, and other infrastructure that would destroy the Xucuru's gardens, fields, and sacred places. The Indians oppose the project. What they want, they say, is to continue to cultivate the land they have lived on and struggled to hold for centuries.

The Xucuru have paid a heavy price for their resistance. They have lost many members of the group, much of their land, and most of their traditional culture. But still they struggle to defend what they have managed to preserve.

A Ritual of Remembrance

On a breezy afternoon in August 2002, hundreds of Xucuru and Indians from neighboring tribes gathered to commemorate the first anniversary of the death of one of their leaders, Chico Quelé. He and two others have

Everybody is plugged in; Pataxó Hã–Hã–Hãe reserve, Bahia, 2002. Photo by Linda Rabben.

been assassinated in recent years as a result of their efforts to reclaim their ancestral territory.

The Indians and a few nonindigenous guests ascend a narrow path that opens onto broad expanses of smooth rock plateaux. Quietly they walk across the rocks and descend into a hole in the forest. There, in the middle of a dark grove, are the graves where the three leaders are "planted." The Xucuru use this metaphor thinking of the seeds from which future crops grow. Planted in the tomb in the center of the grove is Xicão, who led the Xucuru for about twelve years, from the mid-1980s until his assassination in 1998. Across from the tiled tomb is an enormous, pear-shaped rock, about twenty feet high from its broad bottom to its tapered top, stained by moss and lichens. This is a very sacred place for the Xucuru. For many years they carried out their rituals in secret here, because the local powers-that-be made it illegal for them to practice their traditional religion in public.

One at a time, Xucuru men and women approach Xicão's tomb, kneel, and touch his photograph, mounted under glass on the tiled front. They pray silently, heads bowed.

Standing next to Xicao's tomb, the Xucuru religious leader, or *pajé*, weeps as he chants the prayers. One of the victims of the struggle for land was his son. Then the *Toré* begins. The Toré is a dance Indians do all over northeastern Brazil. Marcos de Araújo, the Xucuru's new *cacique*, or political leader, explains the role the Toré plays in their culture: "The Toré is always the main event, the main reason why we meet. It's the part of our religion and our tradition that gives us strength. The resistance of the Xucuru comes from the Toré. We can never allow ourselves to lose this part of our culture and tradition" (interview with the author, August 2002).

Men, women, and children line up abreast, or sometimes singly. They walk or run rhythmically in a circle, chanting as they go. Their feet beat steadily on the compacted earth: BEAT–beatbeat–BEAT–beatbeat–BEAT. Bystanders shake gourd rattles, making a heavy rain of sound. The songs are about saints, or about how good it is to be Xucuru. One of the songs says, "Saint Joan of Arc, the warrior, rules this sacred place."

After about two hours of singing and dancing, the Indians leave the grove and walk back across the rocks and down the narrow path to the village. They climb into cars or on the backs of trucks and travel home over deeply pitted dirt roads in the gathering twilight.

Marcos explains how he was chosen to be the new cacique: "When I was about 12 or 13, I already knew, through the enchanted ones, that I would succeed my father as leader. . . . The enchanted ones are our ancestors, and they speak through our pajé, possessing his spirit. And that was how I learned that I would succeed my father." He did not think he would become the cacique for a long time; but his father, Xicão, was assassinated while he was still a teenager. Marcos became the leader of twenty-three villages and 8,500 people when he was twenty-one.

The Xucuru are Catholic but have preserved their traditional animistic religion and say they worship nature. Marcos bases his work in this traditional belief system. "I do my work in collaboration with the entire community, to ensure that we respect sacred Nature, the forest, the waters, the stones, to make the community aware as we seek our rights together. Every Indian needs to know what his duty is to our Mother Earth. We always say it's from Mother Earth that we get our health, our education, our subsistence." But he admits that when Xicão first started teaching him how to be a leader, "I didn't even know what an Indian was."

Dona Zenilda de Araújo is Marcos' mother and an important leader in her own right. She says she knew from early on that Marcos would be a leader, though he was not Xicão's oldest son. She could tell he had "the gift" that makes some people special.

Zenilda speaks with assurance about the Xucuru heritage:

> Our ancestors didn't have much contact with the church or the whites. They were more in touch with nature, in immediate contact, that kind of faith, and we also have that. . . . These days we see many priests who don't support our struggle. We don't want to listen to that type of priest. We want to hear priests who support grassroots movements. . . . I myself am Catholic, linked directly to God, and I also have my indigenous religion—the faith of our ancestors. We sense their presence. Not everybody feels it—only those who have the gift that they're born with. We feel that strength and it gives us powerful energy. (Interview with the author, August 2002)

The Xucuru's religious faith permeates their lives—their political activities as well as their medical practices and their schools, where they teach traditional lore in addition to the standard Brazilian curriculum. Their faith supports their determination to control their land, preserve their customs, and teach their children how good it is to be Xucuru.

A History of Resistance

The Xucuru are first mentioned as a discrete group in Portuguese records around 1700. They participated in a guerrilla war against invading ranchers in Pernambuco from the late 1600s to the 1720s. Catholic missionaries gave the defeated Indians a kind of refuge in villages called *aldeamentos*, as Brazilian colonists moved onto their traditional lands. Like the colonists, some of the religious orders enslaved the Indians to work on their cattle ranches or in the fields.

In the middle of the eighteenth century, the aldeamentos were transformed into *vilas* administered by members of the Brazilian elite. Members of many different groups were brought together in the vilas. Slavery of Indians was officially ended, but they lived in conditions little better than bondage. They were encouraged (or forced) to marry members of other indigenous groups, so that they would lose their tribal identity and become "civilized." They were not allowed to use indigenous names or speak their traditional language and were given Portuguese surnames.

The rulers of the vilas forced the Indians to build Brazilian-style houses divided into rooms, to prevent "vices." The Indians had to wear clothes. The Brazilians called them "Tupi" or "Tapuyos," generic names for Indians. Later they were called *caboclos*, a pejorative term that means hillbilly or half-breed. Indians who resisted Brazilian control were called ferocious barbarians and treated with ruthless brutality.

Northeastern Indians resisted these forms of domination as best they could, holding onto their traditional practices, especially religious rituals. Over the generations, as they married slaves of African ancestry, they looked less like the Indians the Portuguese had first encountered. A complicated system of racial categories developed to describe the mixed-race people of the Northeast, but some groups managed to preserve their tribal names, stay on their traditional lands, remember some of their traditional languages and customs, and keep dancing the Toré.

Brazil's oligarchs consistently passed laws designed to take indigenous land from the Indians and redistribute it to elite families and their dependents. For example, under the provisions of the 1850 land law, "small farmers and many indigenous villages were excluded from the land registry because they lacked documents proving their ownership. The land law increasingly encouraged invasions of indigenous lands" (Silva 1999: 14). Also in 1850, the emperor of Brazil issued a proclamation giving non-Indians access to lands of Indians who were dispersed in the general population and considered "civilized." In these ways, time and again the Brazilian government tried to legislate northeastern Indians out of existence.

But the Xucuru and other indigenous groups continued to resist. As late as 1894, a punitive expedition went into Xucuru territory to end their raids on ranches; they fought back with bows and arrows.

Nonetheless, the Xucuru were part of Brazilian society. They were recruited or conscripted to fight in the Paraguayan War (1865–70) and claimed years later that the government had given them title to part of their traditional territory to reward their military service. In 1948, the government gave pensions to the daughters of the Xucuru Paraguayan War veterans, thus acknowledging the group's continuing existence.

It was convenient for Brazilians to consider Indians a "vanishing" or "degenerate" race in the nineteenth and twentieth centuries. The vila system was done away with because, as a nineteenth-century provincial governor observed, their inhabitants "are mixed into the population, have forgotten their primitive customs and live in continual conflict with the usurpers of their lands" (Silva 1999: 19). The state's definition of an Indian became more and more narrow, making it easier to take land from people the state decided were no longer Indians. That is, the government took it upon itself to determine who was Indian and who was not.

Even so, the Xucuru and other northeastern indigenous groups continued to consider themselves Indians. They repeatedly traveled to the provincial capital or even the national capital of Rio de Janeiro to press their land claims, or sent letters and petitions denouncing the theft of their land to the authorities. Their struggle for their land has been continual, as shown in Brazilian archives as well as the Indians' oral histories.

Invisible Indians

But it became dangerous to identify oneself as Indian, and over the years the government declared many northeastern groups "extinct." Marcos, the Xucuru's young cacique, told an interviewer, "We were forbidden to conduct our ritual. Many relatives died because they would not obey. So many Xucuru stopped saying they were Indians. They were afraid because the ranchers would kill them" (CIMI 2001a: 82).

Thus the Xucuru became invisible for decades. But they still remembered where they had come from. An anthropologist in the 1930s found fifty Xucuru who could remember their traditional language. He wrote, "They know perfectly well that they descend from the Xucuru tribe that occupied that region, are proud of their ancestry and define themselves as superior to the other inhabitants, hiding their bitterness at the whites for having taken their lands" (Silva 1999: 25).

Despite the Indians' invisibility, the Indian Protection Service did recognize several northeastern indigenous groups from the 1920s on. In 1944 the SPI said the Xucuru numbered 2,191. They were still enduring persecution—the police forbade them to perform their rituals, including curing ceremonies. They complained to the SPI about invasions, threats, and harassment. In 1953, three Xucuru walked to Rio de Janeiro—it took three months—to complain to the federal government about the corruption of the SPI and the violence of local ranchers. On their return they received death threats. At that time they had an officially recognized reserve of 6.75 hectares, about 16 acres.

Brazil's military dictatorship, which began in 1964, was especially repressive in the Northeast, cracking down first on rural grassroots movements that were seeking land reform. In alliance with traditional regional elites, the military denounced these movements and their leaders as communist-inspired. Even so, the Catholic Church formed agencies, the Pastoral Land Commission and the Missionary Indigenist Council, that began working with homesteaders, the landless, and Indians in the early 1970s.

Instead of proselytizing indigenous people, CIMI "accompanied" their struggles for land. Lay pastoral agents, priests, and nuns lived and worked with Indians in every region of the country. They "sought to reinforce tribal institutions, traditions and identities" (Warren 2001: 146). In some regions and among some groups, such as the Kayapó, the church people did not manage to establish themselves. But in the Northeast, where the population had identified itself as Catholic for centuries, they have had considerable success. CIMI has a broader vision, too. The agency "has almost single-handedly financed and coordinated the creation of pan-Indian organizations" over the past two decades (ibid., 147). CIMI provides lawyers, organizes campaigns, publishes periodicals, sponsors meetings, advises indigenous organizations, lobbies government on all levels, and secures international support for indigenous initiatives and projects. Without its "accompaniment" over thirty years, many indigenous groups might have faded into oblivion. But with the advice and encouragement of CIMI staff, groups in northeastern and eastern Brazil have emerged from invisibility, reassuming their indigenous identity and mobilizing to regain their traditional territory.

In the early 1970s, twelve indigenous groups had been identified in the Northeast. By 2000, forty-one groups—some 80,000 people—had emerged from the "caboclo ghetto." The Northeast now has the second highest indigenous population of any Brazilian region.

The road to recognition has been rough. Many groups report similar histories of persecution. For the Pankararé of Bahia,

> conflicts with homesteaders began in the mid-1940s. . . . Aware that if the Pankararé also had their indigenous identity recognized, they would regain their territorial rights, the homesteaders set about preventing them from conducting any rituals. To get away from the threats and persecution, the Indians had to move to Pernambuco to conduct the Toré and the Praiá rituals. . . . The conflicts with the homesteaders worsened in the early 1970s, when the Pankararé finally decided to make public their identity and fight for the rights over their lands. . . . Groups of homesteaders accompanied by politicians and police . . . would invade the Toré grounds each time, beating and arresting the Indians. . . . The conflicts became increasingly more serious, until they resulted in the killing of the cacique. . . . The persecution . . . continued even after FUNAI recognized their ethnic identity. In the mid-1980s . . . violence was carried out intentionally to terrorize the Pankararé and prevent demarcation of the area, which FUNAI kept postponing. . . . Nowadays the Pankararé try to conduct their rituals in the forest. . . . And they avoid doing them in the middle of the village, since they still receive threats from homesteaders who have invaded their lands. (CIMI 2001a: 83)

Routes of Resurgence

Indigenous groups and their allies point to several landmark events that have spurred indigenous mobilization over the past forty years. In the mid-1960s, national and international outcry hastened the end of the SPI, which had become notorious for killing or betraying the Indians it was supposed to protect. In 1978, a national and international campaign prevented the adoption of a law to "emancipate" Brazil's indigenous people. The law would have ended legal protections for threatened Indian groups.

During the military dictatorship, a few indigenous groups and spokesmen gained national attention, despite the repressive climate. Mario Juruna, a Xavante who was elected to Congress, became famous for carrying a tape recorder to meetings so he could hold officials accountable for their promises. The Union of Indigenous Nations (UNI) was started by a small group of Indian students, including one from an "extinct" northeastern tribe. Juruna and UNI clashed publicly with the authorities and won.

After the end of the dictatorship in 1985, indigenous groups became increasingly visible and politically active. With the assistance of NGOs and the Catholic Church, indigenous organizations participated in the Constituent Assembly that drew up the Constitution of 1988. Kayapó warriors in battle dress attended most sessions, lobbied, and held colorful demonstrations that gained considerable attention. Many other indigenous groups also participated in the proceedings. They gained provisions in the new Constitution that greatly improved their legal position and protected their "preferential use and control" of their traditional territories.

Their experience in the Constituent Assembly has served indigenous leaders well—as has their contact with other activists at meetings, demonstrations, and other events in Brazil and abroad. Their organizing, lobbying, and campaigning have become ever more sophisticated and effective over the past two decades. Davi Kopenawa, Paulinho Payakan, Raoni, and a few others have been the most visible among them. Younger and lesser-known activists got their start at the Constituent Assembly or at the indigenous conference in Rio in 1992. They were ready to speak out against the Yanomami massacre of 1993 and Decree 1775/96. Throughout the 1990s, they asked for international help in denouncing policies and laws that might hurt indigenous people in general. Some got to know indigenous leaders from other countries by attending international meetings and have maintained contact with these counterparts over the years. Others have established relationships with international NGOs such as Survival International and the World Rainforest Movement.

Among the young indigenous activists who participated in the Constituent Assembly were representatives of the Pataxó Hã-Hã-Hãe of central Bahia in the Northeast. Like the Xucuru, the Pataxó Hã-Hã-Hãe have a long history of resisting Brazilian domination. They trace violence suffered in the 20th century back to 1936, when state police invaded their recently demarcated territory in search of "an alleged communist cell" (Aldeia Caramuru Paraguaçu 2000: 1). In the 1940s they experienced expulsions, jailings, beatings, and battles over land with homesteaders and police. The violence worsened in the 1950s and 1960s, with killings of Pataxó leaders and full-scale invasions of their land. During the military dictatorship, several leaders were sent to a special prison farm for indigenous "troublemakers." In the 1970s, the state government illegally gave land titles to invaders of Pataxó territory as a political favor.

In 1982, the Pataxó summoned the courage to take a legal action to annul the titles to Brazil's Supreme Court. They still were awaiting a decision twenty years later. In the meantime, local politicians and landlords hired gunmen or sent state police to terrorize the Indians and try to drive them off the land. A "Chronology of Violence" the Pataxó drew up includes many reports like the following, from 1991: "Twenty-nine Indians violently attacked. Seven sent to hospital, including three pregnant women who were beaten and had their clothes torn off. One 13-year-old girl suffered a rape attempt, and other girls were beaten" (ibid., 2).

In twenty years of continuous conflict over their land, eighteen Pataxó leaders have been killed by hired gunmen or police. No one has been brought to justice for these crimes. Tired of waiting for justice, the Pataxó decided they would have to retake their demarcated territory. Over the past decade, unarmed groups of men, women, and children have occupied farmsteads inside their 54,000-hectare reserve. As the Brazilian invaders became more violent, federal police patrolled the reserve, and state police set up roadblocks at the entrances to the indigenous area, to prevent gunmen from entering. But, the Indians said, the gunmen already were living inside the reserve; and more often than not, the police took the opportunity to harass and beat Indians as they left or entered their territory.

Pataxó Martyr

In 1997, in an effort to pressure FUNAI to remove the invaders, a delegation of Pataxó Hã-Hã-Hãe went to Brasilia. Among them was Galdino Jesus dos Santos, whose brother had been killed in the struggle over land. Because he could not get into the guesthouse where he was staying, he went to sleep on a bench at a bus stop. At about 5:30 A.M. on the day after the Day of the Indian, a national holiday, a crew of young men spotted him and decided to have some "fun." They went to a gas station and bought a bottle of fuel. Then they returned to the bus stop, threw the fuel on the sleeping man and set him alight. A passerby took dos Santos to the hospital, where he died. A man on his way to work witnessed the crime and noted the license plate number of the young men's car. Five were arrested, including one minor. One of the youths turned out to be the son of a federal judge. All were upper middle class.

Despite attempts by their families to get them off, the youths were convicted of homicide. But because they were wealthy and had no previous criminal records, their conditions of imprisonment were easy, and it was unlikely they would serve their full sentences. Brazilians were horrified by this depraved and senseless crime — and by the little-known fact that the burning of homeless people as they sleep happens from time to time in Brazil's big cities. They also were mortified by the negative international publicity that followed the killing.

The president of FUNAI went to the Pataxó Hã-Hã-Hãe reserve in Bahia to attend dos Santos' funeral. Pataxó leaders grabbed him, took him to a ranch inside the reserve, and forced him to participate in a *retomada*, or retaking of territory. Soon after, the demarcation of Pataxó Hã-Hã-Hãe land was finally completed. A few years later, a large school was built with federal funds not far from dos Santos' grave. As of August 2002, the Indians had retaken about 12,000 hectares of their territory. But the violence continued — and would continue as long as the government did not carry out its constitutional responsibility to remove invaders from demarcated indigenous areas and compensate them according to the law.

The Pataxó remained grimly determined to continue their struggle:

> When we seek justice, we get assassination attempts and deaths of our relatives. Those who do not own our land, the invaders, are always enriching themselves at our expense. . . . We will no longer remain silent, we will speak out to try to improve the situation so that they treat us with respect and dignity because of the rights we have, since we want only what is ours; we aren't asking for what belongs to others. (Aldeia Caramuru Paraguaçu 2000: 5)

The burning of Galdino dos Santos had a galvanizing effect on indigenous people throughout Brazil. After Xicão Xucuru was murdered about a year later, Indians redoubled their efforts to protect themselves and defend their interests. Also in the late 1990s, verdicts of genocide were handed down in the massacres of fourteen Ticuna in 1988 and sixteen Yanomami in 1993. As increasing numbers of indigenous groups gained access to information about these and other events from radio and television, they saw their local struggles as part of something much larger.

Indigenous Mobilization

According to CIMI, in 2000 about 250 indigenous associations and organizations were active in Brazil. (One newspaper report claimed 400 such organizations existed.) The best-known include CIR, in Roraima, and regional groups, such as COIAB in Amazonia and APOINME in the Northeast. A national organization, CAPOIB, created in 1992, now claims hundreds of members—101 indigenous groups and 55 organizations—and has its office in the national capital, Brasilia.

Indigenous women began organizing their own associations in the 1990s. The First Meeting of Eastern Indigenous Women took place in 1998. At their second meeting in 1999, fifty-eight representatives from eleven indigenous groups drew up a manifesto in which they called for special educational programs to teach traditional knowledge to children; regular meetings in villages and among peoples; demarcation of all indigenous lands; and investigation and punishment of crimes against indigenous groups, including assassinations of leaders and sterilization of women. They ended the manifesto with a call for "construction of a 'new country,' whose guiding principles would be solidarity, justice, and respect for cultural, ethnic, and gender diversity" (CIMI 2001a: 141).

The indigenous women's manifesto also called for nonparticipation in the official commemorations of the 500th anniversary of the first Portuguese landfall in Brazil. Instead, the women vowed to "protest and celebrate our resistance and our struggles" (ibid.). They were part of what became a nationwide movement in the literal sense of the word, as thousands of Indians took buses from their homelands across Brazil to the site of the 500th anniversary commemorations on the northeast coast.

In 1999 a coalition of indigenous and other grassroots organizations started organizing a march and demonstration to protest the triumphalistic celebration of the 500th anniversary, scheduled to take place April 22, 2000, near Coroa Vermelha, Bahia, where the Portuguese had first encountered indigenous people. The coastal Pataxó, a different group from the Pataxó

Hã-Hã-Hãe, are still struggling to gain rights to their traditional territory in this area.

Starting in early April 2000, representatives of more than 150 indigenous groups began wending their way from every part of the country to Bahia. First they arrived by foot, canoe, car, and bus at regional capitals, where they demonstrated publicly, participated in teach-ins, and gave interviews to the national and local media. They called the march "The Other 500."

As the groups were beginning their journey, the authorities made their first response. On April 4, some 200 heavily armed state police invaded indigenous land at Coroa Vermelha and destroyed a monument the Pataxó were constructing in memory of Indians massacred over the previous 500 years. According to an indignant press release from CIMI, the police "shouted at the Indians, 'The government is in charge here until April 26,' and 'Globo [television network] wants the area cleared'" (CIMI 2000b). Near where the Indians' wooden memorial had stood, the official celebration's organizers erected a huge, stainless steel cross.

Meanwhile, about 2,000 indigenous people were converging on Bahia from around the country. Some, from the interior of Amazonia, would see the ocean for the first time; others came from just a few miles away. The Kayapó came in force, the Yanomami sent Davi Kopenawa and other representatives, and 156 other peoples and one group from neighboring Peru also arrived. The greatest numbers came from the Amazon states of Amazonas, Mato Grosso, Pará, and Rondônia, but twenty-one of Brazil's twenty-seven states were represented.

On their way to Bahia, some groups stopped in Brasilia, where they held public meetings, demonstrated in front of Congress, and sent a delegation to President Fernando Henrique Cardoso, Congress members, and other officials. The Indians also paid homage to Xicão Xucuru, whose widow spoke "in memory of all the indigenous martyrs killed in the struggle for land" (CIMI n.d.).

Participants disagreed as to whether they should participate in the official events in Bahia. Most wanted to protest outside. Some did not like the Catholic Church's attempts to build a coalition of protesters with Afro-Brazilian and landless groups. The presence of the landless movement—which the government regarded as much more dangerous than the indigenous movement—might have been what made officials decide to suppress the demonstrations.

When the Indians arrived in Bahia, they found they could not get anywhere near the site of the official commemoration. According to Amnesty International (2001: 1),

> On the day of the anniversary, demonstrators from black and indigenous groups as well as popular activists, politicians, students and many others tried to march from Coroa Vermelha to Porto Seguro. Military police blocked the road, then reportedly used excessive force to break up the peaceful demonstration, attacking marchers with tear gas, rubber bullets and batons. Numerous witnesses alleged that the police attack was unprovoked and apparently designed to prevent the marchers from reaching Porto Seguro, where the presidents of Brazil and Portugal were leading the official celebrations.

At the front of the march were Congress members, dozens of Catholic missionaries, and a local judge, who had handed down an injunction allowing the protest. When the missionaries were arrested, the judge

> demanded their release. However, he too was arrested. Colonel Muller [the commander of the operation] ordered that all remain under arrest and that the road be blocked. The judge and the colonel began a fierce discussion. [The judge] ordered the arrest of the colonel, but the order was not respected. Arrogantly, the colonel asked who would dare to arrest him. The judge was then surrounded by 400 police. (Amazon Alliance 2000)

As the police, wearing battle gear and teargas masks, marched along, pushing the demonstrators back, a lone Terena man confronted them in the middle of the road, his arms outstretched. When he lay in their path, the police walked right over him. The pictures of him lying on the rain-soaked highway were transmitted around the world.

For the participants and many others, these incidents exemplified the Brazilian government's attitude toward Indians, grassroots movements, human rights, and the rule of law. One indigenous leader said, "This is the true face of Brazil, 500 years later." Another commented, "This is Brazil for all the world to see" (Astor 2000).

More than two years later, the Federal Prosecution Service announced it was suing the federal government, the state of Bahia, and Colonel Muller on behalf of those injured in the repression of April 22, 2000. At about the same time, coastal Pataxó conducted a retomada in their territory near Coroa Vermelha. CIMI reported:

> The Indians have requested that FUNAI take measures to prevent a conflict. . . . they report that armed men are circulating in the area at night, firing at the indigenous families' encampment. The Pataxó request the presence of Federal Police in the area to avoid a confrontation and demand immediate action by the federal government to complete the demarcation of their lands. (CIMI 2002a)

So the same drama keeps repeating itself.

Rediscovery of Indianness

Brazil's Indians and their allies could not forget their march across the country or the violent government reaction to their protest in April 2000. Perhaps this and other highly publicized incidents in recent years have contributed to the growing sympathy for indigenous people in Brazil. Perhaps they led thousands of Brazilians to declare themselves Indians in the 2000 census.

Astonishingly, according to the census, Indians are Brazil's fastest-growing population group. From 1990 to 2000, their population more than doubled, from about 350,000 to 700,000 — that is, more than twice as many people identified themselves as indigenous to census takers. More than half may live in urban areas and do not identify what tribe they are part of, probably because they do not know. They are called "generic Indians."

Anthropologist Marta Azevedo, of the Instituto Sócioambiental, questioned the accuracy of the count but agreed that the indigenous population had increased:

The decade of the nineties was very good for the Indians. At the Constitutional Convention and the Earth Summit, they appeared in the media in a positive light. As the environmental issue grew in prominence, they emerged as defenders of the environment. In addition, the Federal University of Minas Gerais did a DNA study in 1997 that showed 45 million Brazilians have indigenous ancestry. These things reinforced ethnic identity and made people increasingly proud of being descended from indigenous people. (Nogueira 2002)

Brazil's Indians are emerging, then, in more ways than one. But they still comprise a tiny proportion (less than 1 percent) of the national population, and they still constitute the poorest of the poor.[1] CIMI estimates that in 1998, "at least 174,000 Indians were hungry and depended on the distribution of food by the federal government to survive. . . . That year, half of the indigenous population lived below the poverty line" (CIMI 2001a: 97). FUNAI's assistance budget suffered cuts of 41 percent that year.

The health situation of Indians on the reserves is

extremely grave. . . . About 50 percent of deaths were among children under age five. Most frequent causes were contagious diseases, especially acute respiratory infections, intestinal parasites, malaria and malnutrition. External causes, especially violence and suicide, were the third greatest cause of death, especially among populations in Mato Grosso do Sul and Roraima. (ibid., 99)

Tuberculosis rates are particularly high among Indians. Incidence is exacerbated by lack of basic sanitation, deterioration in living conditions resulting from invasions, lack of access to health care, and lack of treatment follow-up.

In 1999, the indigenous infant mortality rate was a very high 200 per thousand; 60 percent of the indigenous population suffered from some illness; 60 percent of those illnesses were cases of malaria. Overall mortality was as much as five times higher than the national median. Life expectancy was forty-eight years for Indians, sixty-five for non-Indians. CIMI may not be exaggerating when it calls these statistics a sign of "a new and reinvigorated process of extermination . . . which could be characterized as a gradual and silent genocide" (ibid., 99).

Given this reality, when Indians make their protests, they first demand land, from which they draw their sustenance; then medical care, to attend to the urgent health problems they confront daily; then education, to train the next generation of leaders who will represent them. These are the human rights that are most important to them. Asked about their vision of the future, the women are the most eloquent: They want their children to grow up in peace.

When the Xucuru, Pataxó, and other groups do gain control of their land, how will they live, and can they prosper? They say they want to be left alone to cultivate their fields, as they have done for centuries. But clearly, the world will not leave them alone. It still wants their resources and their labor. The emerging indigenous peoples of the Northeast (and Brazil's other regions) will have to find viable ways to be part of the global economy. Like the Kayapó and the Yanomami, they will have to choose, again and again, how to develop their land, preserve their culture, and live with—and in—the outside world.

9 / Fit for What?

PREDICTING THE END OF AN INDIGENOUS GROUP IS ALL TOO easy. Experts have been doing so for hundreds of years, and they have often been wrong. As a result of the systematic, massive depredation of the world's tropical rainforests during the past forty years, however, it is not unreasonable to fear the end of the indigenous peoples who live in them.[1] Hundreds of indigenous groups already have disappeared, and many more struggle to maintain their traditional ways of life against tremendous odds. They live with disease, hunger, violence, and poverty, not only in Brazil but in Indonesia, Siberia, Australia, the United States, and many other countries. Destroy their means of subsistence, and what (or who) can stop them from vanishing completely?

Governments, multilateral lenders, multinational corporations, private banks, and other institutions may not be counting on the convenient disappearance of indigenous peoples who get in the way of their ambitious development plans, but they often act as if they are. In April 1997, the presidents of Brazil and Venezuela ceremonially inaugurated a road-building project to connect Caracas with Manaus. The road threatened the well-being of at least eight indigenous groups and the environments from which they drew their sustenance (InterPress Service 1997a). The following month, the Pemon Indians of southern Venezuela forced workers to stop constructing high-tension power-line towers across a national park where they live. According to an Internet report from the EnviroNews Service (Hamilton 1997), "The action came as a result of the state-owned company CVG-EDELCA and INPARQUES [the Venezuelan Parks Institute] failing to reply to letters from the Pemon pleading for information and consultation."

Ticuna family in 1993, near the site of the 1988 massacre. Photo by Linda Rabben.

By law, the authorities were required to respond to affected communities within fifteen days.

Also in 1997, twenty Venezuelan environmental groups protested the federal government's "gross abuse of power and deceitful manipulation of public opinion" in granting mining concessions in a forest reserve in the same region, where the Pemon and several other indigenous groups live (Centeno 1997). The Indians and environmentalists said these projects contravened federal laws protecting forest reserves, national parks, and indigenous rights. In both cases, the government failed to notify or consult those affected by its plans. Every month, similar stories come out of countries from Papua New Guinea to Cameroon.

Under years of unremitting pressure from grassroots groups and non-governmental organizations, governments and the giant institutions that dominate the world's economic life have created international agreements, regulatory regimes, laws, and policies to protect vulnerable environments and people. Yet they continue to plan and carry out mega-projects that may lead to the destruction of those fragile communities and their environments.

A report by Amazon Watch (Soltani and Osborne 1997) analyzed eleven giant development projects proposed or in progress in seven Amazon countries: highways, dams, oil and natural-gas pipelines, electric power lines, industrial waterways, and railroads with construction costs in the billions of dollars. Most facilitate production and export of minerals, agricultural commodities, and timber to world markets, but are unlikely to improve the lives of these countries' poor majorities, who lack balanced diets, adequate sanitation, clean water, health care, decent housing, sufficient wages to feed their families, and basic education. Multinational corporations, capital investors, national elites, and Northern consumers are the main beneficiaries. The immediate and long-term environmental and social costs of devastating large areas and numerous communities to build these projects have not been fully calculated.

Publicly funded institutions like the World Bank may have changed their method of participation in such projects, but not their development model. "The private sector now accounts for more than 75 percent of project financing in the developing world while the MDBs [multilateral development banks] play the role of mobilizers of capital [rather] than that of direct lenders," notes the Amazon Watch report (ibid., 7). The MDBs have spurred privatization programs that decentralize the process of development funding. Consequently, the report warns, "pressuring MDBs and governments is no longer sufficient to stopping destructive projects." Since loans often go to unaccountable corporations instead of governments, "disclosure and community consultation policies do not apply," and "these institutions do not adhere to the hard-won environmental and social lending policies of the traditional MDBs" (ibid., 7).

Like the Kaingang Indians who attacked telegraph workers in the 1920s, indigenous groups have tended to confront the shadowy forces of international development on the ground, where they experience the projects' direct effects. In February 1997, for example, the Krikati of Maranhão, on the eastern edge of the Brazilian Amazon, set fire to two electric transmission towers. Fed up with invasions of their territory, whose demarcation they had sought for thirty years, they waited with bows and arrows for the police. Two days later, the Xokleng of Santa Catarina state, in southeastern Brazil, invaded a dam site and opened four sluices, threatening to flood cities downstream. They were demanding indemnification for 856 hectares of flooded land (CIMI 1997a). In July 1997, the Pankararu of Pernambuco, Northeastern Brazil, cited the Krikati as their inspiration when they threatened to bring down transmission towers that supplied electricity to six states. They had been waiting ten years for FUNAI to compensate and resettle homesteaders in their territory (Ricardo 2000: 551). These actions forced the federal and state governments to pay attention to the Indians' grievances, but there was no guarantee the problems would be resolved once the spotlights turned off. In recent decades, the pattern has been for the government to respond under pressure with promises of immediate corrective action, after which nothing has happened. In the 1980s the Kayapó and other groups took to videotaping their meetings with authorities, so they would have evidence of government commitments to use in court proceedings or public confrontations.

The Kayapó Method

The Krikati and Xokleng might have been following the Kayapó's example. Over two decades, the Kayapó have been staging spectacular actions against government officials and others who tried to enter or take their land without their permission. Each time, the outsiders backed down, if only for the moment. In "going international," by mobilizing Sting, visiting world capitals, and influencing global public opinion, the Kayapó showed other indigenous groups and the general public that such tactics could also work.

Over time the Kayapó changed their strategies for gaining the material benefits of "civilization" without abandoning the traditional ways they valued or destroying the environment that sustained them. For many years they raided their neighbors, but this was an inefficient means of obtaining the goods they wanted. Later, when selling off resources to outsiders brought adverse consequences, they expelled miners and loggers from their territory. This action did not usher in an era of sustainable development, however.

The Kayapó are still struggling to earn sufficient money to buy the goods they want, provide education in Portuguese for their children, and health care for all community members. As of 2002, despite federal court rulings, pressure from state politicians and private interests had prevented the demarcation of a sizable part of traditional Kayapó territory called Baú.

In addition, the threat of flooding of a significant portion of the largest Kayapó reserve was revived with the reactivation of the Belo Monte dam project. It was halted temporarily in late 2002 but still could resume at any time.

For the Kayapó and other indigenous groups, the challenges and dangers of "integrating" into Brazilian society while preserving their culture will not end. The Indians need to prepare themselves for repeated confrontations and crises. This means having adequate resources (and a social structure) to mobilize leaders and participants. Readiness also requires cultivating allies in the outside world. The Kayapó have succeeded in doing all these things—indeed, they seem to have an aptitude for coordinated political action. And they have operated independently, which may work for them but not for others.

Groups with fewer resources, like the Krikati and Xokleng, have sought help from the Indigenist Missionary Council and other non-Indian allies, but they also may need to join forces with other indigenous groups and create regional political coalitions. To give an example of such collaboration, in mid-1997, the Tupinikim joined with the neighboring Guarani of Espírito Santo, Brazil, to send representatives to Europe to urge investors there to sell their stock in a multinational cellulose company that was challenging their demarcation rights under Decree 1775/96 (World Rainforest Movement 1997). In Brazil's Northeast, other "resurgent" indigenous groups like the Xucuru, the Pankararu, and the Potiguara are uniting in statewide and regional pan-indigenous associations to pursue and protect their common interests.

Indians throughout Brazil have begun to pay attention to the defense of their natural patrimonies and their traditional knowledge. In December 2001, thirty indigenous leaders met to discuss "The Wisdom and Science of the Indian and Industrial Property." They signed a declaration that their traditional knowledge is "not merchandise that can be sold like any object in the market"; it cannot be separated from their identity, customs, value system, and cosmology. They asked the federal government to give indigenous people a seat on the national Council for the Management of Genetic Patrimony; to pass laws regulating access to genetic resources in consultation with indigenous people; to ratify the United Nations indigenous rights declaration; to oppose patenting of traditional knowledge for commercial gain and punish theft of biodiversity; and to develop policies that would protect biodiversity, including sustainable development for indigenous groups, among other things. The declaration concludes, "Concerned about the advance of bio-prospecting and the future of humanity, our children and grandchildren, we affirm to governments our clear recognition that we are holders of rights and not only interests" (Carta de São Luis 2001: 2).

It is clear from the language of rights, international law, and self-determination that Indians now use that they have learned much from their contacts with international advocacy organizations—and one another—at international meetings like the annual U.N. Indigenous Working Group sessions in Geneva. And it seems likely that they will keep forming intertribal coalitions, councils, and other collaborative structures to increase their political and economic power regionally, nationally, and internationally. Such complex organizational efforts require much time, energy, and human—as well as financial—resources.

Yanomami Dilemmas

The Yanomami have begun to unite to defend their land and culture only in recent years. The perils facing them are formidable:

- Epidemic and chronic diseases that kill potential leaders, weaken the population and disaggregate society
- Inadequate medical and educational assistance, especially across international borders
- Geographic remoteness that impedes communication (it took six weeks for news of the 1993 massacre to reach the outside world, and another two to three weeks to determine the number of victims and whereabouts of survivors)
- Lack of protection against armed invaders
- Lack of political leadership and support—allies are too few and too far away
- No effective control over economic resources

The Yanomami are fortunate in having Brazilian and international supporters who have devoted themselves to the Indians' welfare, who are managing to obtain financial support for development, health, and educational initiatives, and who encourage them to organize. It is uncertain, however, if the Yanomami can pull together to fight the next series of battles against the next generation of bilateral and multilateral mega-projects to threaten their existence as a people.

The Bases for Caring

Why should we care about what happens to the Yanomami and the other indigenous groups that struggle to survive civilization? What difference would it make if they disappeared? Aside from sentimental and humanitarian reasons for supporting indigenous people, there are strong political, environmental, and scientific reasons for defending their cause.

After hundreds of years of destroying peoples who got in their way, the world powers contemplated Auschwitz and recoiled, if only temporarily, from their death-dealing arrogance in 1948. They wrote and signed the Universal Declaration of Human Rights, which established the foundation of a new political order, based on the rule of law and respect for all human beings. It is worth reviewing the first three paragraphs of the Universal Declaration's preamble:

> *Whereas* recognition of the inherent dignity and of the equal and inalienable rights of all members of the human family is the foundation of freedom, justice and peace in the world,

> *Whereas* disregard and contempt for human rights have resulted in barbarous acts which have outraged the conscience of mankind, and the advent of a world in which human beings shall enjoy freedom of speech and belief and freedom from fear and want has been proclaimed as the highest aspiration of the common people,

> *Whereas* it is essential, if man is not to be compelled to have recourse, as a last resort, to rebellion against tyranny and oppression, that human rights should be protected by the rule of law. . . . (Center for the Study of Human Rights 1992: 6)

Article 3 of the Universal Declaration declares, "Everyone has the right to life, liberty and security of person." Other articles outlaw slavery, torture, arbitrary arrest, and detention, and guarantee equal protection of the laws. Most of the world's nations have ratified this document, which has become the foundation of international human rights law.

The noble sentiments of the Universal Declaration and the international covenants of civil, political, economic, social, and cultural rights have not been realized, but they do provide the bases for actions to protect and defend basic human rights around the world. And indigenous peoples have the same human rights as other human beings. Additional agreements, such as International Labor Organization Conventions 107 and 169, guarantee indigenous groups' rights to live on their traditional lands and follow their traditional customs.[2] Governments have committed themselves to protecting those rights, both through international treaties and in their national laws.

So when a multinational oil company signs a concessionary contract with a government and then takes over part of an indigenous community's land without adequate consultation or compensation, it and the government are violating international and national law. This fact in itself makes nothing happen. The United Nations sends no troops, the Inter-American Commission on Human Rights makes no protest, the U.S. Government does not break diplomatic relations with the country, and the International Chamber of Commerce does not criticize the company's action.

In one such case, the U'wa indigenous community of Colombia campaigned for years with the help of international environmental and indigenous-support organizations. The group threatened collective suicide if a multinational corporation did not respect their decision not to allow oil exploration on their land. Internet users sent letters to Colombian officials, the company's directors, the European Parliament, and U.S. Congress members, calling for action to protect the U'wa's human rights. Finally, in 2002, the corporation pulled out of U'wa territory. Soon after, however, the U'wa had to restart their campaign because a national oil company tried to take over the project. Similar cases have happened and continue to happen in Ecuador, Brazil, Guyana, Venezuela, Suriname, and other countries. By pressuring governments in these ways, indigenous people, allied with citizens of many nations, are seeking to implement principles enunciated in international law.

In a statement to the World Bank and International Monetary Fund,

Amnesty International pointed out that "development is all too often pursued at the expense of human rights" and urged the multilateral financial institutions "to take civil and political rights as seriously as economic and social rights, and recognize the indivisibility of all human rights" (Amnesty International 1997).

Like other indigenous groups, Brazil's indigenous peoples have basic human rights, guaranteed in international agreements and the nation's Constitution, which uphold their control over their traditional territories and their entitlement to the same services and protection the Brazilian government is legally obligated to provide to all its citizens. They have begun to take action based on their recognition of these rights.

Economic Reasons for Protecting Indigenous Peoples

For those who do not consider moral reasons for supporting indigenous peoples sufficiently compelling, ecologists have calculated the monetary value of what used to be called "externalities": environmental costs associated with large-scale exploitation and consumption of natural resources often found on or in indigenous lands.

Stanford University ecologist Gretchen Daily has pointed out that "goods and services" provided by natural ecosystems—including purification of air and water, recycling of wastes, generation and maintenance of soil fertility, pollination, and foods—are worth trillions of dollars. "Humanity came into being after most of these services had been in operation for hundreds of millions to billions of years. They are so fundamental as to make them both easy to take for granted and hard to imagine disrupting beyond repair, as human activity threatens to do today." Although Daily admitted "it would be absurd to try to estimate the value of natural processes in strictly economic terms," she wanted decision makers to be aware of nature's incalculable importance for all societies (Environmental News Service 1997).

Do Indians Save the Environment?

Traditionally, Indians exploited the forest without destroying it. Some anthropologists and biologists believe their shifting cultivation methods over the centuries have preserved and even enlarged the forests. Steve Schwartzman, an anthropologist and senior scientist at Environmental Defense, points out, "If you put together satellite images of all the fires burning in the Amazon, you can see the outline of the indigenous areas just from that. Where Indian land starts is where the fires stop" (Rohter 2002b).

Environmental justifications for defending indigenous rights are not always clear-cut, however. Increasingly, Indians are not left to their own devices. Once in contact with outsiders, indigenous groups may not do any better than others at protecting and sustainably developing their land and natural resources. Given the opportunity to share in the profits, the Kayapó allowed gold miners and loggers to depredate their territory. Other indigenous groups have made similar deals with predatory outsiders in exchange for short-term gain. They seek medical services, schools, access roads, electricity, clean water, and other necessities, and if the government does not fulfill its legal responsibility to provide these things, they may turn to private companies for them. The experience of the Kayapó and other groups shows that selling off resources may bring immediate benefits, but the long-term damage caused by logging, mining, and other industrial extractive activities harms people's health and the environment. To ensure a prosperous future in a relatively unspoiled environment, indigenous peoples need incentives to stop selling off their natural patrimony, as well as workable development plans and support to carry them out.

The Scientific Case for Indigenous Rights

Recent scientific research indicates that tropical deforestation is one of several causes of global climate change, which may have devastating effects around the world.[3] Indigenous efforts to use the environment sustainably (and thereby reduce or slow global climate change) deserve support, not only for their sake but for ours. Northern donations and tax monies back the private, governmental, and intergovernmental programs that finance these initiatives. That makes every taxpayer a funder who needs to know how his or her money is being spent and to what end. Stockholders in corporations that invest in projects affecting indigenous people also need to know the results of their investments. According to our legal and moral codes, if we take resources (whether mahogany, natural gas, diamonds, or tropical fruit) from other people, we owe them equitable compensation in return. We have no rights to steal from anyone.

In all these ways northerners are involved in and responsible for what happens to indigenous people and are therefore accountable to them. Whether or not we think about them as we drink coffee from areas indigenous people have lost to invaders, or as we drive cars powered by petroleum extracted from indigenous lands in Mexico, Ecuador, or Venezuela, they are certainly affected by our consumption patterns. And all human beings share an interest in the future of the earth, our only home.

Furthermore, if we allow indigenous people to disappear, abetting the process of extinction by investing in projects that ruin their environment, we lose the promise of diversity that is our birthright. As Darwin pointed out, "During the modification of the descendants of any one species, and during the incessant struggle of all species to increase in numbers, the more diversified the descendants become, the better will be their chance of success in the battle for life" (Darwin 1963: 125).

According to paleontologist Rick Potts, humans evolved in response to extremely unstable climatic and environmental conditions. "Human adaptation to novel contingencies . . . means that our unique social behaviors, mental capacities and ecological strategies are not attached to strict limits defined in our past." As a species we have an enviable flexibility. "The strange buoyancy of the hominids is in us, a hopeful heritage of response to novel environmental dilemmas" (Potts 1996: 277).

Most modern societies, however, see themselves in opposition to, separate from, and outside nature, conceived of as an unchanging obstacle to human dominion, something to be conquered, exploited, and controlled. Many members of these societies take a short-term view of human actions, unable to imagine consequences beyond their lifetime. Yet, under the impact of human activity, things seem to be changing almost too quickly to cope with. Evolutionary change takes place over thousands of generations, but in a few generations we seem to have altered fundamentally our relationship to nature. In contrast, indigenous peoples represent a less destructive form of adaptation that seems like an Eden we cannot return to.

Human beings still comprise an extremely diverse species, thanks to our highly developed capacity for learning from the particular experiences of our ancestors and passing along cultural knowledge to our descendants.

Depending on local conditions, human populations have created myriad ways of adapting to or altering and controlling their surroundings. Northerners tend to consider their technological domination of the environment as evidence of superiority over people with simpler ways of life. I daresay we would have considerable difficulty adapting to the Kayapó or Yanomami environment if we were suddenly deprived of our material aids, however. And since evolution is an open-ended process, we cannot know what parts of our species will be most successful in the long run. Modern civilization could be a mere "flash in the pan," to be remembered as we recall the vanished glories of the Inca or Mycenae. Or it could become a monumental catastrophe, if the changes we have set in motion turn out to be overwhelmingly destructive or unsustainable. We indulge in a self-serving illusion if we think that the short-lived success of civilization constitutes evidence of "natural selection."[4]

Anthropologist Adam Kuper can summon only guarded optimism about our species' prospects:

> This changing, growing, converging world we now live in is the long-term product of the cumulative and accelerating development of culture, which began only some 40 millennia ago. . . . And yet it is not easy to be sanguine about our future. Human beings have been their own worst enemies . . . but it is not too optimistic to believe we have the means to survive, and perhaps to make things better. (Kuper 1994: 244)

Potts emphasizes, "We are part of nature's ongoing process," and thus dependent on it. Whatever we do to it, we do to ourselves.

As civilization's creations and customs spread throughout the world and overwhelm local forms, diversity—whether cultural or biological—suffers. What looks in the short term like successful adaptation may be the harbinger of decline. A few varieties of hybrid seeds crowd out the many local forms that could give rise to robust new varieties. Disease bacteria may become resistant to lifesaving drugs faster than we can develop new cures. Babies die because their mothers give them infant formula mixed with contaminated water, instead of breast-feeding them. When we neglect, scorn, or do away with local variations in culture, no matter how remote or "primitive" they seem, we may deprive our own descendants of options for a good life.

Indigenous people can teach us much about what is useful. But they also have an intrinsic right to live that does not depend on what they can teach us. In defending their rights, we exercise and uphold our own. Despite the commonness of selfish, corrupt, and immoral acts among human beings, we can still hold onto a sense of our species' common good and act to protect and advance it.

When human populations were small and isolated from one another, living off the land by hunting and gathering, they often applied the idea of the common good only to themselves and their relatives. Groups like the Yanomami and the Kayapó did not define others, who spoke different languages and followed different customs, as fully human. Although our species' social universe has expanded geometrically during the past 10,000 years, to include billions instead of dozens or hundreds of others, we still have difficulty in comprehending others' humanity. Unlike some other species, we carry on a high level of internecine conflict.[5] Especially during the past 10,000 years, we have destroyed as much as we have created.

At the same time, we depend on human beings thousands of miles away from us to supply us with the materials we need to construct and maintain our extremely elaborate way of life. Many denizens of civilization work long hours to create tangible and intangible goods and the means to transport them to people they never see or know. We have created extraordinarily complex social, economic, and political arrangements that link us to other humans in myriad ways. This economic and political interdependence affects people, animals, and habitats in the remotest corners of the world. We can use our unparalleled learning and teaching capabilities to transcend both our biological limitations and the unintended consequences of our inventiveness, but we are neither omniscient nor omnipotent. Rushing along the edge of a precipice, we seem to pay scant attention to the faraway consequences of our actions until it is almost too late. We are "too clever by half."

Seeking More than Mere Survival

After oil has spilled or mercury has entered the food chain, indigenous and other traditional groups are often left to cope with the consequences of outside impingements. But that is not all they have to do. They also struggle to sustain themselves, preserve their traditions, and benefit from the changes that have come unbidden to them. Their response to the outside world has been not only to redefine and assert their identity but also to organize to protect their interests. Community, regional, national, and international movements founded and run by indigenous people now defend indigenous rights. For example, in Brazil, CIR defends the interests of the Macuxi and neighboring groups in the northern Amazon. CAPOIB's indigenous staff represents indigenous interests before Congress and government agencies. Indian organizations in all eight Amazon basin nations have banded together with international NGOs in the Amazon Alliance, whose offices are in Washington, D.C.

Allied organizations offer these groups financial and moral support. The Indian Law Resource Center (ILRC) of Washington, D.C., started providing legal help to the Yanomami in 1978. Since then the center has gone to the Inter-American Commission on Human Rights, the United Nations Commission on Human Rights, and U.N. Working Group on Indigenous Populations, among other intergovernmental bodies, on the Yanomami's behalf. In 1989 and 1990, when genocide was raging, ILRC appealed for U.N. Secretary General Perez de Cuellar's intervention. In April 1991 the Center arranged for Davi Kopenawa to meet with Perez de Cuellar as well as U.S. State Department, World Bank, and Inter-American Commission officials. Brazil's president responded to the international pressure by ordering expulsion of the garimpeiros and ratifying the demarcation of the Yanomami reserve. Now the ILRC is assisting the Yanomami in their effort to reclaim the blood samples taken from them more than thirty years ago.

Alliances between the people on the ground and sympathizers far away are not easy to establish or maintain, but they have become necessary vehicles for indigenous self-preservation. A Washington office with a long e-mail list, or a well-timed letter to U.S. Congress members, can sometimes accomplish more than a group of warriors burning electrical transmission towers. The warriors may gain more attention at first, but their political allies may work for years to secure long-term benefits in the world capitals where policymakers make the decisions that determine their fate.

For the most part, indigenous people gain little attention from northern media or policymakers, and Brazil disappears from the international news for months at a time, except when a massacre or scandal hits the headlines. Since the 1993 Haximu massacre, the Yanomami have received sporadic media coverage. Once Payakan fell from grace, the Kayapó ceased being symbols of ecological wisdom and largely disappeared from public view. In general, feature stories about Indians tend to focus on bad news. A few headlines prove the point: "Rape by Decree" (*The Guardian*), "Decree Endangers Survival of Brazilian Indians" (*Christian Science Monitor*), "Indians of Brazil Live 5.6 Years Less" (*Folha de São Paulo*). Even the positive headlines are qualified by pessimism: "For Once, A Victory for Indians" (*The Washington Post*), "Latin American Indians Organize to Improve Lives Even Worse than in U.S." (*The New York Times*). It is not surprising, then, that many people think of Indians as pathetic remnants of once-great cultures, soon to disappear forever.

And yet the Indians continue fighting to survive. Despite the frequent predictions of extinction, their persistence in following their traditions testifies to their "fitness" for what Darwin called "the battle for life." A man of his time, Darwin expressed repulsion at the "savage who delights to torture his enemies, offers up bloody sacrifices, practices infanticide without remorse, treats his wives like slaves, knows no decency, and is haunted by the grossest superstitions" (1981: 404–405). Montaigne or Léry might have used these same phrases to describe Europeans at many moments in their bloody history.

Adam Kuper observed that the inhabitants of Tierra del Fuego, to whom Darwin was referring in this passage, "would have been . . . appalled to learn that the Anglo-Saxons had the effrontery to claim kinship to them, yet nevertheless practiced slavery and mechanized warfare, flogged women in public, sent their children away from home in early childhood, and believed that their god had been born to a virgin" (Kuper 1994: 62).

Yet Darwin managed to transcend his Victorian prejudices when he contemplated the awe-inspiring grandeur of life on earth, in which "endless forms most beautiful and most wonderful have been and are being evolved." He also recognized that creation could grow out of destruction. "Each at some period of its life, during some season of the year, during each generation or at intervals, has to struggle for life and to suffer great destruction," he wrote. "The vigorous, the healthy and the happy survive and multiply"

(Darwin 1963: 462). Indigenous ways of life have thrived during most of the history of our species. Five-hundred years of assaults upon them by what we call civilization may amount to but a season of destruction. Their fate, and ours, is still in the making.

It is poignant now to remember Davi Kopenawa's sad instructions to Bruce Albert, "Tell them . . . how we were, how we had good health, how we weren't dying so much, we didn't have malaria. Tell how . . . we hunted, how we held feasts, how happy we were." In contrast, the sight of the Kayapó in fighting gear, dancing in front of the Brazilian Congress to defend their interests, exhilarates. "I have never taken so much pleasure," Léry wrote, "as I delighted then in seeing those savages do battle." Unlike Léry's Tupinambá, the Kayapó use their fearsome reputation to gain their objectives mostly without bloodshed, by fighting their battles ritualistically. They and the Yanomami have learned difficult but valuable lessons through experience, and they are changing in order to survive. So must we. Only time—and the countless acts and events that constitute cultural and biological evolution—will tell who is most fit, and for what.

Notes

1 / Setting the Scene

1. According to the Brazilian Constitution of 1988 (my translation): Lands traditionally occupied by the Indians are reserved for their permanent possession, and the exclusive use of the riches of the soil, the rivers and the lakes existing on them falls to them. . . . Acts with the object of occupation, control and possession of lands referred to in this article, or exploitation of the natural riches of the soil, rivers and lakes are null and void and without juridical effect. . . . To indigenous advocates, this provision makes Decree 1775/96 (and several other measures) unconstitutional.

2. In 2002, a constitutional amendment prohibiting indigenous reserves from occupying more than half the area of any state was making its way through the Brazilian Congress. The state of Roraima, where most of the Brazilian Yanomami live, would be among those affected by this bill's passage.

2 / In Search of the Other

1. Caminha quotations translated by Linda Rabben.

2. In the mid-fifteenth century, Pope Nicholas V gave the kings of Portugal and Spain "full and free permission to invade, search out, capture and subjugate enemies of Christ wherever they may be and to reduce their persons into perpetual slavery." This authorization was extended from Africa to the Americas in 1493.

3. Villas Boas quotations translated by Linda Rabben.

4. The neighboring Juruna called the Kayapó "wooden lips" because the men wore wood plates in their lower lips. Few do today.

5. Anthropologist Dominique Gallois, who studies the Waiapi Indians of Amapá state, and other anthropologists have criticized FUNAI's continued use of the "attraction" method to make contact with "isolated" Indians. She believes it establishes an unhealthy relationship of domination and dependence (Grupioni 1994: 121–134).

6. At the beginning of the twentieth century, about 300 indigenous groups lived in Brazil. By the end of the century, about 220, speaking 180 languages, survived. Most groups have fewer than 1,000 members.

7. According to the tax records of the Yanomamö Survival Fund, which are available for public inspection according to U.S. law, the fund has been inactive since at least 1993. I found no record of either the Yanomamö Survival Fund or the American Friends of Venezuelan Indians having supported development or relief projects for the Yanomami or other indigenous groups. My written request to Chagnon for information in mid-1997 went unanswered. On December 31, 1998, Chagnon and his wife filed a form with the California state government, closing down the Yanomamö Survival Fund, but did not fill in their signatures on the form.

8. Michael Heckenberger's archaeological research in the Xingu region in 1996 uncovered defensive earthworks from 1350 to 1450 C.E., implying that Amazonian indigenous groups were making war upon one another well before contact with Europeans started. The Xingu is far from Yanomami territory, but such evidence may affect future theorizing on the causes of indigenous bellicosity.

9. Chagnon hated this analysis. In his 1996 review, he commented, "Ferguson comes uncomfortably close to claiming that my presence among the Yanomamo, especially between 1964 and 1970, 'caused' the wars I described. . . . Ferguson adds machetes to his argument as a material supplement to my vileness and trading caprice" (Chagnon 1996: 671).

10. Bruce Albert (1997b) contends: "Yanomami war-making cannot be reduced to a matter of contact and access to tools (just as it cannot be reduced to any other purely material cause, whether proteins or genes). These factors can certainly affect the intensity of warfare (in the sense of raiding), but the fact remains that Yanomami warfare (as a system of values and a ritual-political device) is above all part of a complex social totality, outside of which it cannot be understood."

3 / The People from Between the Waters

1. The Kayapó call themselves Mebengokre, the people from between the waters; indigenous enemies gave them the derisive name "Kayapó," which means "monkey-like."

4 / Payakan: A Cautionary Tale

1. In June 1997 the Xavante stopped one of the federal government's new mega-projects, the Araguaia-Tocantins-Rio das Mortes Waterway, by obtaining (with the help of ISA) an injunction from a federal judge. The judge's decision was based on the fact that IBAMA had not granted an environmental license to carry

out the work on the waterway, and the constitutional demand that Congress must authorize construction of such waterways passing through indigenous areas after consulting the communities concerned, was not adhered to. Two Xavante communities of approximately 1,600 people live near the waterway's proposed route (SEJUP 1997c). The struggle by indigenous, environmental, and community groups to stop the waterway continued in 2002.

2 A Kayapó leader threatened to sue the Body Shop in 1996, accusing the firm of using his image for commercial purposes without compensating him.

5 / Yanomami Apocalypse

1. The Brazilian government offered to sell the world's largest niobium deposit to private buyers in 1997 for a mere u.s.$600,000. The low price was attributed to the mineral's oversupply in the world market and the deposit's remote location, in a national park and state bio-reserve near Yanomami territory (Figueiredo 1997: 3). The welfare of indigenous groups living near the niobium deposit apparently was not considered. However, IBAMA sought to stop the sale on the grounds it would be unconstitutional. This is an example of how conflicting policies and mandates lead Brazilian government agencies to work against one another.

2. In the mid-1990s CEDI merged with NDI to become ISA.

3. Yanomami leaders from Brazil and Venezuela met in an assembly for the first time in late 1997. They expressed strong opposition to mining and proposed mega-projects that threaten their communities and environment.

6 / Davi

1. In this interview, Davi refers to Xawara as feminine, while on other occasions he identifies it as masculine.

2. Quotations from Albert (1991) translated by Linda Rabben.

3. For a description of Salesian missionary schools for the Yanomami in Venezuela, see Salamone (1997: 89–106).

8 / Emerging Indians

1. CIMI estimated Brazil's indigenous population in 1999 at 551,991. According to CIMI, 65 percent lived in villages and 35 percent lived in towns and cities.

9 / Fit for What?

1. According to a 1996 report by the World Wildlife Fund, the proportion of the earth covered by forests has dropped from 40 to 26 percent since the Industrial

Revolution. The most rapid and sustained destruction has occurred since 1950. About 15 million hectares of tropical forests disappear each year. During the 1980s, Brazil and Indonesia accounted for 45 percent of the global loss. Since the 1992 Earth Summit, forest destruction in Brazil has increased substantially.

2. The U.N.'s Draft Declaration on the Rights of Indigenous Peoples, which has been in the works for more than fifteen years, goes even further in specifying the responsibilities of governments to protect indigenous land, cultural, political, labor, and other rights.

3. Most climatologists agree that the heating of the earth's atmosphere, resulting from human activities producing increasing emissions of carbon dioxide, may lead to flooding, droughts, and other damaging climactic events around the world. In recent years, people living in or near deforested areas in Brazil have reported local climatic changes that make their subsistence more difficult.

4. Stephen Jay Gould (1997a: 35) insisted, "Selection cannot suffice as a full explanation for many aspects of evolution . . . in domains both far above and far below the traditional Darwinian locus of the organism." Like many anthropologists, Gould believed that "the passage of acquired traits to subsequent generations," or cultural evolution, supercedes much slower Darwinian evolution among humans. As geneticist Steve Jones (1997: 41) puts it: "Our evolution is unique in that it is mainly in the mind."

5. In their provocatively titled book, *Demonic Males*, Richard Wrangham and Dale Peterson (1996: 251) suggest that humans can reduce their violence, which seems to have reached a terrifying level across the species, by reducing the dominance of males over females. "Male demonism is not inevitable. Its expression has evolved in other animals, it varies across human societies, and it has changed in history. . . . We can have no idea how far the wave of history may sweep us from our rougher past."

Bibliography

Abreu, João Batista de. 1996. "Ingleses acusados de enganar os caiapós." *Jornal do Brasil* (Rio de Janeiro), February 23: 7.

Ação pela Cidadania. 1989. "Roraima, Brazil: A Death Warning." *Cultural Survival Quarterly* 13(4): 59–67.

Agência Ecumênica de Notícias. 1993. "Commitment of Brazilian Authorities to Uphold Rights of Indigenous People Called into Question by AI." January 21.

Albert, Bruce. 1989. "Yanomami 'Violence': Inclusive Fitness or Ethnographer's Representation." *Current Anthropology* 30 (5): 637–40.

———. 1991. "Xawara: O ouro canibal e a queda do céu." In *Povos Indígenas no Brasil 1987/88/89/90*. São Paulo: Centro Ecumênico de Documentação e Informação.

———. 1995. "O ouro canibal e a queda do céu: Uma crítica xamânica da economia política da natureza." *Série Antropologia* 174. Brasília: Universidade de Brasília.

———. 1996. "O massacre dos yanomami de Haximu." In *Povos Indígenas no Brasil 1991/95*. Edited by C.A. Ricardo. São Paulo: Instituto Sócioambiental.

———. 1997a. "'Ethnographic Situation' and Ethnic Movements." *Critique of Anthropology* 17(1): 53–65.

———. 1997b. Personal communication.

———, ed. 2001. *Research and Ethics: The Yanomami Case (Brazilian Contributions to the "Darkness in El Dorado" Controversy)*. Documentos Yanomami N.2. Brasília: Comissão Pró-Yanomami.

Alcântara, Euripedes. 1995. "Índio também é gente." *Veja*, December 6: 7–10.

Aldeia Caramuru Paraguaçu. 2000. "Cronologia da violência praticada contra os Pataxó Hã-Hã-Hãe."

———. 2002. "Relatorio das lideranças Pataxó Hã-Hã-Hãe à Procuradoria da República—Ilheus, BA."

Alencar, José de. 1975. *Iracema: Lenda do Ceará*. Rio de Janeiro: Livraria Francisco Alves Editora.

Alonso, George. 1995. "Disputa deixa índios morrerem sem assistência." *Estado de*

São Paulo, November 13.

Amazon Alliance. 2002. "Local Organizations Request Letters Regarding Amazon Pipeline." Listserve, September 13.

Amazon Watch. 2000. "Thousands Participate in Indigenous March in Brazil in Protest of Official 500 Year Celebrations." Amazon Alliance listserve, April 21.

American Anthropological Association (AAA). 1991. "Report of the Special Commission to Investigate the Situation of the Brazilian Yanomami."

———. 2002. "El Dorado Task Force Papers," vols. 1 and 2, May 18. www.aaanet. org.

Amnesty International. 1992. "Brazil: 'We Are the Land.' Indigenous Peoples' Struggle for Human Rights." London.

———. 1993. "A Shameful Legacy: Human Rights Violations against the World's Indigenous Peoples." *Focus,* May: 3–6.

———. 1997. "Statement by Amnesty International on the Occasion of the World Bank/International Monetary Fund Annual Meetings, Hong Kong, September 1997." London.

———. 2001. "Brazil: A Year On and Still No Justice." *Amnesty International News* vol. 31, no. 2, March: 1.

Anaya, S. James. 1994. "International Law and Indigenous Peoples, Historical Stands and Contemporary Developments." *Cultural Survival Quarterly,* Spring: 42–44.

Andersen, Martin E. 1994. "Turning Our Backs on Those Who Were Here First?" *Washington Times,* November 24: A17.

Associação Vida e Ambiente (AVA). 1994. "Plano de ações para a elaboração de propostas para as áreas indígenas—Baú/Mekragnoti."

———. 1995a. *Boletim da AVA* 1(2).

———. 1995b. "Relatório sobre o momento kayapó e perspectivas."

———. 1995c. "Subsídios para discussão sobre projetos alternativos para as áreas Mebengokre."

Associated Press. 2001. "With Controversy Swirling Around Them, Yanomami Have Other Worries." Amazon Alliance listserve, February 13.

Astor, Michael. 2000. "Brazil 500th Anniversary Protested." *Associated Press.* Amazon Alliance listserve, April 24.

Barsh, Russel L. 1994. "Making the Most of ILO Convention 169." *Cultural Survival Quarterly* 18(1): 45–47.

Bermann, Célio. 2001. "O Brasil não precisa de Belo Monte." Unpublished ms.

Berwick, Dennison. 1992. *Savages: The Life and Killing of the Yanomami.* London: Hutchinson.

Biocca, Ettore. 1970. *Yanoáma: The Story of Helena Valero, a Girl Kidnapped by Amazonian Indians.* New York: Dutton.

Borofsky, Robert, ed. 2001. "Yanomami Roundtable Forum." www.publicanthro
pology.org.

Braga, Teodomiro. 1991. "Cresce chance de ajuda americana à Amazônia." *Jornal do Brasil*, December 5.

Brasil, Amazonas. 1995. "Violência contra a soberania nacional. Tentativas de internacionalização da Amazônia." *O Diário* (Boa Vista), December 23: B1.

Brasilians. 1997. "Calls for Adoption of a Declaration to Protect the Rights of Indigenous People." January: 5E.

Brasiliense, Ronaldo. 1993. "Complô armado. Sydney Possuelo atribuí sua queda da presidência da Funai a pressões militares e econômicas e a intrigas palacianas." *IstoÉ*, May.

————. 1995. "Caiapós endividados tomam posto da Funai." *Correio Braziliense*, November 15.

Brazilian Embassy (Washington, D.C.). 1993. "Brazilian Policy on Indigenous Population." *Current Issues 3.*

Brazil Network (U.K.). 1992–97. Newsletter.

Brooke, James. 1990. "Rain Forest Indians Hold Off Threat of Change." *New York Times*, December 3: A4.

————. 1993a. "Brazil Is Evicting Miners in Amazon." *New York Times*, March 8: A7.

————. 1993b. "Gold Miners and Indians: Brazil's Frontier View." *New York Times*, September 7: A4.

————. 1993c. "Crackdowns on Miners Follow Indian Killings." *New York Times*, September 19: 10.

————. 1995a. "Amazon Indians' Battle for Land Grows Violent." *New York Times*, June 11: 3.

————. 1995b. "Atrocity Case in Amazon Is Botched." *New York Times*, June 29: A6.

————. 1995c. "Asphalt Ribbon Binds Brazil and Venezuela." *New York Times*, September 24: 11.

————. 1995d. "Proposed Cuts in Indian Programs Hit Those Who Rely Most on Federal Aid." *New York Times*, October 15: 16.

Buchanan, Rob. 1993. "The Rain Forest Rape." *Details*, March: 46–56, 214.

Bugge, Axel. 2001. "Saving Forest Is Top Priority in Amazon." Reuters News Service, Amazon Alliance listserve, June 11.

Burns, E. Bradford. 1993. *A History of Brazil.* 3d ed. New York: Oxford University Press.

Caminha, Pero Vaz de. 1974. "Carta." In *Brazilian Literature 1.* Edited by C. L. Hulet. Washington, D.C.: Georgetown University Press.

Campanha pela Demarcação das Terras Indígenas na Amazônia. 1992. "Índios mudam estratégia e lançam campanha publicitária."

"Carta de São Luis do Maranhão." 2001. June.

Castilho, Ela Wiecko Volkmer de. 2002. Ofício No. 115/2002/CaDIM/MPF. *Boletim Yanomami* no. 25. CCPY listserve, April 3.

Centeno, Júlio César. 1997. "The Management of Corruption in Venezuela." Amazon Coalition listserve, June 5.

Center for Economic and Social Rights (CESR), Oxfam America, Rainforest Action Network. 1996. "Oil in the Rainforest: The Impacts of the Responses to Texaco's Operations in the Ecuadorian Amazon."

Center for the Study of Human Rights. 1992. *Twenty-Four Human Rights Documents.* New York: Columbia University.

Centro Ecumênico de Documentação e Informação (CEDI). 1991. *Povos indígenas no Brasil 1987/88/89/90.* São Paulo.

Chagnon, Napoleon A. 1983. *Yanomamö: The Fierce People.* 3d ed. New York: CBS College Publishing.

———. 1988. "Life Histories, Blood Revenge and Warfare in a Tribal Population." *Science* 239: 985–992.

———. 1990. "On Yanomamö Violence: Reply to Albert." *Current Anthropology* 31(1): 49–52.

———. 1992. *Yanomamö: The Last Days of Eden.* New York: Harcourt Brace Javonovich.

———. 1995. "L'ethnologie du déshonneur: Brief response to Lizot." *American Ethnologist* 22: 187–89.

———. 1996. "Review of *Yanomami Warfare.*" *American Anthropologist* 98(3): 670–72.

———. 1997. *Yanomamö.* 5th ed. Fort Worth, TX: Harcourt Brace College Publishers.

Chernela, Janet. 1988. "Potential Impacts of a Proposed Amazon Hydropower Project." *Cultural Survival Quarterly* 12(2): 20–23.

Cipola, Ari. 1996. "Índios do Brasil vivem 5,6 anos menos." *Folha de São Paulo,* June 7: 8.

Clay, Jason. n.d. [1991]. "Resource Wars: Nation and State Conflicts of the Twentieth Century." Unpublished ms.

Coalition for Amazonian Peoples and Their Environment. 1996. "Annual Meeting Report, June 26–July 1, Quito, Ecuador."

Colchester, Marcus and Fiona Watson. 1995. "Venezuela: Violations of Indigenous Rights. Report to the International Labor Office on the Observation of ILO Convention 107."

Comissão pela Criação do Parque Yanomami. 1993. *Update* 70, August 23.

———. 1995. "The Survival of the Yanomami." *Yanomami Urgente,* April 17.

———. 1997. *Update* 97, December 8.

Comissão Pro-Yanomami (CCPY). 1993. *Jornal de Urihi* 16, March.

————. 2001a. *Haximu: Foi genocídio!* Documentos Yanomami N.1.

————. 2001b. *Jornal de Urihi*, March.

————. 2002. *Boletim* nos. 25–32. On proyanomami listserve, May–November.

Conferência Nacional dos Bispos do Brasil. 2001. *Por uma terra sem males. Fraternidade e povos indígenas. Texto-base da Campanha da Fraternidade 2002.* São Paulo: Editora Salesiana.

Conklin, Beth A. and Laura R. Graham. 1995. "The Shifting Middle Ground: Amazonian Indians and Eco-Politics." *American Anthropologist* 97(4): 695–710.

Conselho Indígena de Roraima (CIR). 1994. "Situação fundiária das terras indígenas de Roraima."

————. 1995. "Relação dos inquéritos policiais que apuram crimes praticados contra ou entre índios em Roraima, 1991 a 1994."

————. 2001. "Documento da reunião no Ajarani." June 2.

————. 2002. "Nós existimos!" October 10.

Conselho Indigenista Missionário (CIMI). 1987. "Doctrine of National Security Threatens Brazil's Indians." *Cultural Survival Quarterly* 11(2): 63–65.

————. 1993a. "Madeireiras apressam a retirada de mogno de área indígena." In ax.brasil computer conference, October 10.

————. 1993b. "Governo brasileiro permite que militares interfiram na demarcação das terras indígenas." In ax.brasil computer conference, October 28.

————. 1993c. "Pelo menos 42 índios foram assassinados no Brasil em 1993." In ax.brasil computer conference, December 23.

————. 1994a. *1993: A violência contra os povos indígenas no Brasil.* Brasília: Conferência Nacional dos Bispos Brasileiros.

————. 1994b. "Exploração de madeira provoca danos aos povos indígenas." In ax.brasil computer conference, January 14.

————. 1994c. "Índios yanomami no Brasil são prostituídas em troca de comida." In ax.brasil computer conference, September 19.

————. 1994d. "Índios kayapó expulsam 2000 garimpeiros de suas terras." In ax.brasil computer conference, September 22.

————. 1995. "Organizações indígenas—um novo sujeito político." In brasil.noticias computer conference, May 4.

————. 1996a. "Yanomami em assembléia chamam FHC e o Ministro Jobim de medrosos e irresponsáveis." In ax.brasil computer conference, January 18.

————. 1996b. "Povo Tembé: Uma história que é o retrato da situação dos 350 mil índios no país." *Porantim*, June/July: 7–10.

————. 1996c. "Condenados cinco acusados do massacre Yanomami." In ax.brasil computer conference, December 20.

————. 1996d. "Army and FUNAI Accused of Helping to Decimate the Yanomami." Amazon Coalition listserve, December 23.

———. 1997a. "Índios reagem ao descaso do governo federal." In ax.brasil computer conference, February 17.

———. 1997b. "Áreas indígenas são alvo das empresas madeireiras internacionais." In ax.brasil computer conference, June 20.

———. 2000a. *Campanha internacional pela regularização do território Pataxó Hã-Hã-Hãe.* Itabuna, BA: Diocese de Itabuna.

———. 2000b. "A tropa colonial continua viva." April 5.

———. 2001a. *Outros 500: Construindo uma nova história.* São Paulo: Editora Salesiana.

———. 2001b. "Newsletter No. 449." Amazon Alliance listserve, March 6.

———. 2002a. "Newsletter No. 528." Amazon Alliance listserve, September 6.

———. 2002b. "Justiça para Galdino." www.cimi.com.

———. n.d. *Marcha e conferência indígena, abril de 2000.* Brasília.

Correio Braziliense. 1995. "Edital de leilão judicial juízo federal da terceiro vara." May 21: 39.

Coulter, Robert T. 1994. "The Draft Declaration on the Rights of Indigenous Peoples: What Is It? What Does It Mean?" Washington, D.C.: Indian Law Resource Center.

Cox, Larry. 1991. Letter to the editor. *Brasilians* (New York), December.

Cristaldo, Janer. 1995. "Uma teocracia na Amazônia." *Folha de São Paulo,* February 12: B1.

CSL Films. 1996. *Warriors of the Amazon.* Television documentary. Produced by Chris Curling.

Cubel, Kátia. 1993. "Garimpeiro também é vítima, diz ministro." *Folha de São Paulo,* August 20.

Cultural Survival Quarterly. 1989. "The Kayapó Bring Their Case to the United States." 13(1): 18–19.

———. 1996. "Genes, People and Property." Special issue, 20(2).

Daes, Erica-Irene. 1994. "Introductory Statement on the United Nations Draft Declaration on the Rights of Indigenous Peoples, Working Group on Indigenous Populations, Subcommittee on Prevention of Discrimination and Protection of Minorities, 46th Session, 22 August." Geneva: United Nations.

———. 1996. "Introductory Statement. 14th Session of the Working Group on Indigenous Populations, 29 August." Geneva: United Nations.

Darwin, Charles. 1963. *The Origin of Species.* New York: Dutton.

———. 1981. *The Descent of Man, and Selection in Relation to Sex.* Princeton, NJ: Princeton University Press.

Davis, Shelton. 1977. *Victims of the Miracle: Development and the Indians of Brazil.* New York: Cambridge University Press.

Distrito Sanitário Yanomami. 1991. "Primeiro relatório do Distrito Sanitário Yanomami." Boa Vista: Fundação Nacional de Saúde.

Durning, Alan. 1991. "Native Americans Stand Their Ground." *World Watch*, November/December: 10–17.

Eakin, Marshall. 1997. *Brazil: The Once and Future Country.* New York: St. Martin's Press.

Earth Times. 1997. "Rainforest Roads: A 'Compound Disaster.'" April 16–30: 11.

Environmental News Service. 1997. "Nature's Services Worth Trillions, Scientists Told." Ecological Enterprises computer conference, 17 February.

Epstein, Jack. 1996. "Decree Endangers Survival of Brazilian Indians." *Christian Science Monitor*, March 7: 6.

Escobar, Gabriel. 1996a. "Indians of Ecuador Coalescing in Quest for Political Power." *Washington Post*, July 23: A12.

———. 1996b. "For Once, a Victory for Indians." *Washington Post*, September 24: A13.

Estado de São Paulo. 1993. "Conselho nacional da Amazônia é instalado." December 4.

———. 2002. "Amazonia Loses 18,000 Square Kilometers of Forest in One Year." Amazon Alliance listserve, June 14.

Estanislau, Maria. 1995. "Funcionários da Funai são mantidos como reféns no Pará." *Folha de São Paulo*, November 15.

Farnsworth, Clyde. 1997. "Australians Resist Facing Up to Legacy of Parting Aborigines from Families." *New York Times*, June 8: 18.

Feeney, Patricia. 1997. "Dehumanizing Growth. The Cost of Brazil's Stabilization: Eroding Indians' Rights." Oxford: Oxfam United Kingdom and Ireland.

Feijó, Atenéia, and Marcos Terena. 1994. *O índio aviador.* São Paulo: Editora Moderna.

Ferguson, R. Brian. 1995. *Yanomami Warfare: A Political History.* Santa Fe, NM: School of American Research.

Ferrer, Yadira. 1997. "Suicide Threat by Indigenous Group." InterPress Service, ips.english computer conference, June 19.

Figueiredo, Lucas. 1997. "Ibama quer impedir venda de jazida no AM." *Folha de São Paulo*, October 7.

Fisher, William H. 1991. "The Institutional Roots of Indigenous Environmental Protest: The Kayapó and Macrodevelopment in Pará, Brazil." Unpublished ms.

———. 1994. "Megadevelopment, Environmentalism and Resistance: The Institutional Context of Kayapó Indigenous Politics in Central Brazil." *Human Organization* 53(3): 220-232.

———. 1995. "Kayapó Social Organization and the Central Brazilian Frontier: Dualism and Authority." Paper delivered at the Latin American Studies Association meeting, September 28–30.

Folha de Boa Vista. 1997. "Projeto que permite mineração será votado na próxima semana." August 22.

Folha de São Paulo. 1991a. "Autor de 'Raoni' processa dois brasileiros." November 21: 12.

————. 1991b. "Retrato falado: Sting." December 8.

————. 1992. "Começa este mês demarcação do maior território do país." July 5: 15.

————. 1995. "Começa hoje nova retirada de garimpeiros." June 5.

Fundação Mata Virgem (FMV). n.d. [c.1990]. "Biografia, Megaron Txucarramãe."

————. 1990. "Unified Health Care Program in Xingu National Park."

————. 1991. Untitled memo on sterilization of Payakan's wife, Irekran.

————. 1992. *Folha da Mata Virgem,* May.

————. n.d. [1992a]. "Background Information—Menkragnoti Indigenous Area."

————. n.d. [1992b]. "Program for Scholastic Education in the Xingu Indian Park."

————. n.d. [1992c]. "Term of Reference for Getting Intruders Out of Kayapó, Mekragnotire and Bau Indian Areas."

————. 1993a. "Texto a ser proferido pelo líder indígena Megaron Txucarramãe em audiência pública do Congresso dos Estados Unidos da América." July.

————. 1993b. "Spring Expedition Trip to Menkragnoti Area," November.

————. 1993c. "Third and Final Operational Report on Demarcation of the Menkragnoti Indian Area." November 16.

————. 1994a. "ONG exige indenização para kayapós contaminados por mercúrio." March.

————. 1994b. "Plano de ação imediata para a área menkragnoti (PAI)." April.

————. 1995. *Relatório de atividades, 1989–1994.*

Fundação Nacional do Índio (FUNAI). 1994. "Termo de referência para desintrusão das áreas indígenas kayapó, Menkragnoti e Baú."

————. 1995. "Informação No. 007/CPTI/DPI."

Gabeira, Fernando. 1991a. "Brasil discute com G7 verbas para preservar a Amazônia." *Folha de São Paulo,* December 7.

————. 1991b. "G7 concede US \$250 mil a projeto-piloto para Amazônia." *Folha de São Paulo,* December 9.

Galé, Nelino. 1997. "Agrava-se a situação na área yanomami." CIMI listserve, July 29.

Galvão, Eduardo. 1967. "Indigenous Cultural Areas of Brazil, 1900–1959." In *Indians of Brazil in the Twentieth Century.* Edited by J. Hopper. Washington, D.C.: Institute for Cross-Cultural Research.

Gay, Kathlyn. 1993. *Rainforests of the World.* Santa Barbara, CA: ABC-CLIO.

Gazeta Mercantil (São Paulo). 1994. "Proibida exploração de madeira em área indígena." In brasil.noticias computer conference, April 9.

Geertz, Clifford. 2001. "Life Among the Anthros." *New York Review of Books*, February 8: 18–22.

Goering, Laurie. 1996. "Rain Forest Residents Sue Texaco." *Washington Post*, July 16: A16.

Gomes, Laurentino. 1992. "A cegueira verde. Movidos pelo fanatismo, os ecoxiitas recusam as evidências de que Paiakan é culpado de estupro." *Veja*, June 17: 82–84.

Gomes, Laurentino, and Paulo Silber. 1992. "A explosão do instinto selvagem. Paiakan, o cacique-simbolo da pureza ecológica, estupra e tortura uma adolescente." *Veja*, June 10: 68–73.

Gomes, Severo. 1990. *No meio do caminho*. Brasília: Centro Gráfico do Senado Federal.

Gomez, Gail Goodwin. 1997a. "The Impact of Gold Mining on Yanomami Health." Paper delivered at American Anthropological Association annual meeting, November.

———. 1997b. Personal communication.

Gonçalves, Francisco. 1994. "Garimpeiros invadem a reserva ianomami." *Jornal do Brasil*, August 9.

Gould, Stephen Jay. 1997a. "Darwinian Fundamentalism." *New York Review of Books* 44(10): 34–37.

———. 1997b. "Evolution: The Pleasures of Pluralism." *New York Review of Books* 44(11): 47–52.

Gregor, Thomas, and Daniel Gross. 2002. "Anthropology and the Search for the Enemy Within." *Chronicle of Higher Education*, July 17.

Gross, Daniel. 1996. "The World Bank in Brazil." *Anthropology Newsletter* 37(5): 2.

Gross, Daniel, and Stuart Plattner. 2002. "Anthropology as Social Work: Collaborative Models of Anthropological Research." *Anthropology News*, November.

Grupioni, Luís Donisete Benzi, ed. 1994. *Índios no Brasil*. Brasília: Ministério da Educação e do Desporto.

Guardian (London). 1997. "New Hope for Forests. But the Chainsaw May Win in the End." March 10.

Gutkowski, Cris. 1994. "Paulinho Paiakan é absolvido," "Polícia temia conflito se houvesse condenação," "Justica absolve Paiakan de estupro." *Folha de São Paulo*, November 29: B1.

Hamilton, Dominic. 1997. "Pemon Indians Paralyze Powerlines." EnviroNews Service. In hr.indigenous computer conference, June 4.

Heck, Egon. 2002. "Números, mascaras e esperança." *Porantim*, June/July: 3.

Hemming, John. 1978. *Red Gold: The Conquest of the Brazilian Indians*. Cambridge, MA: Harvard University Press.

———. 1987. *Amazon Frontier: The Defeat of the Brazilian Indians*. London: Macmillan.

Hume, Douglas. 2001. "El Dorado." www.anth.uconn.edu/gradstudents/dhume/
darkness_in_el_dorado/index.
Indian Law Resource Center (ILRC). 1990. "Statement to Inter-American Com-
mission on Human Rights on Case #7615: Violations of the Human Rights of
the Yanomami Indians."
Instituto dos Estudos Sócio-Econômicos (INESC). 1994. "Yanomami: os limites da
cidadania." *Informativo* no. 50: 10.
Instituto Sócioambiental (ISA). 1995. "Xicrin rompem com modelo predatório e
defendem manejo sustentável." In ax.brasil computer conference, June 13.
———. *Parabólicas.* 1996–2000.
International Labor Office (ILO). 1991. *Convention No. 169. Convention Concerning
Indigenous and Tribal Peoples in Independent Countries.* Geneva: United Nations.
InterPress Service. 1993. "Yanomami Massacre Becomes National Security Issue."
In ips.english computer conference, August 27.
———. 1994. "Estudios muestran contaminacion de indigenas con mercurio." In
ips.espanol computer conference, July 26.
———. 1997a. "Caldera y Cardoso vuelven a verse." In ips.espanol computer conference, April 5.
———. 1997b. "Presencia de 3.000 'garimpeiros' amenaza a yanomamis." In
ips.espanol computer conference, August 16.
Johnson, George. 1996. "Dispute over Indian Casinos in New Mexico Produces
Quandary on Law and Politics." *New York Times,* August 18: 24.
Johnston, Barbara R., ed. 1997. *Life and Death Matters: Human Rights and the Environment at the End of the Millennium.* Walnut Creek, CA: Alta Mira Press.
Jones, Steve. 1997. "Go Milk a Fruit Bat!" *New York Review of Books* 44(12): 38–41.
Jornal do Brasil. 1991a. "Fazendeiro não deixa índio assumir reserva." November
19.
———. 1991b. "Collor demarca área indígena com 9,4 milhoes de hectares." November 29.
———. 1991c. "Exercito e Ibama vão impedir garimpo no Pico da Neblina." November 29.
———. 1991d. "Mata Virgem ajudará demarcação." November 30.
———. 1993. "Ricúpero buscará recursos externos para a Amazônia." In
brasil.noticias computer conference, September 10.
Jornal do Comércio (Rio). 1993. "Militares povoarão a Amazônia." In brasil.noticias
computer conference, October 6.
Kayapó, A'Kjabor, et al. 1993. Letter to AIMEX (Associação Exportadoras da Madeira do Estado do Pará). May 17.
Klintowitz, Jaime. 1995. "A culpa é do índio." *Veja,* September 20: 66–68.
Kuper, Adam. 1994. *The Chosen Primate: Human Nature and Cultural Diversity.*

Cambridge, MA: Harvard University Press.

Leão, Eduardo. 1994a. "Garimpeiros são expulsos por Kayapó." *Porantim*, September: 15.

———. 1994b. "Mercúrio contamina kayapó." *Porantim*, October: 13.

Leary, Warren E. 1992. "Explorers of Amazon Branch Retrace Roosevelt Expedition." *New York Times*, April 10: A12.

Leitão, Ana Valéria Nascimento Araújo. 1994. "Indigenous Peoples in Brazil." *Cultural Survival Quarterly*, spring: 48–50.

Léry, Jean de. 1990. *History of a Voyage to the Land of Brazil, Otherwise Called America*. Translated by Janet Whatley. Berkeley: University of California Press.

Lévi-Strauss, Claude. 1967 (1955). *Tristes Tropiques*. New York: Atheneum.

Lewan, Todd. 1997. "Brazil Shifts Use of Foreign Funds to Restore Native Atlantic Glory." *Washington Times*, March 17: A12.

Lewis, John. 1990. "Non-Governmental Organizations and International Human Rights." *New York Law Journal* 203(71): 1, 4.

Liberal, O. 2002. "Federal Police Seize 1,990 Illegal Mahogany Logs in Pará." Belém: Amazon Alliance listserve, September 6.

Lindee, Susan. 2001. "A Tangled Web in More Ways Than One." *Pennsylvania Gazette*, January/February.

Lizot, Jacques. 1985. *Tales of the Yanomami: Daily Life in the Venezuelan Forest*. Cambridge: Cambridge University Press.

———. 1994. "On Warfare: An Answer to N.A. Chagnon." *American Ethnologist* 21(4): 845–862.

———. 1996. E-mail communication. "Yanomami health problems in Venezuela." December 6.

Machado, Marina. 1993. "The Health Situation of the Kubenkokre and Pukanu Tribes." New York: Rainforest Foundation International.

MacMillan, Gordon. 1995. *At the End of the Rainbow? Gold, Land, and People in the Brazilian Amazon*. New York: Columbia University Press.

Magalhães, Edgard D. 1995. "Breve notícia e relato histórico da situação sanitária e violência contra as populações indígenas de Roraima: em especial o caso Yanomami." Boa Vista: DSY/FNS.

———. 1996. "Memorando," "Saúde Yanomami—1995."

Mansur, Alexandre. 2002. "Somos índios." *Época* 218, July 24.

Marks, Jonathan. 2002. *What It Means to Be 98% Chimpanzee: Apes, People, and Their Genes*. Berkeley: University of California Press.

Marques, Jairo. 2002. "Ação de ONGs baixa mortalidade de índios." *Agência Folha*, September.

Martins, Américo. 1993. "Comandante diz que reserva é ameaça ao país." *Folha de São Paulo*, August 20.

Martins, Leda. 2002. "Commentary on the El Dorado Task Force Report." *An-*

thropology News, November.

McIntyre, Loren. 1991. *Amazonia: Photographs and Text*. San Francisco: Sierra Club Books.

Medeiros, Alexandre. 1995. "Amazônia em dois tempos/2." *Jornal do Brasil— Domingo*, October 29: 75–85.

Melloni, Eugenio. 1997. "Xingu Dam Plan to Be Revived." *Gazeta Mercantil*, March 31. In hr.indigenous computer conference. Translated by Glenn Switkes. April 11.

Michaels, Julia. 1992. "Rape Trial Highlights Brazilian Native Rights." *Christian Science Monitor*, June 19: 6.

Ministério Público. 1992. "Laudos periciais." Silvia Letícia da Luz Ferreira. Belém: Estado do Pará.

Mongiano, Aldo. 1995. Letter to Fernando Henrique Cardoso, President of Brazil, August 23.

Montaigne, Michel. 1984. *Essays*. New York: Penguin.

Monteiro, Joaquim. 1995. "Mogno roubado dos caiapós vai a leilão." *Correio Braziliense*, May 30: 4.

Moreira, Memélia. 1991. "A estratégia do genocídio yanomami," "Cronologia de um genocídio documentado." In CEDI, *Povos indígenas no Brasil 1987/88/89/90*: 162–164, 172–193.

Movimento dos Atingidos por Barragens. 2001. Interview with Sadi Baron, flyer.

Movimento pelo Desenvolvimento da Transamazônica e Xingu. 2002. Letter to President Fernando Henrique Cardoso, flyer.

NACLA Report on the Americas. 1996. "Gaining Ground: The Indigenous Movement in Latin America." 29(5): 14–43.

———. 1997. "The Body Shop Controversy." Letter of Adrian Hodges and reply of Jan Rocha. 30(4): 4.

Nash, Nathaniel. 1992. "Latin American Indians: Old Ills, New Politics." *New York Times*, August 24: 1, A6.

Nepstad, Daniel, and Eric Davidson. 1993. "'Deforestation's Other Side' Isn't Rosy." Letter to the editor. *Washington Post*, October 8: A26.

Nogueira, Pablo. 2002. "A multiplicação dos índios." *Galileu* 132, July. www.globo.com.

Núcleo de Direito Indígena (NDI). 1994. "Relatório de viagem, Área Indígena Kayapó," "Comunidades indígenas conseguem importantes vitórias na defesa de suas terras." *Informativo*, March/April: 3–4.

O'Connor, Geoffrey. 1993. Unpublished interview with Sting.

Oliveira, Claudio Esteves, and Deise Alves Francisco. 1994. *Report on Health Activities in the Yanomami Area*. Boa Vista: CCPY.

Oliveira, Edmundo. 1991. *A vitimização dos índios na Amazônia*. Belém: CEJUP.

Oliveira, Luíz Rodrigues de. 1995. "Mudanças no decreto 22/91 ameaçam PP-G7."

Jornal do Brasil, March 2: 4.

Onis, Juan de. 1992. *The Green Cathedral: Sustainable Development of Amazonia.* New York: Oxford University Press.

Paiakan, Paulinho. n.d. "Project Proposal. Aukre Village Kayapó Nation Brazil."

Pereira, Euclides. 1994. "Roraima: Um estado de violência institucionalizada." Boa Vista: CIR.

Pietricovsky, Iara, and Ricardo Verdum. 1995. *Mapa da fome entre os povos indígenas no Brasil (II).* Brasília: INESC/PETI-MN/ANAI-BA.

Pinagé, Luíz Carlos. 1991. "The Current Status of Development and Environment—Brazil." Paper presented at International Forum on Sustainable Development.

Pinto, Lúcio Flávio. 2001. "Xingu também será fechado." *Jornal Pessoal*, July 1–14.

Pisani, Elizabeth. 1991. "Opposition Mounts to the New Yanomami Reserve." *Guardian*, December 27: 26.

Plant, Roger. 1991. "Land Rights for Indigenous and Tribal Peoples in Developing Countries." World Employment Programme Working Paper. Geneva: ILO.

Podesta, Don. 1993. "Efforts to Save Rain Forests Raise Suspicions in Brazil." *Washington Post*, October 11: 1, 23.

Porantim. 1992a. "Caso Paiakan. Não foi julgado mas já é culpado." June: 6.

————. 1992b. "A morte do coronel kayapó." July/August: 13.

————. 2002a. "Governo federal extingue Funasa." March: 13.

————. 2002b. "Pistoleiros matam mais um líder Pataxó Hã-Hã-Hãe." August: 5.

Posey, Darrell A. 1995. "Sustainable Characteristics of Kayapó Society." Paper presented at LASA meeting, September.

Potts, Rick. 1996. *Humanity's Descent: The Consequences of Ecological Instability.* New York: William Morrow.

Priest, Dana. 1996. "American Radar Aiding Drug Fight." *Washington Post*, January 7: A22.

Queiroz, Antônio Carlos. 2002. "Mineradores derrubam presidente da Funai." *Porantim*, June/July: 4.

Rabben, Linda. 1988. "Land, Debt, and Democracy." *Nation*, April 30: 597–601.

————. 1990. "Brazil's Military Stakes Its Claim." *Nation*, March 12: 341–342.

————. 1992a. "Notes on Demarcation Procedures." New York: Rainforest Foundation International.

————. 1992b. "Memo on Payakan." New York: Rainforest Foundation International.

————. 1993. "Demarcation—and Then What?" *Cultural Survival Quarterly*, summer: 12–14.

————. 1995. "Kayapó Choices: Short-Term Gain vs. Long-Term Damage." *Cultural Survival Quarterly*, summer: 11–13.

———. 1998. *Unnatural Selection: The Yanomami, the Kayapó and the Onslaught of Civilisation.* London: Pluto Press; Seattle: University of Washington Press.

Rainforest Foundation International. 1991. "The Rainforest Foundation and Fundação Mata Virgem Urge Pres. Collor to Demarcate All Indian Territories as Foundation Releases First Annual Report."

———. 1992a. "Jungle Operation Begins Demarcation." August 21.

———. 1992b. "Mercury Project at SBPC." August 25.

———. 1992c. "News Update." Winter.

———. n.d. [c.1992]. Mekragnoti Indigenous Area—Background.

———. 1993, 1994. *Quarterly Journal.*

———. 1996. *Out of the Forest.* Newsletter, summer.

Rainforest Foundation United Kingdom. 1995. *Annual Report 1994–95.* London.

Rainforest Foundation United States (RFF). 2002. *2001 Annual Report.* New York.

Ramos, Alcida Rita. n.d. [c.1988]. "Área indígena Yanomami." Unpublished ms.

———. 1990a. "Indigenismo de Resultados." *Série Antropologia* 100. Brasília: Universidade de Brasília.

———. 1990b. "Ethnology Brazilian Style." *Cultural Anthropology* 5(4): 452–472.

———. 1991. "Os direitos do índio no Brasil. Na encruzilhada da cidadania." *Série Antropologia* 116. Brasília: Universidade de Brasília.

———. 1992. "Sobre la utilidad social del conocimiento antropologico." *Antropologicas*, July: 51–59.

———. 1994. "The Hyperreal Indian." *Critique of Anthropology* 14(2): 153–171.

———. 1995a. "A profecia de um boato." *Série Antropologia* 188. Brasília: Universidade de Brasília.

———. 1995b. "Por falar em paraíso terrestre." *Série Antropologia* 191. Brasília: Universidade de Brasília.

———. 1995c. *Sanumá Memories: Yanomami Ethnography in Times of Crisis.* Madison, WI: University of Wisconsin Press.

———. 1995d. "Seduced and Abandoned: The Taming of Brazilian Indians." In *Questioning Otherness: An Interdisciplinary Exchange.* Edited by V. R. Dominguez and C. M. Lewis. Iowa City, IA: Center for International and Comparative Studies, University of Iowa.

———. 1998. *Indigenism: Ethnic Politics in Brazil.* Madison, WI: University of Wisconsin Press.

Reuters. 1997. "Church Says Brazilian Indians under Attack by Whites." Ecological Enterprises listserve, March 13.

Ribeiro, Berta. 1990. *Amazônia Urgente. Cinco séculos de história e ecologia.* Belo Horizonte: Itataia.

Ribeiro, Darcy. 1967. "Indigenous Cultures and Languages of Brazil." In *Indians of Brazil in the Twentieth Century.* Edited by J. Hopper. Washington, D.C.: Institute for Cross-Cultural Research.

Ricardo, Carlos Alberto, ed. 1996. *Povos indígenas no Brasil 1991/1995*. São Paulo: Instituto Sócioambiental.

———. 2000. *Povos indígenas no Brasil 1996/2000*. São Paulo: Instituto Sócioambiental.

Robbins, Jim. 1997. "For Indians, Environment Becomes New Battleground." *New York Times*, February 9: 32.

Rocha, Jan. 1991. "Prospectors Bring Malaria Back to Brazil's Indians." *Guardian*, July 7: 10.

———. 1996a. "Rape by Decree." *Guardian*, January 31.

———. 1996b. "Burning Ambition." *Guardian*, November 20.

———. 1997. "Influx of Asian Timber Giants Threatens Efforts to Manage Rain Forest." *Washington Times*, March 17: A12.

———. 1999. *Murder in the Rainforest: The Yanomami, the Gold Miners and the Amazon*. London: Latin America Bureau.

Rohter, Larry. 2002a. "Deep in Brazil, a Flight of Paranoid Fancy." *New York Times*, June 23.

———. 2002b. "Amazon Forest Still Burning Despite the Good Intentions." *New York Times*, August 23.

———. 2002c. "A New Intrusion Threatens a Tribe in Amazon: Soldiers." *New York Times*, October 1.

Roque, Atila. n.d. [1996]. "Social Watch: Brazil. Poverty Again at the Center of Debate." Rio: FASE/IBASE. www.chasque.apc.org/socwatch/genebra.

Rousseau, Jean-Jacques. 1950. "A Discourse on the Origin of Inequality." In *The Social Contract and Discourses*. London: Dent.

Saffirio, John, and Raymond Hames. 1983. "The Impact of Contact: Two Yanomami Case Studies. The Forest and the Highway." *Cultural Survival Occasional Paper 11*, November.

Sagoff, Mark. 1997. "Do We Consume Too Much?" *Atlantic*, June: 80–96.

Sahlins, Marshall. 2000. "Jungle Fever." *Washington Post Book World*, December 10: 1, 3, 5.

Salamone, Frank. 1997. *The Yanomami and Their Interpreters: Fierce People or Fierce Interpreters?* Lanham, MD: University Press of America.

Saldanha, Patrícia. 1992. "FNS abandona sanitaristas na selva." *Porantim*, June: 5.

Saldanha, Patrícia, and Eduardo Leão. 1992. "Eco-92 garante a demarcação." *Porantim*, June: 4.

Schemo, Diana Jean. 1995a. "Hope for Amazon Rain Forest: New Fruit." *New York Times*, September 24: 12.

———. 1995b. "Amazon Is Burning Again, as Furiously as Ever." *New York Times*, October 12: A3.

———. 1996a. "In Brazil, Indians Call on Spirits to Save Land." *New York Times*, July 21: 1, 6.

———. 1996b. "Indians in Brazil Wither in an Epidemic of Suicide." *New York Times*, August 25: 1, 6.

———. 1996c. "Brazil Indefinitely Postpones Ruling on Indian Land Claims." *New York Times*, October 11: A5.

———. 1996d. "Legally, Now, Venezuela to Mine Fragile Lands." *New York Times*, December 8: 1, 22.

Schmink, Marianne, and Charles H. Wood. 1992. *Contested Frontiers in Amazonia.* New York: Columbia University Press.

Schomberg, William. 1996. "Brazil Wins Funding for Amazonian Highway." *Washington Times*, September 14.

Schwartzman, Stephen. 1986. "World Bank Holds Funds for Development Project in Brazil." *Cultural Survival Quarterly* 10(1): 25–27.

Serviço de Justiça e Paz (SEJUP). 1994. "Foreign Minister Asked German Embassy to Omit Demarcation Funding from Programa Piloto Grant." News from Brazil, sejup.news computer conference, March 24.

———. 1996. "Gold Prospectors Return to Indigenous Area." News from Brazil, sejup.news computer conference, August 22.

———. 1997a. "Indians Regroup in a Shantytown in São Paulo." News from Brazil, sejup.news computer conference, March 5.

———. 1997b. "Indigenous Lands Bargained for Votes in Favor of Reelection." News from Brazil, sejup.news computer conference, May 22.

———. 1997c. "Work on Waterway Halted by Court Order." News from Brazil, sejup.news computer conference, June 26.

Silva, Edson. 1999. "Notas para uma história Xucuru." Unpublished ms.

———. n.d. "O povo Xukuru é um só!" Unpublished ms.

Smole, William J. 1976. *The Yanoama Indians: A Cultural Geography.* Austin, TX: University of Texas Press.

Soltani, Atossa, and Tracey Osborne. 1997. *Arteries for Global Trade, Consequences for Amazonia.* Malibu, CA: Amazon Watch.

Sponsel, Leslie. 1992. "Amazonia as an Ecosystem: General Overview." Paper presented at "Transforming the Amazonian Rain Forest" symposium, March.

———. 1994a. "The Killing Fields of the Brazilian and Venezuelan Amazon: The Continuing Destruction of the Yanomami and Their Eco-Systems by Illegal Gold Miners, Future Scenarios and Actions." Paper presented at American Anthropological Association annual meeting, December.

———. 1994b. "The Yanomami Holocaust Continues." In *Who Pays the Price? The Sociocultural Context of Environmental Crisis.* Edited by B. R. Johnston. Washington, D.C.: Island Press.

———. 1997. "The Master Thief: Human and Environmental Impacts and Rights in Relation to Gold Mining and Mercury Contamination in the Amazon." In *Life and Death Matters.* Edited by B. R. Johnston. Walnut Creek, CA: Alta

Mira Press.

———. 2000–2002. Personal communications.

———. 2002a. "A Summary of the International Conference." American Anthropological Association Web site. "Comments on the work of the AAA El Dorado Task Force." April. www.aaanet.org.

———. 2002b. "Yanomami Studies: Past, Present and Future." Paper presented at the American Anthropological Association annual meeting, November.

Storto, Luciana. n.d. "A Report on Language Endangerment in Brazil." Unpublished ms.

Survival International. 1992. *Indians of the Americas: Invaded but Not Conquered.* London.

Switkes, Glen. 1997. "Victory! Judge Halts Dam on Indian Land." In ax.brasil computer conference, March 29.

Tanaka, Nair. 1994. "Health Trip to Mekragnoti." Rainforest Foundation International.

Tierney, Patrick. 2000. *Darkness in El Dorado: How Scientists and Journalists Devastated the Amazon.* New York: W. W. Norton.

Tullberg, Steven M. 1994. "Indigenous Peoples, Self-Determination and the Unfounded Fear of Secession." Unpublished ms. Washington, D.C.: Indian Law Resource Center.

———. 1996. "Statement on Behalf of the Indian Law Resource Center by Steven M. Tullberg to the Briefing of the Congressional Human Rights Caucus on Brazil's Decree 1775/96."

Turner, Terence. 1978. "The Txukahamãe Kayapó Are Alive and Well in the Upper Xingu." *Survival International Review* 3(2): 18–21.

———. 1988. "History, Myth and Social Consciousness among the Kayapó of Central Brazil." In *Rethinking History and Myth.* Edited by J. Hill. Urbana: University of Illinois Press.

———. n.d. [1989]. "Five Days at Altamira." Kayapó Support Group.

———. 1990. "Role of Indigenous Peoples in the Environmental Crisis." Unpublished ms.

———. 1991a. "The Mebengokre Kayapó." Unpublished ms.

———. 1991b. "Representing, Resisting, Rethinking Historical Transformations of Kayapó Culture and Anthropological Consciousness." In *Colonial Situations. Essays on the Contextualization of Ethnographic Knowledge.* Edited by G. W. Stocking, Jr. Madison, WI: University of Wisconsin Press.

———. 1992a. "Os Mebengokre Kayapó: História e mudança social." In *Historia dos indios no Brasil.* Edited by M. Carneiro da Cunha. São Paulo: Secretaria Municipal de Cultura.

———. 1992b. "Viagem aos Kayapó, 11–24 julho 1992." São Paulo: ISA.

———. 1994. "The Yanomami: Truth and Consequences." *Anthropology Newslet-*

ter, May: 46, 48.

———. 1995a. "Indigenous Rights, Environmental Protection and the Struggle over Forest Resources in the Amazon: The Case of the Brazilian Kayapó." Unpublished ms.

———. 1995b. "A sociedade Kayapó." São Paulo: Instituto Sócioambiental.

———. 1995c. "The Kayapó Revolt against Extractivism: An Indigenous People's Struggle for Socially Equitable and Ecologically Sustainable Production."

———. 1996a. "Brazil: Indigenous Rights vs. Neoliberalism." *Dissent*, summer: 67–69.

———. 1996b. "Association Protests Threat to Indigenous Land Rights." *Anthropology Newsletter* 37(5): 22.

———. 2000–2002. Personal communications.

———. 2001a. "Eugenic Ideas in James Neel's Conception of 'Primitive Society.'" Paper presented at the University of Michigan Colloquium "Science–Ethics–Power: Controversy over the Production of Knowledge and Indigenous Peoples."

———. 2001b. "The Yanomami and the Ethics of Anthropological Practice." Occasional Paper of the Center for Latin American Studies Program. Ithaca, NY: Cornell University.

Turner, Terence, and Davi Kopenawa Yanomami. 1991. "I Fight Because I Am Alive." *Cultural Survival Quarterly*, summer: 59–64.

Turner, Terence, and Leslie Sponsel. 2000. "In Re: Scandal About to Be Caused by Publication of Book by Patrick Tierney." E-mail, August 31.

United States Department of State. 1997. "1996 Human Rights Report: Brazil." Washington, D.C.: Bureau of Democracy, Human Rights and Labor.

Urihi. 2000–2002. *Jornal da Urihi*. Boa Vista.

Verdum, Ricardo. 1994. "A fome e os povos indígenas: Luzes no fim do túnel." *Informativo* no. 53: 10. Brasília: INESC.

Verswijver, Gustaaf. 1978. "Séparations et migrations des Mekragnoti, groupe Kayapó du Brésil Central." *Société Suisse des Américanistes, Bulletin* 42: 47–59.

Viana, Virgílio, and Isabelle Gianini. 1994. "Plano diretor da reserva Kayapó-Xicrin do Cateté." São Paulo: ISA.

Villas-Boas, André. 1993. *"Green Gold" on Indian Land: Logging Company Activities on Indigenous Land in the Brazilian Amazon*. Sao Paulo: CEDI.

Villas Boas, Orlando, and Claudio Villas Boas. 1994. *A Marcha para o Oeste. A epopéia da expedição Roncador-Xingu*. 4th ed. Rio de Janeiro: Editora Globo.

Wallace, Scott. 1993. "Rape and Politics in the Rain Forest." *Penthouse*, November.

Warren, Jonathan. 2001. *Racial Revolutions: Antiracism and Indian Resurgence in Brazil*. Durham, NC: Duke University Press.

Warrick, Joby. 1997. "Checkup Time for the Environment." *Washington Post*, June

22: A6.

Werner, Dennis, et al. 1979. "Subsistence Productivity and Hunting Effort in Native South America." *Human Ecology* 7(4): 303–315.

———. 1982. "Variation in Swidden Practices in Four Central Brazilian Indian Societies." *Human Ecology* 10(2): 203–217.

Wiggins, Armstrong. 1990. "Violations of the Human Rights of the Yanomami Indians. Statement of the Indian Law Resource Center, September 28, 1990, Case No. 7615, Inter-American Commission on Human Rights." Washington, D.C.: ILRC.

Wilford, John Noble. 1991. "Oldest Pottery in Americas Is Found in Amazon Basin." *New York Times*, December 13.

Wilson, Richard A. 1997. "Human Rights, Culture and Context: An Introduction." In *Human Rights, Culture and Context, Anthropological Perspectives*. Edited by R. A. Wilson. London: Pluto Press.

World Conference of Indigenous Peoples on Territory, Environment and Development. 1992. "Kari-Oca Village Declaration."

World Rainforest Movement. 1997. "Brazil: Tupinikim and Guarani Indigenous Peoples vs. Aracruz Cellulose." *Bulletin*, WRM listserve, June 3.

Wrangham, Richard, and Dale Peterson. 1996. *Demonic Males: Apes and the Origins of Human Madness*. Boston: Houghton Mifflin.

Yanomami, Davi Kopenawa. 1989. "Letter to All the Peoples of the Earth." *Cultural Survival Quarterly* 13(4): 68–69.

Zacquini, Carlo. 1993. "Yanomami Air Strip is Inaugurated on Mayday." *CCPY Update* 66, May 3.

Index

Illustrations are indicated in bold face.

Breinigsville, PA USA
03 December 2010
250617BV00002B/3/P